The Mahathir Legacy

*A nation divided,
a region at risk*

Ian Stewart

ALLEN&UNWIN

First published in 2003

Allen & Unwin
83 Alexander Street
Crows Nest NSW 2065
Australia
Phone: (61 2) 8425 0100
Fax: (61 2) 9906 2218
Email: info@allenandunwin.com
Web: www.allenandunwin.com

National Library of Australia
Cataloguing-in-Publication entry:

Stewart, Ian, 1928- .
   The Mahathir legacy : a nation divided, a region at risk.

   Includes index.
   ISBN 1 86508 977 X.

   1. Malaysia - Politics and government. 2. Malaysia -
   Economic conditions. 3. Malaysia - Social conditions. I.
   Title.

320.9595

Set in 11/13 pt Bembo by Bookhouse, Sydney
Printed by South Wind Production Services, Singapore

10 9 8 7 6 5 4 3 2 1

Contents

Preface   iv
Introduction   1

Chapter 1   An ambitious crown prince   11
Chapter 2   Battle lines drawn   31
Chapter 3   Tensions rise between 'best of friends'   47
Chapter 4   Protégé outfoxed by mentor   64
Chapter 5   The axing of an heir   85
Chapter 6   Sexual shocks for a prudish people   104
Chapter 7   Black eye provokes outrage   119
Chapter 8   A citizen and a government on trial   134
Chapter 9   The semen-stained mattress   149
Chapter 10   Long jail terms end dazzling career   166
Chapter 11   Foe's defeat comes at a cost   182
Chapter 12   Clinging to power   204
Chapter 13   Terrorists at the gates   221

Index   238

Preface

The revelations in January 2002, that terrorist cells based in South-East Asia and linked to Osama Bin Laden's al-Qaeda Islamic organisation had selected US, British and Australian diplomatic missions in Singapore for future bomb attacks, and the murderous assault on a Balinese nightclub packed with Australians in October 2002 demonstrated that the region faced a security threat more serious than Western governments had envisioned in their strategic scenarios. For Australia, especially, they showed a need to re-evaluate the stability of the countries to its north and to determine how it should respond to the growing peril of Islamic militancy. While the activities of insurgent Islamic groups in Indonesia and the Philippines had long been cause for concern, the disclosure that Malaysia and Singapore had given birth to their own militants intent on murdering people perceived to be enemies of Islam meant Canberra could no longer assume these were two countries it did not have to worry about. Singapore, of course, has the will and the power in its tough laws to tackle internal militants. However, the links of local Malays in Singapore to a regional terrorist network underlined the country's vulnerability as a Chinese island in a Malay Muslim sea. The most disturbing aspect of the information released about terrorist activities was the extent to which al-Qaeda had penetrated Malaysia, where the rapid growth of Islamic fundamentalism is providing fertile ground for the development of extremist ideas. Malaysia was one of a number of countries in which al-Qaeda members held meetings ahead of the attacks on America on September 11, 2001, US Federal Bureau of Investigation Director Robert Mueller said on a visit to Kuala Lumpur in March 2002.

Malaysia was a bastion of Islamic moderation and political stability for many years. But uncertainties now cloud its political future and questions are being raised about whether its moderate Muslims will be swamped by a new breed of zealots, intolerant of non-Muslims at home and hostile to those abroad. Much of the blame for this change in Malaysia's outlook lies with Dr Mahathir Mohamad, Prime Minister since July 1981. Dr Mahathir, ironically, has been a proponent of Islamic moderation and, until 1997, was credited with providing the leadership that, it was then thought, would ensure his country remained politically stable and economically strong for some time to come.

Part of the problem lies in the way Malaysia has developed over the past two decades. Its growth, reflected in economic statistics, has been dramatic, especially in the ten years up to 1997, when the Asian economic crisis ended the boom. During that period, Malaysia's gross domestic product grew at a rate of more than 8 per cent annually. By 1997, total external trade reached more than US$158 billion, making Malaysia the world's 18th biggest exporting nation and 17th biggest importer; per capita income, which had been US$300 at the time of independence, had risen to US$4000. But the benefits of the growth did not permeate to poor rural areas or the urban underprivileged.

Kuala Lumpur, Malaysia's capital, exhibits the exuberant expansion of the boom years. Towering office blocks, decorated at night with glittering coloured lights, fill the city centre. Motorways and light rail transport systems intersect the capital. But beneath the glitter there are flaws. In his column in *New Sunday Times* on 8 July 2001, A. Kadir Jasin, former group editor of the *New Strait Times*, complained that Kuala Lumpur hosted the world's tallest buildings and had the appearance of a First World city, the people responsible for its upkeep had a Third World mentality. He asked: 'What good does it do to have the world's tallest building when from its windows we see slums and ghettos?' Neglect of the slums contributed to an outbreak of racial conflict in March 2001, which was the first serious violence between races since 1969.

Dr Mahathir has every reason to be proud of the growth he presided over in the 1990s and for setting out a vision for Malaysia to become a fully developed nation by 2020. But his preoccupation with showing the world that 'Malaysia Boleh'—Malaysia can—through his encouragement of architectural spectacle in Kuala Lumpur, and the expenditure of billions of dollars on such 'mega-projects' as the new administrative centre in Putrajaya south of Kuala Lumpur, was not matched by a similar enthusiasm for tackling some basic urban and rural problems.

He strongly championed two ventures—the creation of a national car, the Proton Saga and its subsequent variations, and a steel industry—which channelled funds and energy into subsidised products that were more symbolic of nationalist aspirations than meaningful contributions to the nation's wealth. And just as more attention was paid to giving the capital an ersatz glamour than the major make-over it required, so too was there more focus at the national level on growth statistics than overcoming the backwardness of many rural areas—in both peninsular Malaysia and the Borneo states—and dealing with growing social problems. It is in the slums of the capital and in poor rural areas that Islamic fundamentalism is flourishing with its potential to produce extremist groups.

Malaysia's growing segregation of the races is another reason for anxiety. It is dimming the prospect of a unifying Malaysian identity emerging in the near future. Malays and other indigenous people account for more than 60 per cent of the Malaysian population, Chinese just under 26 per cent and Indians about 7 per cent. Older generation Chinese and Malays recall having close friends of both races when they were young but note that today's youth seem to stick with their own kind. An important cause of racial segregation is the increasing pressure on young Malays—from nationalists and radical ulama (clerics)—to be more Islamic and culturally aware. This leads them to shun non-Malays. Removed from the influence of other races, young Malays have become more vulnerable to radical Islamic ideas.

In a speech in July 2002, Dr Mahathir conceded that steps to integrate the races had failed and extremism was on the rise. He said this could lead to the electoral defeat of the ruling National Front alliance, which he heads and added: 'There will be a lot of tension and what happened in 1969 [when Kuala Lumpur was racked by racial riots] can happen again.'

Young Chinese, for their part, resent the continuing privileges accorded Malays in education and in the work place. They feel their race is being marginalised. They complain that the Chinese have been forced into a political partnership with the United Malays National Organisation (UMNO), the dominant government party, which leaves them with no real say in government. At the same time their lifestyle is under threat from the fundamentalism preached by the opposition Parti Islam se-Malaysia (PAS) and favoured by some UMNO members.

The introduction of the New Economic Policy (NEP) in 1972 established quotas for places for Malays in universities and employment and allocated them shares in listed companies with the aim of raising their proportion of national wealth from 2 per cent to 30 per cent. The policy at first angered many Chinese, but they learned to live with the rules and worked harder to make enough money to send their children overseas for a tertiary education when they lost out to less qualified Malays in university selection. They told themselves the NEP would eventually be discontinued or modified. However, nearly 30 years after the NEP's introduction, it is still in place and the Chinese community is asking when, if ever, all races will be treated equally and a true Malaysian identity evolve. Young Chinese, especially, are increasingly dissatisfied with their 'second-class' status.

Their discontent was intensified recently by the disclosure of a serious flaw in the quota system which allocates 35 per cent of places in universities to Chinese and 10 per cent to Indians, with the rest going to bumiputras—Malays and other indigenous people. Each year, hundreds of Chinese with the highest academic qualifications are turned away from universities because the Chinese quota has been filled. Administrators have now revealed that the bumiputra allocation is never fully taken up, but no one has offered the vacant places to Chinese or Indians. It is no wonder that Chinese youth have been strong supporters of calls by Suqiu, a Chinese activist group, for an end to the Malays' special privileges.

A survey taken by Malaysia's *New Straits Times* in mid-1999 highlighted the depth of racial segregation among the nation's youth. A 16-year-old Indian girl told the newspaper she had no Malay friends, declaring that Malays hated her. The study found Malays thought Chinese were 'crafty and sly', while Indians and Chinese described Malays as bodo (stupid). A Chinese boy denied that he was 'anti-Malay' but said he did 'not really like Malays'. Other studies found that university students socialised with members of their own race and seldom mingled with other ethnic groups on campus.

The government announced that, in a move to check the increasing polarisation of the races, universities would require students of different races to share dormitory rooms. But Malays and Chinese resisted the change. In July 2000, the authorities announced plans for 'Vision Schools', which would bring together national, Chinese and Tamil schools in a single complex, where they would share a playground, assembly hall and canteen. Their common use of these facilities, it was claimed, would lead to greater integration of the races. National schools, where Malay is the teaching language, cater mainly to Malays, although they are open to Chinese and Indians. But most Chinese and Indian parents prefer to send their children to schools where lessons are given in Chinese and Tamil.

Chinese community groups and educationists immediately objected to the plan for Vision Schools, with some people expressing concern that they were a first step in the abolition of Chinese schools and Chinese culture. Dr Mahathir attacked the opponents of the Vision Schools as strongly as he had condemned Suqiu which he called 'extremist'. While he realised the need to keep on side with the Chinese, whose votes have become important in preserving the ruling National Front's stranglehold on Parliament, he risked alienating Malays by giving in to Chinese demands. As a result, there is a risk of an exodus of many disillusioned younger Chinese at the same time as the proportion of Chinese in the population is falling. Any emigration of bright young Chinese is a worry, since the Chinese have been the driving force behind the nation's economic growth, and Malaysia must find a new crop of Chinese entrepreneurs if it is to attain Dr Mahathir's 2020 development goal and overcome the wealth disparities helping to foster Muslim radicalism.

Dr Mahathir sought to inculcate an entrepreneurial spirit in young Malays by encouraging them to study international scientific journals which are written in English. But the English of most young Malays is so poor that they cannot follow basic written instructions. This shortcoming is further isolating Malays from the mainstream of modern Western thought, and alarming educationists. The standard of English has deteriorated sharply at every level, from senior officials in government offices to employees in department stores, over the last 30 years. This has resulted from demands by Malay nationalists that English be subordinated to Malay. From the beginning of the 1970s, Malay became the official medium of instruction in national schools and the use of English was relegated to special subjects. Educationists have said the decline in English speaking among Malaysians began with the scrapping in 1971 of the requirement for students to obtain a pass in English to qualify for the School Certificate.

Unfortunately, the reasonable goal of ensuring Malay was accorded the importance it deserved as the national language was pursued to the point where Malaysians lost the advantage their previous excellence in English had given them in international commerce, diplomacy and tourism.

Abdullah Ahmad, an executive of the New Straits Times group and former special envoy to the United Nations, declared that the standard of English was 'getting worse by the day among all races', and that he was worried about 'Malaysia's capacity to participate actively in the global economy and international relations'. A columnist for another Malaysian newspaper *The Sun on Sunday*, K. Pathmanabhan, commented that the passion for Malay had 'unfortunately led to the shutting of children's minds from the world, as well as keeping global developments out of the reach of most adults'.

While the problems outlined above have created strains in Malaysian society, the most serious dislocation has resulted from divisive actions taken or initiated by the Prime Minister, beginning with the sacking of Anwar Ibrahim, his deputy, in 1998. The fateful decisions Dr Mahathir made at this time and their repercussions for the nation and the region are discussed in the following pages.

Introduction

The demonisation of Dr Mahathir Mohamad by Western governments over the Anwar affair reflected more than outrage over what they perceived as unfair treatment of the former deputy prime minister. It highlighted a widespread antipathy among foreign leaders and officials towards the Malaysian Prime Minister, arising from his sometimes abrasive personality and non-conformist policies. In the year before Anwar Ibrahim was sacked from government, Dr Mahathir had railed against foreign stock market and currency speculators, and alienated the US administration and like-minded governments with his criticism of Western democracy and his jaundiced view of human rights activism. As he increasingly championed Third World, or South, causes and warned developing countries to be on guard against 'neo-colonialism'—read United States—his antagonists in Washington grew.

Dr Mahathir is always courteous to foreign visitors but often appears detached—as if he were still a medical practitioner meeting a patient for the first time. His manner is friendly but he displays warmth only to close friends and family. Yet he is not an insensitive person. He can be overcome with emotion when speaking of matters about which he feels strongly, such as his desire to make Malays more goal-oriented and competitive. Nevertheless, he often comes across as aloof. Armani-suited Anwar, on the other hand, presented a congenial image to the West. Foreign leaders found him charming and personable. He was seen as the liberal face of the Malaysian government, who would bring change and a more Western brand of democracy to Malaysia. United States and European government heads chose to ignore the many contradictions in Anwar's personality and his radical Islamic background, which made it questionable whether he would steer the nation in a direction favourable to the West, far less prove to be a better leader than Dr Mahathir. The deputy prime minister and finance minister's chameleon-like practice of projecting himself as the person his audience would like him to be won him ardent followers among people as disparate as conservative anti-Western Malay Muslim youths and the chiefs of the capitalist West's iconic International Monetary Fund (IMF) and World Bank. But few among his admirers thought to wonder who the real Anwar might be. His intellect, good humour and penchant for quoting a wide range of Asian and Western sages and philosophers was sufficient to secure their devotion.

Besides, it was easy to dislike Dr Mahathir. He did not pander to the interests of the West. On the contrary, he took on the mantle of leader of the developing countries, urging them to resist the blandishments of foreign capitalists and their governments. Of course, there was a certain dichotomy here since his government had created an attractive investment climate which had prompted leading multinational corporations to set up manufacturing operations in Malaysia. He had also personally approached Microsoft chairman Bill Gates and other new-economy entrepreneurs on visits to the United States and persuaded them to give their support to his innovative plan for a Multimedia Super Corridor, extending south from Kuala Lumpur, which he envisioned as an information technology test bed along the lines of California's Silicon Valley. But it was his anti-West character that was dominant as the economic crisis that had begun with the collapse of Thailand's currency rocked South-East Asia.

The year 1997 should have been triumphant for Dr Mahathir. Malaysia was set to celebrate its 40th anniversary of independence (on 31 August) and play host to the annual meeting of foreign ministers of the Association of South-East Asian Nations (ASEAN), 30 years after it was founded. The Malaysian Prime Minister had decided early in 1997 that with the Malaysian economy showing no signs of weakening after a decade of growth at an annual rate of more than 8 per cent and the National Front coalition in firm political control, the time was approaching when he could step down and let his deputy, Anwar, take over. Dr Mahathir had also set his mind on bringing all the nations of South-East Asia into the regional association so that the 30th birthday party would be a celebration of the 'ASEAN 10'. He had been the driving force behind the decision of Malaysia and its partners—Brunei, Laos, Indonesia, Philippines, Singapore, Thailand, Vietnam—to include Burma, despite US and European opposition, and was now keen to see Cambodia join the team.

Amid preparations for the ASEAN meeting, Malaysia unveiled a new logo of ten rice sheafs. But Hun Sen's blatant seizure of power in Phnom Penh, reneging on his agreement to share government with the elected Funcinpec party following the 1993 Cambodian elections, made it impossible for ASEAN to observe its policy of non-interference in members' internal affairs or to turn a blind eye to the malefactions of the leader of potential member number ten. Malaysia was prepared to welcome Cambodia at the forthcoming foreign ministers' meeting, but the Philippines and Thailand raised objections which ended Dr Mahathir's expectation of opening an ASEAN 10 conference.

The 1990s had been a period of relative political and economic stability throughout South-East Asia but suddenly the situation had changed. Not only was there the onset of conflict between the joint prime ministers in Cambodia, but in 1997 there was a dramatic plunge in Asian currencies and stock markets. Dr Mahathir's frustration over the forced depreciation of the ringgit and sudden end to Malaysia's decade-long economic boom prompted him to attack currency traders as 'international crooks' trying to undermine Malaysia's economy. He singled out US financier George Soros, blaming him personally for the ringgit's fall. Soros' denial that any of the funds he administered had engaged in speculation against the ringgit was supported by other market players, but Dr Mahathir nevertheless compared him with drug traffickers and called him a moron. Dr Mahathir conceded that his language was 'intemperate' but seemed overwhelmed by what he saw as the injustice of specu-lators being able to damage the economy which Malaysia had successfully developed over the 40 years of its independence. His outbursts put the stock market into a steeper dive and further alien-ated the US administration.

Despite this, Dr Mahathir maintained his rage. He made it clear he would not allow himself to suffer the perceived humiliation that had befallen Indonesia's President Suharto. The Indonesian leader had been shown in a widely published photograph signing away inde-pendent economic action in exchange for IMF assistance, as the IMF's chief, Michel Camdessus, stood over him with folded arms—like a headmaster watching a pupil complete a detention exercise. Dr Mahathir referred to 'sinister powers' who were using their economic might to weaken developing countries. These neo-colonialists wanted nations like Malaysia to 'bow down and end up being debtors to them' so they could dictate what Malaysians should or should not do. He accused the West of a conspiracy to bring down governments in South-East Asia. Interestingly, in October 2000, with Malaysia's economy in good health again and his own position secure, he modified his stand. He conceded there was 'no conspiracy' and that attacks against the East Asian economies 'were not orchestrated'—more likely 'rogue currency traders just saw an opportunity to make a pile for themselves'. But in 1997 and 1998, the fury of the frustrated Malaysian Prime Minister allowed for no such reasonableness.

During this period also he found himself increasingly at odds with the man he had selected to be his successor. Anwar and offi-cials in his Finance Ministry and Bank Negara, the central Malaysian bank, believed Malaysia would be better off seeking help from the IMF and World Bank than going it alone. But their economic argu-ments were ineffectual against Dr Mahathir's determination to preserve Malaysia's independence of action. Having lived under the

proactive – reactive
constructive intervention

brutal Japanese occupation of Malaysia and experienced discrimination as a young Malay doctor working in post-war British-ruled Malaya, he has made it clear he regards any form of foreign interference as abhorrent. According to a Malaysian journalist present at the time, he once told an audience of rural Malays: 'Never trust a white man.'

Anwar had also begun to position himself as a champion of change in ASEAN, to the annoyance of Dr Mahathir. In an article written for *Newsweek*, Anwar said ASEAN must 'move from being a largely reactive organisation to being a proactive one'. He wrote that it needed to intervene before simmering problems erupted into full-blown crises like the one that was unfolding in Cambodia. Anwar suggested it was time for ASEAN 'to seriously consider the idea of "constructive intervention"'. Such a new framework would 'not violate the [ASEAN] principle of non-interference in the internal affairs of another state'. But it seemed to promise just that by going significantly beyond the existing and ineffective ASEAN policy of 'constructive engagement'.

The kind of change envisioned by Anwar was anathema to Dr Mahathir. In an interview with Bernama, the national news agency, on the eve of the 30th ASEAN Ministerial Meeting in Kuala Lumpur, Dr Mahathir defended the group's policy of constructive engagement and said it had produced 'tremendous results'. In his opening speech at the meeting on 24 July 1997, he said it was 'regrettable' that Cambodia's entry had been blocked, inferring his ASEAN partners had buckled to Western pressure. Declaring that ASEAN must resist and reject such attempts at coercion, he said they were 'not part of the ASEAN way'.

The ASEAN meeting, which was followed by the usual discussions between the group and its dialogue partners, which include the United States, Russia, China, Japan and the European Community, highlighted the growing animosity between Dr Mahathir and the US Government. Dr Mahathir angered the Americans by attacking Soros directly in the Bernama interview and indirectly in his ASEAN speech. He said 'rogue speculators'—a term he had previously applied to Soros—whom he also described as anarchists and brigands, wanted to destroy weak countries and force them to 'submit to the dictatorship of international manipulators'.

The US Government leapt to Soros's defence. Speaking on 'currency fluctuations' at the ASEAN Post-Ministerial Conference, where the dialogue partners had their say, Stuart E. Eizenstat, US Under Secretary of State for Economic, Business and Agricultural Affairs, disputed Dr Mahathir's thesis. He said experience suggested that market movements were 'not dominated by a small number of currency speculators', let alone one person who happened to be a US citizen. Eizenstat also responded to another Mahathir contention that the United Nations Declaration on Human Rights was outdated since it did not represent the views of the developing nations and should be reviewed. Asked to comment on the Malaysian Prime Minister's stand, Eizenstat said it was 'remarkable' that anyone would want to 'dilute' the UN declaration. This was seen as a slight to Dr Mahathir not only by Malaysians but by most of the other ASEAN foreign ministers at the press conference, who presented a united front in supporting the Malaysian leader. Eizenstat's perceived affront was returned when the Malaysian Foreign Minister, Abdullah Badawi, closed the press conference without allowing him to reply to an attack on the United States by China's Vice-Premier and Foreign Minister, Qian Qichen, leaving the American clearly frustrated.

It was the most dramatic and out-of-character ending to an ASEAN meeting in the group's history. In the past, any differences that threatened to mar press conferences were cloaked with a determined cordiality. This time the Americans were left smarting. Secretary of State Madeline Albright, who two years later was the most vigorously vocal senior US critic of Malaysia over the jailing of Anwar, took a swing at Dr Mahathir on her way home from the ASEAN meeting through Singapore. Ms Albright, who angered her Malaysian hosts with a strong attack on ASEAN member Burma, described the Malaysian leader as 'a case of his own', while praising Senior Minister Lee Kuan Yew, Singapore's former prime minister, for having the 'most modern and most strategic vision' she had encountered for a long time.

Singapore's government has ensured an opposition cannot thrive, curtailed the freedom of a former politician, Chia Thye Poh, through imprisonment or a form of house arrest for more than 30 years, and displeased Washington by allowing the caning of a US teenager for vandalism. Yet despite the fact that Lee has made clear his disregard for free-wheeling Western democracy, he is admired within the US administration while Dr Mahathir is reviled. The explanation lies in the fact that while the Singapore leader may have been an authoritarian prime minister, he was in most instances a staunch supporter of the United States on defence issues and an advocate of a US military presence in Asia. Dr Mahathir on the other hand was publicly suspicious of Washington's intentions in the region. Additionally, Singapore provided the United States with a 'logistics' presence in Singapore after it was ejected from its base in the Philippines. The United States was also more at ease with a country that had close ties with Israel than one led by Muslims who supported the Palestinian cause. Singapore had turned to Israel for help in creating a defence force after its separation from Malaysia in 1967. Malaysia did not recognise Israel.

Towards the end of 1997, Malaysia–US relations worsened significantly. Malaysia was infuriated by US efforts to halt a US$2 billion gas project in Iran involving the Malaysian oil corporation Petronas, French petroleum company Total and Russia's Gazprom. Washington warned that Malaysia could face reprisals under the 1996 *Iran–Libya Sanctions Act*, which sought to penalise non-US companies investing more than US$40 million in the oil and gas sectors of Iran or Libya. The Malaysian Government and its supporters were also angered by a move by Congressman Robert Wexler to have the US House of Representatives approve a resolution calling on Dr Mahathir to resign or apologise over alleged anti-US and anti-Semitic remarks. This related to Dr Mahathir's suggestion that a Jewish conspiracy was behind the regional financial turmoil and subsequent explanation that he was only drawing attention to the coincidence that two of the nations affected—Indonesia and Malaysia—had mainly Muslim populations while, Soros, the man he blamed for the crisis was Jewish.

Members of the youth wing of the United Malays National Organisation (UMNO), the dominant government party headed by Dr Mahathir, protested outside the US embassy against the Wexler resolution and the threat of sanctions over the Petronas deal. The embassy said it had received two telephone calls threatening harm to US citizens and advised Americans in Malaysia to 'maintain a high level of security awareness'. Dr Mahathir dismissed American fears of violence, declaring, 'It is only an expression of anger of the people in Malaysia,' and that Malaysians were 'not a violent people'. But the rising anti-American sentiment prompted the outspoken US ambassador, John Malott, to issue a statement complaining strenuously about the 'America-bashing', and calling for efforts to control 'the ugly atmosphere'. He said he was concerned about 'the growing tendency to blame everything that is happening on foreigners, usually Americans, or on the foreign press, usually American-owned'. Dr Mahathir brushed aside the American diplomat's complaint, declaring that Malaysians had a right to speak their minds and express their feelings about issues.

Malott, who retired from government service in 1999, later became a strong defender of Anwar, although the then deputy prime minister had dutifully joined the chorus of criticism against the United States and had also introduced a motion in parliament expressing confidence in Dr Mahathir. In February 2001, when Anwar was in hospital for treatment of a back ailment—having been moved there from his jail cell in November—Malott wrote to the *Washington Post* to express his concern about the former deputy prime minister, whom he described as a political prisoner and 'a continuing nemesis of Prime Minister Mahathir Mohamad'. He asked whether one could be certain that any operation performed in Malaysia was 'risk-free', outraging Malaysian doctors.

In the final months of 1997, the stress of events began to take their toll on Dr Mahathir, who is renowned for his stamina despite undergoing a multiple coronary by-pass operation in 1989. He suffered a series of colds and looked tired and drawn in contrast with his usual robust appearance. As a new year dawned, the pressures on him intensified. Share prices and the ringgit continued to fall in value. Differences over economic policy between the Prime

Minister and his Finance Minister became sharper. Interest rates were a contentious issue, with Dr Mahathir thinking they should be held down to protect businesses in contrast with the view of the IMF and Anwar that they should be allowed to rise. Unusually, the Prime Minister became a target of thinly veiled criticism at home in the establishment media, as well as of harsh attacks abroad. Anwar exuded confidence. When asked about the conflicting statements on economic policy by him and Dr Mahathir, Anwar said he was 'in charge'.

But the beleaguered Prime Minister was not about to give ground. Two developments in January 1998 signalled his determination to assert his authority. One set the stage for the eventual removal of an editor who had written critical articles about him. The other was the creation of a National Economic Action Council, headed by the Prime Minister as chairman, to help the government deal with the growing economic crisis. Anwar appeared to have an important voice in the council as deputy chairman, but the appointment of Daim Zainuddin as executive director tilted control in favour of Dr Mahathir. Daim, who has been Dr Mahathir's most trusted colleague for at least twenty years, was already economic adviser to the government and treasurer of UMNO. As Finance Minister from 1984 to 1991, he introduced policies that helped Malaysia recover from an earlier economic downturn. Dr Mahathir also publicly sought the help of a group of 'veterans', including the former deputy prime minister and UMNO deputy president, Ghafar Baba, to serve as a liaison group between the government and public on the economic crisis. Ghafar had resigned as deputy president rather than contest the 1993 UMNO elections against Anwar's money-fuelled campaign. He was a fierce foe of his successor.

In June, Daim's role was augmented when he was appointed as Special Functions Minister, who would be 'entrusted with the tasks related to economic development'. Anwar saw himself being sidelined and his influence eroding and knew he needed to act before he was eased out of office. The resignation of Indonesian President Suharto under public pressure in May spurred him to draw parallels between Indonesia and Malaysia and imply it was time for a change in the Malaysian leadership. Apparently believing the turbulent events in Indonesia provided him with an opportunity to force Dr Mahathir's early retirement, he induced his protege, Zahid Hamidi, UMNO Youth chief, to call for UMNO to reject nepotism, cronyism and corruption, the same three transgressions attributed to the Suharto regime by Indonesian students in their street demonstrations.

Zahid's rallying cry caused a stir but no immediate groundswell of support to oust Dr Mahathir. A veteran of many party battles, the Prime Minister, who was also UMNO president, moved quickly to outsmart his deputy by releasing lists of hundreds of 'cronies' who had benefited from the party's policy of providing business opportunities for Malays. They included members of Anwar's family, who had acquired substantial holdings in a number of leading corporations. Anwar tried to save himself by sacrificing his pawn, Zahid. But Dr Mahathir was not about to let Anwar retain the positions of deputy prime minister or UMNO deputy president from where he might stage another attempt to seize power. His sword fell swiftly on his overambitious crown prince. On 2 September Dr Mahathir sacked Anwar, who was subsequently arrested, tried on charges of corruption and sodomy, and jailed.

Anwar was a victim of the ruthless machinations of Malaysian politics, but he had planned to be the victor. In these circumstances, the West's demonisation of Mahathir and canonisation of Anwar did not accurately reflect the situation. But while Dr Mahathir may have believed his merciless removal of Anwar justified, it proved to be a blunder of Malaysia-shaking proportions, dividing the nation, turning Malay against Malay and providing new impetus to an Islamic radicalism spreading throughout the country. This is Dr Mahathir's legacy.

1 | An ambitious crown prince

It appeared to be a perfect union, before the explosive rupture and extraordinary events that put one of the partners behind bars. The nation's leader, a pragmatic and respected visionary, had taken under his wing a charismatic younger man with an outstanding intellect and new-generation approach which, it was believed, would enable him to meet the challenges of the future while building on the gains of the past, when the time came for him to succeed his mentor. Throughout Asia and the world, the partnership of the Malaysian Prime Minister, Dr Mahathir Mohamad, and the Deputy Prime Minister, Anwar Ibrahim, was acclaimed as an example for less well led countries in the region. It marked Malaysia as a politically stable nation with a settled line of succession. Then, suddenly, in the middle of 1998, the situation changed dramatically.

Given the disparate natures of the two men, it is perhaps surprising that the relationship lasted as long as it did, flourishing to the point of Dr Mahathir annointing Anwar as his heir. Both men were rebels in their early years, going against the established UMNO leadership. But they had little else in common. Moreover, Anwar was an impatient leader-in-waiting, a scheming prince who coveted the crown of the ruler while constantly proclaiming his loyalty. In 1995, amid growing evidence that he was building up grassroots support for a move against the Prime Minister, Anwar declared that he had never had any problems with the man who nominated him as the next head of government. He said he looked up to Dr Mahathir as his 'leader and father' in his political struggle.

Although he was an anti-establishment radical in his student days, Anwar had had a cosseted upbringing. He was no kampung (village) boy. Born in Penang in 1947, he received his secondary education at the Malay College Kuala Kangsar, an elite school, which has produced many government and business leaders. In his book *The Asian Renaissance*, a compilation of his speeches and articles, he recalled how as a child he 'read with enthusiasm Asian history and literature, autobiographies and the Books of Mencius from a small collection of [his] father's . . . taking copious notes in the process'. He wrote: 'Exposure to the English public school tradition at the Malay College Kuala Kangsar in the 1960s enabled me to gain familiarity with the English language, its literature and the thoughts of its great writers.' Anwar graduated from the University of Malaya in 1971 with a Bachelor of Arts honours in Malay studies.

In his university days Anwar rose to national prominence as a student activist and an eloquent speaker on social, economic and political issues, decrying rural poverty and corruption and advocating wealth redistribution. Known as Pak Sheikh, he attracted a devoted band of followers, who saw him as the standard bearer for Malay nationalism and Islamic fundamentalism. In 1972, Anwar founded the Islamic Youth Movement of Malaysia—known by its Malaysian acronym as Abim—and became its first president. Abim, whose inaugural members included Fadzil Noor, the former president of Parti Islam se-Malaysia (PAS), the largest opposition party, and other dedicated Islamists, was launched with the stated aim of promoting Islam as a way of life and extending spiritual and material support to needy Malay Muslims. But Abim's dakwah, or missionary role, was subordinated to a politically driven programme of anti-government activism spearheaded by its leader, Anwar. This led to his detention in 1974 under the *Internal Security Act* for organising anti-government student demonstrations in support of poor farmers. Fadzil Noor assumed the position of acting president of

Abim until Anwar's release in 1976, when he again became head of the body.

Abim showed an increasing political bias towards PAS and supported it in the 1978 election after the fundamentalist party had ended an alliance with UMNO. Fadzil and other Abim leaders became leading PAS party members and Anwar was expected to join them. But in a move that shocked his Abim colleagues, Anwar accepted an invitation from Dr Mahathir to join UMNO in 1982. In that year's election he won the Permatang Pauh parliamentary seat in Penang state.

Interviewed before the 1999 general election at PAS headquarters in Alor Star, Kedah, Fadzil, who died in June 2002 after undergoing heart bypass surgery, told me that, before Anwar's surprising embrace of UMNO, it was believed that he would join PAS. Although they had worked as a team in Abim, after 1982 Fadzil and Anwar 'had contact, but were not very close'. That is not surprising. One could not imagine Fadzil abandoning his Islamic radicalism and donning designer-label clothing or hobnobbing with the rich and famous of the world in the manner of his one-time friend. His usual garb was the gown and white skullcap that he and his associates wore to affirm their role as religious leaders. But if he felt any bitterness over Anwar's choice of UMNO over PAS, Fadzil put it behind him in 1998 and joined other opposition leaders in supporting the claim of his jailed former Abim partner that he was framed and calling for his release. In the interview, Fadzil, 63, affirmed PAS's backing for the opposition parties' stated plan to make Anwar prime minister if it won the election. Gazing steadily at me through steel-rimmed glasses set above a white mustache and goatee, with his white skullcap resting on the table in front of him, Fadzil declared: 'Anwar will become prime minister after we have settled all the legal requirements for his release.' At the time I found it hard to believe that Fadzil would ever abdicate the leadership that would be his by virtue of PAS's standing as the largest opposition party in favour of the man whom some of his Abim comrades believe betrayed them and PAS by dealing with the devil. The ideological distance between PAS and UMNO is underscored by their respective headquarters in Alor Star. My interview with Fadzil was in a small sparsely furnished room, three flights up a narrow wooden stairway in an old, shabby building. Visitors leave their shoes at a landing before mounting the last section of stairs, which is carpeted. The Kedah office of UMNO is in a shiny, modern building, where elevators whisk visitors to a meeting room and nobody removes their shoes.

Anwar's defection to the enemy was especially startling to his Abim associates because Dr Mahathir was Minister of Education at the height of the 'campus revolution' in 1974, pitted against his future protégé until the younger man was removed from the scene of battle to spend two years as an ISA detainee. But Dr Mahathir recognised the student activist's potential as a future political leader with a strong base of loyalists, and successfully steered him into UMNO. His success in persuading the radical young rebel to join UMNO 1982 and run for parliament just two weeks before his first general election as Prime Minister was seen as a major political stroke.

Anwar rose rapidly in UMNO and in the government with Dr Mahathir's patronage. He underwent a remarkable transformation from scruffily dressed, anti-government terror to meticulously groomed, immaculately attired establishment figure with a powerful political base at home and friends in high places abroad. He was elected president of UMNO Youth, the party's youth wing in 1982, the same year in which he joined the party and was elected a member of Parliament. Dr Mahathir immediately brought Anwar into government as a deputy minister in the Prime Minister's Department. He was subsequently appointed Minister of Culture, Youth and Sports in 1983, and Minister of Agriculture in 1984, and then given the prestigious education portfolio in 1986. In 1991, he replaced Daim Zainuddin as Minister of Finance. In 1993, he steam-rollered his way to the position of UMNO deputy president having garnered enough support from UMNO divisions to ensure his election at that year's party elections but winning unopposed when the incumbent, Ghafar Baba, withdrew.

Dr Mahathir had wanted Ghafar to remain as Deputy Prime Minister and UMNO deputy president and had made this clear to those around him. Anwar seemed to go along with his leader, denying he had any designs on the number two post. But he and his supporters worked assiduously at the grassroots to set in motion an unstoppable wave of support for his candidacy as deputy president, spending money freely to win the divisional nominations that destroyed any chance Ghafar had of retaining the post. Anwar also formed a 'Vision Team' of senior party figures to add strength to his power bid, despite Dr Mahathir's stated opposition to the establishment of teams. After Anwar's defeat of Ghafar, Dr Mahathir named him Deputy Prime Minister in accordance with party tradition, which allots the top two government positions to the UMNO president and deputy president. Anwar's aggressive push for power, however, had made him many enemies, who would later work actively against him or support the Prime Minister despite their misgivings about the political fallout from his sacking.

Many Malaysians interpreted the striking change in the persona of Anwar Ibrahim—which had become even more pronounced after he was made a deputy minister in the Prime Minister's Department—as evidence of a self-serving expediency. The new Anwar was viewed with suspicion by those Chinese who had regarded his Malay Muslim radicalism as a threat to racial harmony. He was also distrusted by intellectuals and members of the business community, who remembered him as the leader of Malay Muslim students who smashed English signs at the University of Malaya, and as the Islamist who had close links with leaders of the world's most conservative Islamic countries. Anwar worked hard to counter the doubters. His speeches began to explore multicultural themes and include quotations from Confucius and other Chinese philosophers. They also took on a regional flavour and featured Indian scholars and Philippine revolutionary heroes such as Jose Rizal. He cultivated the media and eventually gained control of two newspapers and a television station through loyalists in editorial and management positions. One columnist—not a loyalist—wrote that Anwar had joined UMNO to change the system from within but that instead the system had changed Anwar.

A core of Anwar supporters was soon surrounded by people working to make him UMNO president and prime minister. A team skilled in Western-style public relations techniques set about making him an internationally known and admired figure, projecting, through their contacts with foreign correspondents and editors, the image of a progressive, globally concerned intellectual, who was a moderate Muslim with liberal views about the media, free speech and democracy. The smoothly presented assertions of the image-makers, combined with Anwar's speeches and articles, led to him being acclaimed in regional publications as an Asian Renaissance Man, whose broad sweep of knowledge, interests and beliefs marked him as the role model for regional leaders in the 21st century. This glowing picture was reinforced by the title of Anwar's book, *The Asian Renaissance*, as well as its contents. Published in 1995 two years before the shattering events that ended his political career, the book evokes the intellectual breadth of the author in its wide-ranging discussion of such topics as democracy and civil society, justice and law, ethics and economics, Islam in South-East Asia, and the Asia of the future. Anwar ensured the thoughts expressed would be unambiguously identified with him by stating in the preface: 'The ideas in this book are the product of personal reflections on events, writings and encounters with personalities.'

Yet the book, which is loaded with references to philosophers and sociologists from East and West, as well as poets and writers from William Shakespeare to Rabindranath Tagor, and offers nine pages of 'Select Bibliography', reads more like the thesis of an enthusiastic college student eager to demonstrate his erudition than a considered analysis of regional issues. This is not to impugn Anwar's intellect. He has one of the most impressive minds of any leader to emerge in Asia in the past 50 years. He is intelligent, charming, witty and an exciting speaker. Watching him mesmerise an audience of UMNO members with his oratorical skills ahead of the 1993 party election, I was reminded of Sukarno, the first president of Indonesia, whom I saw in action many times. Five years later, on the eve of Anwar's arrest, as I stood among the 40 000 people gathered to hear him speak at the National Mosque in Kuala Lumpur and noted his ability to stir emotions with fiery rhetoric, I wondered if he, like the charismatic Sukarno, was prepared to use demagoguery to achieve a political end. Sukarno, too, was versed in the literature of East and West and sprinkled his speeches with quotations from philosophers and writers. He filled the palace in Jakarta with artworks, mostly from Java and Bali and liked to say that he had an artistic vein inherited from his Balinese mother. Sukarno, in his way, was the Renaissance man of his time. But Sukarno never had a need to promote himself. He had been a key figure in the revolution that wrested the islands called the Netherlands East Indies from the Dutch. Other revolutionaries may have been braver or bolder but he had the aura of a leader and so became one. He was vain, egotistical and boasted to me about his seduction of women. He also quashed democracy in Indonesia. But he was simply Sukarno.

Anwar has often seemed more concerned with creating a multi-faceted personality with wide appeal than with being simply Anwar. In an article co-written with a representative of the Japanese newspaper *Mainichi Daily News* some months after he had sacked Anwar, Dr Mahathir said that his deputy was 'a populist' and that he liked to be praised, 'especially by foreign VIPs'. Dr Mahathir stated: 'He is especially liked by his US counterparts because he always agrees with them. I am afraid I like to speak my mind and some of my views are not popular with foreigners. This is something that I cannot help.'

Dr Mahathir has certainly shown himself to be constant in his beliefs and more transparent emotionally. He can be politically devious and behind his benign smile he may well be plotting your downfall. But he has held doggedly to his political beliefs in the face of fierce criticism and his own expulsion from UMNO. He scolds Malays mercilessly for their failure to do as well as Chinese in examinations but he also proclaims that they—and Malaysians generally—can achieve any goal they set themselves. When he suffered a heart attack in 1989 and his doctors said he would have to undergo open heart surgery, he turned down Singapore Prime Minster Lee Kuan Yew's recommendation to use Victor Chang, the renowned Australian heart surgeon. He wanted local doctors. When Anwar, the ultra-nationalist, was transferred from his prison cell to a hospital in November 2000, suffering severe back pain caused by a disc problem, his family sought permission for him to be flown to Germany for an operation. Anwar may have believed that only foreign surgery could help him, or he may have seen an opportunity in an overseas trip to delay his return to prison, but either way he left himself open to having his nationalism questioned.

'Who is the real Anwar?' is a question that has been asked a number of times by Malaysian journalists exploring the character of the former deputy prime minister. Within days of his sacking he had reverted to the fervent radicalism and street politics of his student days, becoming again Pak Sheik in proletarian pants and short-sleeved shirt. The complex nature of Anwar is reflected in his writing. The idealistic characterisation of the renaissance of Asia contrasts starkly with the grubby money politics of UMNO, in which he was a willing participant. The Asian renaissance, he wrote in his book, 'entails the growth, development and flowering of Asian societies based on a certain vision of perfection; societies imbued with truth and the love of learning, justice and compassion, mutual respect and forbearance, and freedom with responsibility'.

Anwar says his goal has always been the reformation of Malaysian society, which would see the elimination of cronyism, corruption and injustice and make life generally better for Malaysians. He argues that he was destroyed because he wanted to change the system. But UMNO contemporaries are sceptical about whether as leader Anwar would have done anything to weaken the party machinery and government procedures that buttressed his new authority. Even some of his supporters are of a similar mind. Rustam Sani, an academic who turned to opposition politics after Anwar's sacking, conceded to me that the system would have remained intact and unchallenged if Anwar had succeeded Dr Mahathir as planned. He described Anwar's sacking as a blessing in disguise because it prompted him to go on the offensive and become a catalyst for change. Forced to become a rebel again, Anwar gave voice to public grievances, which have become national issues and provided the opposition with a vote-winning platform.

But Anwar enjoyed the fruits of government office for sixteen years—a long time to allow the evils of the establishment to flourish without objection if he believed they should be abolished. In that sense he is no different from other UMNO leaders who talk about the need for change but do not rock the boat for fear of falling—or being pushed—overboard. His family, like the relatives of other

UMNO officials, acquired significant wealth through the allocation of shares to bumiputras (indigenous Malaysians) and privatisation projects favouring Malays. These privileges accorded Malays through the New Economic Plan created a new bumiputra middle-class and a score of multimillionaires but did little for the poor in rural areas, for whom Anwar had fought as a student firebrand.

The complex nature of Anwar is also evident in his book. There he presents himself as a reasonable man taking an even-handed position on East–West issues. In his chapter 'Symbiosis Between East and West', he criticises the condescension of Westerners in castigating Asian countries for being sluggish in effecting societal reforms. But their 'cultural arrogance' should 'not detract from the fact that Asians themselves are guilty of many of the transgressions with which the West has charged them'. In the chapter 'Democracy And Civil Society', he declares that 'power personalised is power plundered from the people'. He goes on to say: 'Democracy is not a luxury that Asians cannot afford, as some would have us believe. On the contrary, it is a basic necessity for responsible and ethical governance.' Statements of this kind, which are not heard from the outspokenly anti-Western Dr Mahathir, have endeared Anwar to some Western leaders. But he qualifies his praise of democracy with a countering tilt to Asian values, writing that the fact that Asian countries were in different stages of economic development suggests that each country will 'negotiate its way to democracy and civil society at its own pace'. The Asian vision of civil society departs 'in a fundamental respect from that articulated by some Western thinkers', and Asia will 'shape its civil society in its own direction'.

The contradictions evident in Anwar extend to religion. In *The Asian Renaissance*, he champions the 'middle path' for South-East Asian Muslims, saying this moderation leads to a pragmatic approach in social, economic and political life. He argues for 'reason and common sense', asserting that 'the proponents of the imposition of Muslim laws or the establishment of an Islamic state are confined to the periphery'. But the hudud laws, with their harsh medieval punishments, and the Islamic state are in the platform of PAS, the fundamentalist party, which he was once expected to join and which is now an ally of the National Justice Party, formed in his name and headed by his wife, Dr Wan Azizah Wan Ismail. Unlike Dr Mahathir, who wants to reform the syariah courts, where the imposition of Islamic law discriminates against women, Anwar has the support of the ulama, Malaysia's religious leaders. Dr Mahathir is berated by ulama in mosques as an apostate. Anwar is the subject of prayers for his release from jail. The ulama clearly believe Anwar is no moderate, but an adherent of the stricter kind of Islam they preach. So do many women's groups.

Anwar's position on women's rights was tested in 1997. In June of that year Selangor state religious authorities arrested and prosecuted three Malay Muslim beauty pageant contestants for dressing indecently. Newspapers carried photographs of the young women being escorted from the stage by Islamic officials as the results of the competition were being announced. They were subsequently convicted and fined. The incident provoked an outcry from women's groups, who vigorously defended the right of women to choose what they wore. The four leading organisations issued a statement condemning the Selangor religious authorities for subjecting the arrested trio to 'public humiliation'.

Anwar, who was acting Prime Minister while Dr Mahathir was overseas, was initially silent on the matter. Even after he was reportedly prodded by the Prime Minister from abroad he avoided a direct rebuke, merely calling on religious authorities to adopt a moderate approach in implementing Islamic law and to be sensitive in matters affecting youth, culture and the arts. His remarks had no apparent effect. A Selangor religious official warned women to cover up or face prosecution. He listed swimsuits, low-cut blouses, high-slit skirts and any body-hugging clothing as prohibited items. Ishak Baharom, the Selangor mufti, or head religious official, said the arrest of the three women was justified and in accordance with syariah law. He said such actions were necessary to 'combat the social ills plaguing society'.

On his return from overseas, Dr Mahathir immediately criticised the action of the Selangor religious authorities. He called on all states to freeze the enforcement of existing religious rulings that reflected 'negatively' on Islam and refrain from implementing any new rulings until a study of the system was completed by the Prime

Minister's Department. He recommended state religious departments should focus their attention on 'pressing problems', such as drug addiction and AIDS. Ishak Baharom was also informed that his contract would not be renewed when it expired at the end of October. As a result, Dr Mahathir came under intense fire in mosques across Malaysia, the clerics preaching that all the problems faced by Malaysia at the time—ranging from thick smoke haze from fires in Indonesia to a fall in the value of the ringgit—were due to the failure of his government to ensure the strict implementation of Islamic laws. Ishak Baharom told a mosque prayer gathering that Dr Mahathir had suffered an erosion of his faith, in effect calling him an apostate.

Anwar's implicit support for rigid Muslim practices is also seen in the depiction of the wearing of the tudung, the head-covering that leaves exposed only a woman's cheeks, nose, mouth and eyes, as an act of true faith which separates the Anwar and Mahathir camps. Siti Hasmah, Dr Mahathir's wife, who is a popular woman, and his daughter Marina seldom wear a head scarf and never the dour tudung. Marina Mahathir is the model of a progressive Malay Muslim woman. In a country where conservative values have obstructed discussion of anything related to sex, she has worked vigorously to make people aware of the spreading scourge of HIV in her role as chairman of the AIDS Council of Malaysia. In the column she writes for *The Star* newspaper she strongly attacked some religious clerics whom she accused of wanting women to be 'at home having babies endlessly and covered head to toe'. On the other hand, Anwar's wife Azizah and their two teenage daughters never appear in public with their heads bared. On no recorded occasion in recent years has Azizah foregone the formal face-encircling garment for a simple scarf. Yet, apart from her conservative appearance, she is a modern, accomplished woman who has practised as an ophthalmologist, raised six children and won a seat in Parliament.

A Malaysian political analyst said he believed Anwar used religion to further his interests. While presenting himself as a moderate to friends in the West, the former deputy prime minister capitalised on his early history as an Islamic radical to win the support of Muslim conservatives in his campaign to unseat Dr Mahathir. His acolytes have long portrayed him as a traditionalist, who wants to make Malaysia more Islamic, and today he is to young Muslim rebels what Che Guevara was to left-wing revolutionaries. He does nothing to counter this image and seems to be seeking to use the rise in Islamic radicalism to his advantage. His image-makers were so successful in portraying the family unit of Anwar, Azizah and their children as the epitome of Islamic piety that after his sacking most clerics unhesitatingly gave their support to him against the man whose faith they considered suspect. Azizah and the children have adjusted less easily than Anwar to the change in their lifestyle. Quiet, well-groomed and well-behaved, the children still bear the stamp of the good years as sons and daughters of a member of the hierarchy. Azizah wears the new mantle of anti-establishment opposition leader uncomfortably. However, Anwar returned to his radical roots as easily as he had fitted into the life of the powerful political elite.

While Anwar's seamless shift from Pak Sheikh to Datuk Seri (an honorary title which he is still given) showed that he was more opportunistic than idealistic, his aggressive efforts to reach the top ranks of UMNO demonstrated another strong trait—ambition. This was especially obvious in 1993 as he used his network of friends, skill as an orator and large cash payments to win enough support to secure the position of UMNO deputy president and replace veteran leader Ghafar Baba as deputy prime minister. For a man who claimed the high ground on moral terms, Anwar was not loath to take advantage of the avarice of his fellow members of UMNO. By the 1990s money politics was rife throughout UMNO, from the smallest branch and division up to the senior ranks of the party, and Anwar used the payment and patronage system to his advantage.

Dr Mahathir repeatedly called on party members to root out money politics, but to no avail. As campaigning for party positions intensified ahead of the 1996 elections, and in defiance of a supreme council ban, he complained that Kuala Lumpur hotels were full of people giving out money for votes and threatened to expose the offenders. Six low-ranking candidates were disqualified for vote-buying and other corrupt practices in the lead-up to the elections but UMNO officials with clean records said that Dr Mahathir needed to make an example of top-ranking people before anything would change.

While Anwar's followers—as witnessed by myself and other journalists—were handing out packets of money to acquire the support of UMNO division leaders in his 1993 campaign against Ghafar Baba, Anwar himself was winning over influential people in the party by promising positions in the administration he would form when he took over from Dr Mahathir. These people included his Vision Team candidates for the three UMNO vice presidential posts—Najib Tun Razak, who had not previously been an Anwar fan, Muhammad Muhammad Taib, and Muhyiddin Yassin. Najib was Defence Minister, and the two other vice presidential candidates were the chief ministers of Selangor and Johor respectively. Anwar also backed Rahim Thamby Chik, Chief Minister of Malacca, for the post of UMNO Youth chief. But Anwar concealed his ambitions for the UMNO post from Dr Mahathir until the middle of 1993. In June, before leaving for a visit to China, Dr Mahathir told reporters that Anwar had decided not to compete for the post of deputy president in the coming party elections. The Prime Minister also criticised people who 'insisted on securing nominations' at the divisional level for Anwar for deputy president. He said they were 'not working for Anwar' but he was wrong. They were not only working for Anwar but under his instructions. The number of divisions giving their nominations for deputy president to Anwar snowballed rapidly. The groundswell of support for him became an avalanche. By August, Dr Mahathir, ever the pragmatist, had changed his stand. He declared himself neutral in the contest for deputy president.

By October, a month before the elections, Anwar had an unbeatable lead. With nominations in from 153 of UMNO's 165 divisions, Anwar had 145 while Ghafar had only seven. (One division, from Dr Mahathir's electorate in Kedah, honoured his neutrality pledge.) Since each divisional nomination was worth ten bonus votes, Anwar had the election wrapped up. The 1800 delegates to the general assembly would normally be expected to vote in accordance with the preference of their divisions but even if there had been a leak of sympathy votes to Ghafar, the bonus votes made it impossible for him to defeat Anwar. On 15 October, Ghafar resigned from the government and announced that he would not defend his position as deputy president of UMNO.

Anwar's defeat of Ghafar was a watershed in more ways than one. It made Anwar the second most powerful man in the country but it also established a group of enemies who would later provide formidable support for Dr Mahathir when he was challenged by his deputy. As well as Ghafar, these included Sanusi Junid, the Agriculture Minister, who became an even more bitter foe when he was dropped from cabinet by Dr Mahathir because of the bad feeling between him and Anwar. (Sanusi's chargrin over his dismissal from cabinet was later assuaged by his appointment as Chief Minister of Kedah.) Another Ghafar supporter was Abdullah Badawi, the Foreign Minister, who later succeeded Anwar as deputy prime minister and UMNO deputy president. Rafidah Aziz, the Minister of International Trade and Industry, had also been a Ghafar supporter. In the aftermath of the 1993 elections, Rafidah and Anwar made no secret of the growing enmity between them. She came under scrutiny when it was disclosed her son-in-law had received a large allotment of company shares under the scheme providing for a proportion of new issues to go to bumiputras. Rafidah, who was later cleared of wrongdoing, responded to her critics by releasing in parliament a six-page document naming relatives of other leading politicians who had received similar allocations. They included Dr Mahathir's son Mirzan and Anwar's brother Marzuki. Rafidah also said Anwar's Finance Ministry had allocated shares in six blue-chip companies to unnamed recipients. In 1995 Anwar told journalists she was 'unpopular in the party' and her support was slipping. But Rafidah held her portfolio in the new cabinet announced by Dr Mahathir following the April general election.

Following his triumphant progress to victory in 1993, Anwar made no effort either to patch up his damaged relations with followers of the vanquished camp or build on the ties he had established with his Vision Team. As a result, when later he needed friends in high places, he found he had none. Even before the UMNO general assembly met, the Vision Team, which was portrayed in the press as four men and Anwar on a rakit, or raft, was looking shaky. A source close to developments reported that about three weeks before the 1993 party elections, the word went out 'the rakit is broken'. It was every man for himself. Or almost. At the last moment, Anwar put his political weight and financial resources behind Vision Team member Muhyiddin for vice president. The Johor Chief Minister, who had been trailing other Vision Team member Najib in nominations for UMNO vice president, won the largest number of votes. This meant that he was effectively the third-ranking leader after the president and deputy president and would be in a strong position to become Anwar's deputy when, as was expected, Anwar succeeded Dr Mahathir. Anwar had never developed a comfortable relationship with Najib, whose pedigree as the son of a former prime minister and member of the Malay aristocracy set him apart from the one-time anti-establishment rebel. They were cut from different batik. Najib was also too self-assured to play a pliable secondary role under Anwar's leadership. Additionally, if Najib held the key number three slot he could be a problem if he chose not to support an Anwar push to oust Dr Mahathir. So Anwar chose Muhyiddin as his de facto deputy without even the pretense of a placatory gesture towards Najib. This was to prove a costly oversight.

Anwar quickly distanced himself from the other two Vision Team members, Rahim and Muhammad Taib, when they had run-ins with the law and did not make up with them after they were cleared of impropriety. Rahim's alleged involvement with a 15-year-old girl, which he has strenuously denied and never been charged over, was first reported in *Utusan Malaysia*, the UMNO-owned newspaper, over which Anwar exerted a strong influence. Under pressure from Anwar and his media friends, Rahim resigned from his posts as party youth chief and Malacca chief minister and became a resolute foe of his former Vision Team leader. But Anwar was a man in a hurry. Almost immediately after assuming the number two posts in government and UMNO, Anwar was planning to shoulder aside Dr Mahathir with the same political machinery he had used against Ghafar and take over as party president and prime minister. Addressing the UMNO general assembly in November

1994, Dr Mahathir gave a clear signal to Anwar that he was under scrutiny, recalling the treachery of Brutus against Julius Caesar. Anwar declared his loyalty to the president but ignored the call for him to curb his ambition

In 1995, amid growing signs of politicking at divisional level by his supporters, Anwar again denied having any designs on the positions held by his mentor. Dr Mahathir publicly fostered the charade of a unified leadership while plotting counter-measures with his lieutenants. Politicians worldwide are frequently economical with the truth, but the UMNO hierarchy has always taken a delight in being as obscure as the story lines of the country's wayang kulit, or shadow plays. Put simply, both Dr Mahathir and Anwar concealed the truth about their relationship. Dr Mahathir played along with Anwar's protestations of loyalty, avoiding a showdown that he might lose. He had not yet changed his thinking that Anwar should succeed him; he merely wanted to keep his deputy in check until he was ready to step down. Anwar, for his part, did not want to alienate the public by seeming to be an ungrateful protégé until he had the UMNO votes he needed and was ready to face down the Prime Minister and demand his retirement. Anwar's team fed stories to the foreign media which were intended to show that Dr Mahathir was on the ropes, while insisting that the Deputy Prime Minister would not force his mentor from office. They suggested Dr Mahathir would soon step aside so that his deputy could take over. The overseas news reports caused Mohamed Rahmat, UMNO secretary-general, Information Minister and staunch Mahathir supporter, to urge Malaysians not to view the foreign media as an authority on Malaysian events, saying they made baseless allegations to create disunity in the country.

Anwar's easy victory over Ghafar had made him overconfident and his intentions were transparent. A senior UMNO official said he believed Anwar's tactic would be to secure nominations for his election as party president from more than 100 divisions and then invite Dr Mahathir to resign to avoid a destabilising contest. But in thinking he could sweep Dr Mahathir aside, Anwar surprisingly underestimated his adversary's prowess in the infighting of UMNO politics, which he had demonstrated repeatedly over three decades.

In the course of his efforts to seize the power that would eventually have been handed to him, Anwar showed a political naivety that not only kept him from his goal but led to his sacking, arrest and imprisonment.

Dr Mahathir was one move ahead of Anwar in the political manoeuvring that followed. First, he acted to placate senior party officials who wanted him to ensure there would be a smooth transition of power rather than a struggle between contenders for the top job as a result of his sudden death or illness. At the 1995 UMNO general assembly, Dr Mahathir said he would retire 'soon', reaffirmed that Anwar was his natural successor and added that he hoped the transition would 'not bring about disastrous repercussions to the party'. Anwar, in his address to the youth and women's wings of UMNO, declared that his loyalty to the president could not be questioned and said that anyone who put him forward as a candidate for the party leadership would be wasting their time. But Dr Mahathir and his supporters were unconvinced of his fealty and persuaded the general assembly to resolve that there should be no contests in 1996 for the positions of president and deputy president. Anwar's people had to go along with the resolution or appear to be out of step with the national interest.

Rumours were soon spreading that the general assembly's decision was unconstitutional and Anwar's challenge would go ahead. In April, Dr Mahathir and his supporters succeeded in getting the UMNO supreme council to pronounce that anyone planning to run for a party post must register as a candidate. It ruled that only registered candidates could be nominated for election at the forthcoming October general assembly. This meant that Anwar would have to register as a candidate for president in order for divisions to give him their nominations. But such an open move could backfire against him since he had repeatedly denied any intention of running against Dr Mahathir. Speculation then mounted that the Anwar camp was planning a blitz of division nominations for their man to embarrass Dr Mahathir and force his retirement. In May, Mahathir's team, under UMNO secretary-general Mohamed Rahmat, came up with a third counter-move. The supreme council decreed that only Dr Mahathir could be nominated for president and only Anwar for deputy president. Anwar was now firmly blocked from an assault on the presidency in 1996.

Before this skirmishing was under way, Anwar's supporters had attempted to show that Dr Mahathir was losing his control of the party, it blocked the appointment of Sanusi as Chief Minister of Kedah. When the plan failed, Dr Mahathir ordered an investigation into the circumstances and found evidence of a link to the Anwar camp. Salamon Selamat, Anwar's political secretary and chief activist, suddenly resigned from his position in what some political analysts saw as a case of the retainer falling on his sword to absolve the master from blame and retribution. (Two years later, in similar fashion, Anwar would sacrifice another ally, Zahid Hamidi, whom he persuaded to lead a new assault to seize the prize that he could not wait to be given.) Anwar humbled himself with another submissive pledge of loyalty to Dr Mahathir and, in a speech from his political base in Penang, called for party unity and an end to the politics of playing off one leader against another—as if it were some third party and not him who was behind the efforts to undermine the Prime Minister. His speech, in which he pledged the state's full support for the continued leadership of Dr Mahathir, signalled his recognition of his newly weakened position. It marked the end of his first putsch—but with his abasement, which many of his followers found acutely embarrassing, he lived to fight another day. For Anwar, self-preservation was more important than loss of face.

Dr Mahathir added salt to the Anwar camp's wounds by announcing that he might seek a further term by standing in the 1999 party election. In early May 1996, he had announced that Tengku Razaleigh Hamzah, who had mounted an unsuccessful challenge against Dr Mahathir in 1987, was returning to UMNO after nine years in opposition as head of his small Semangat 46 party. This prompted speculation that the former UMNO heavyweight might replace Anwar as Dr Mahathir's deputy. In typical Mahathir fashion, the Prime Minister used a press conference to air the speculation while ostensibly quashing it. He said there had been suggestions that he wanted Tengku Razaleigh back in UMNO to balance Anwar's influence and 'undermine and subvert' him. Dr Mahathir said he wished to state categorically that such suggestions were not true.

He said his relationship with Anwar was 'very good', in fact, it was 'the best'. But the Anwar camp saw the press conference as a clear warning. If the Deputy Prime Minister behaved himself, he could expect, eventually, to succeed Dr Mahathir. Otherwise, the Prime Minister would install Tengku Razaleigh or someone else as his heir. Having shown that he was the political master and Anwar a mere apprentice, Dr Mahathir apparently believed that his deputy had learned his lesson and there was no reason to punish him for his impatience. He also thought it was important to create an appearance of unity in the party and reassure senior officials that the smooth transition he had promised would still take place. Besides, he remained convinced at that time that Anwar was the most suitable person to take over the leadership.

In many ways, 1996 was a triumphant year for Dr Mahathir. As he presided over UMNO's 50th anniversary celebrations, the economy was continuing to show the strength that had produced a decade-long boom and optimism was high. In November, Dr Mahathir was automatically re-elected UMNO president and Anwar had to be content with his reaffirmation as deputy president. Mahathir's Malaysia had the appearance of a nation that was both politically and economically stable. Nevertheless, the 1996 UMNO election results were a warning to the Mahathir loyalists that while Anwar had been defeated in his first challenge to the Prime Minister, he was building a power base in preparation for a later assault on the presidency. They could take comfort from the fact that Abdullah Badawi had regained one of the three vice presidential posts by getting more votes than Muhyiddin Yassin, but the Anwar camp more than made up for this setback by placing their people as heads of UMNO Youth and Wanita UMNO, the women's wing of the party. The defeat of Rafidah Aziz by Siti Zahara Sulaiman in a bitterly fought battle shocked Dr Mahathir supporters, but the more significant result, because of the events that would follow, was the election of Zahid Hamidi, as chief of the youth wing of UMNO.

The stage was set for the next clash between the aging ruler and the young pretender to his throne. Their first engagement was more like a game of chess than a battle for power, with no display of open hostility by either side. The second stripped away the façade of friendliness, exposing a raw animosity between the two men. It was a savage struggle, which racked Malaysians emotionally, shattering their complacency and leaving them fractured and uncertain of their destiny.

2 | Battle lines drawn

The financial crisis that began in Thailand in 1997 and spread throughout South-East Asia provided Anwar with the opportunity for a new attempt to unseat Dr Mahathir and become the nation's leader. At the beginning of the year he acted the dutiful number two. But he continued to expand his power base, using his Islamic credentials to establish a core of supporters whose religious conservatism was closer to PAS than the pragmatic Dr Mahathir and his followers. Nazri Aziz, a UMNO supreme council member and former Anwar supporter who was now in the Mahathir camp, said he was concerned that those who were using Islam as their platform were also trying to 'undermine their opponents as being less Islamic'. The chief proponents of the new Islamism were the man and woman he had successfully placed as heads of UMNO Youth and Wanita UMNO. UMNO youth chief Zahid Hamidi was the most vocal champion of the conservative Islamic cause. Rejecting criticism that he and others were using religion to win followers for their faction, he said the emphasis on religion was the wish of members of the party who had 'chosen leaders whom they believed had the [correct] Islamic background'. Anwar among them, presumably.

As the year progressed, Anwar began, in statements and speeches, to underline differences between him and Dr Mahathir, with the apparent intention of presenting himself as the best person to lead Malaysia in a changing world demanding new ideas and policies. In an interview with *Newsweek* in August he said people of his generation 'would like to see greater liberty, access to literature and knowledge, less censorship'. They did not have 'an obsession about the need for order and political stability'. Anwar paid tribute to Dr Mahathir while emphasising the gap between them. Referring to the Prime Minister's criticism of the West, he said: 'It's not actually new but the manner and style of how he puts it provokes debate. That is his strength. If you speak in a nice conciliatory manner like I do in *The Asian Renaissance*, it doesn't provoke that much of a debate. When he does this in such a provocative and combative style, then immediately people listen.' The remarks could be seen as a humorous, approving appraisal of his mentor, but within months Anwar would be setting in motion a major effort to undermine Dr Mahathir's standing and force him to step aside.

In the same interview, he expanded on the point he had made in an article written for *Newsweek* a month before that ASEAN must 'move from being a largely reactive organisation to being a proactive one'. He said it was unfortunate that some people suggested his position in the article was consistent with the US view and insisted he was advancing it as 'an ASEAN position, as ASEAN leadership', adding: 'It is horrifying to learn that every time you talk about justice and order and civil society and democracy you have to be articulating on other people's behalf. Why can't notions like justice and liberty and humanitarian concern be an ASEAN position?'

He failed to elicit a sympathic response from Dr Mahathir who, speaking ahead of the organisation's ministerial meeting, rejected the notion of a more proactive ASEAN. However, in the early part of 1997, Dr Mahathir was preoccupied with other matters, such as promoting the Multimedia Super Corridor (MSC) and preparing to host both the ASEAN foreign ministers' meeting and the heads of government summit. In particular, Dr Mahathir wanted 1997, the 30th year of the organisation's existence, to be the year in which it became the ASEAN 10, including all the governments of the region.

With the UMNO elections out of the way and a national poll not due for another two years, Dr Mahathir decided it was a suitable time to take a two-month break overseas, 'do some writing' and talk to foreign leaders and corporate figures about the MSC. Dr Mahathir was so confident of his support in UMNO and Anwar's acceptance of the status quo that when he headed overseas on 19 May, he left his deputy in charge as acting Prime Minister. It was the first time the Deputy Prime Minister had been given this title in Dr Mahathir's absence abroad. Asked at a press conference ten days before he left if this were to test whether Anwar was capable of succeeding him, Dr Mahathir replied jokingly: 'Yes, he has to sit for an examination. When I come back, I will make him sit down and answer questions. I will then mark the paper.' Then in more serious vein he said Anwar had his 'full trust'. A little more than a year later, Dr Mahathir had radically changed his opinion of his deputy.

The two months in which Dr Mahathir was away passed quietly in Malaysia apart from the Selangor state beauty pageant incident over which Anwar kept a low profile. But it was a time that saw the beginning of the end of Malaysia's boom years. While the Prime Minister was overseas, Thailand's baht plunged in value as investors lost confidence in the country's economy. The currencies of its neighbours also dived, share prices fell in concert and the region was thrown into economic turmoil.

The period in 1997 leading up to the collapse of regional currencies and stock markets proved to have been the economic zenith of Mahathir's Malaysia. For many Malaysian tycoons, it was the peak of their prosperity. In May, the *New Straits Times* listed eleven Malaysian owners of corporate jets, whose high-flying lifestyles pointed up the wealth generated (at least at the top) by a decade of economic expansion. They included Tajudin Ramli, chairman and controlling shareholder of Malaysia Airlines (MAS); Halim Saad, chief of the Renong Group; Ting Pek Khiing, chairman of Ekran Berhad; Ananda Krishnan, the man who gave Malaysia the world's tallest buildings and its satellite capability; Vincent Tan, head of the Berjaya Group; and Daim Zainuddin, government economic adviser, former finance minister and one of Malaysia's richest businessmen. They were all kingpins of Malaysia Inc. and good friends of Dr Mahathir. With other leading business figures, they embodied a controversial cosiness between a segment of the corporate sector and the government. This relationship, as well as questions about some Malaysian business practices and the nation's spending on multibillion ringgit 'mega-projects', were among reasons given by foreign fund managers for their withdrawal from Malaysia as the economic shock waves spread across South-East Asia.

The regional economic crisis brought many of the jet fliers down to earth. Ting was one of the first of the top tycoons to suffer from the sudden change in the financial climate. His company, Ekran, had been chosen as developer of the controversial Bakun dam hydro-electric project in Sarawak state on Borneo island. The scheme involved flooding an area the size of Singapore and laying the world's longest undersea power cables across the South China Sea from Borneo to Peninsular Malaysia. It also called for the destruction of 69 000 hectares of forest and the displacement of about 10 000 members of indigenous tribes. The project was attacked by environmentalists for its devastating impact on these people and the local flora and fauna. It was also questioned by power generation experts on the grounds of cost and practicality. In June 1996, the High Court upheld a suit by people from the area that it contravened environmental laws, but the ruling was quashed by the Appeal Court. In late 1997, Ekran terminated a contract with a consortium led by Swiss-based Asea Brown Boveri and the Finance Ministry took over the project, paying Ting's company a multimillion ringgit package in compensation. But with the economic outlook looking grim, the Bakun dam scheme was temporarily shelved.

Tajudin and Halim were both close to Daim, a lawyer who became a successful businessman and established himself as Dr Mahathir's most trusted adviser. In 1979, Daim took the position of chairman of Peremba, a company he helped set up to manage the property and commercial assets of the Urban Development Authority. The staff he hired for Peremba and a number of other young Malaysians whom be befriended became known as 'Daim's boys'. Virtually all of them eventually earned the right to be called tycoons, and provided Malays role models in their bid to match Chinese corporate wealth. Among them was Wan Azmi Hamzah, whom Daim appointed general manager of Peremba. Wan Azmi went on to become chairman of Land and General, a leading diversified corporation. Two other top recruits were Halim Saad and Samsudin Abu Hassan. Samsudin escaped the financial bruising of the economic crisis by serendipitously falling out with influential members of the establishment and taking off to South Africa, where he made large and profitable investments. Tajudin did not work for Peremba but nevertheless became part of the Daim circle.

Halim Saad built up Renong, a diversified group and flagship of Malaysia Inc., from a core of companies formerly owned by UMNO. He was a major beneficiary of the government's privatisation programme. But Renong was one of the first business empires to stagger under the shock of the regional economic crisis and almost sank under a debt burden of M$8 billion. The internal juggling undertaken to save the group from a disaster that would have shaken the nation's financial system attracted strong criticism at home and abroad. That included the purchase of a large block of Renong shares by a group company, United Engineers (Malaysia), in July as the stock market fell. The acquisition made matters worse by provoking angry investors in Renong to dump their shares. At the end of 1998 a rescue plan was worked out for the debt-ridden corporation under which Renong's wholly owned subsidiary, Projek Lebuhraya Utara Selatan (PLUS), a cash-spinning toll-road operator, would raise M$8.41 billion from 50 local financial institutions by issuing zero-coupon seven-year bonds with an annual interest of 10 per cent. PLUS would lend M$5.45 billion to Renong and the rest to UEM as funds to settle creditors' claims. An analyst quoted by *The Star* newspaper commented: 'The cash cow is being milked by the group. Without PLUS Renong would have collapsed.' The arrangement was endorsed by the Corporate Debt Restructuring Committee set up by the government under Bank Negara, the central bank, to help companies hit by the economic crisis. Officials were at pains to show that the Renong restructuring did not involve official funding but they could not dispel perceptions that Halim had received special consideration. It was not the end of the story as more restructuring of UEM was required in 2001.

In 1994, Tajudin Ramli was given the nod to buy a controlling 29 per cent stake in MAS from Bank Negara through his company Naluri. By 1998 Naluri and MAS were in trouble. The debts of MAS ballooned to M$2 billion. For the 12 months ended 31 March 2000, its third year without a profit, the airline reported a net loss of M$700 million. Nine months later, the government bought back Naluri's stake, paying M$8 a share, the same price at which Tajudin had acquired the airline. The market price of an MAS share was M$3.69 when Tajudin sold his interest. The sale, which provided Naluri with funds to dispose of debts amounting to M$1 billion, drew some of the strongest criticism the government faced over the perceived rescue of the failed businesses of favoured sons. Daim, then Finance Minister, said the deal was 'not a bail-out' but it was questioned even within UMNO.

Rescues or bail-outs involving well-connected business figures were a feature of the Malaysian corporate scene in 1997 and 1998 as the economy worsened. In 1998, the deal that attracted the most adverse reaction from foreign financial analysts was the acquisition of the entire shipping business and assets of Konsortium Perkapalan Berhad (KPB) by Malaysia International Shipping Corporation (MISC), a company in which Petroliam Nasional Berhad (Petronas)—the abundantly cash-endowed national oil corporation—had a 29 per cent stake. MISC financed the purchase by issuing shares to Petronas, which then had a holding of more than 51 per cent in the shipping company. KPB had been 51 per cent owned by Mirzan Mahathir, the eldest son of Dr Mahathir, whose prime ministerial office has direct control over Petronas. Mirzan's company had seen its share price tumble from M$16 in 1996 to M$1.17 at the beginning of 1998. It was reported in the press to have debts of well over M$1 billion. Mirzan and Petronas chairman Mohamad Hassan Marican denied that the deal was a bail-out for KPB, with Hassan saying: 'One has to put the personality issue aside. It's an arms-length deal, which will enhance the value of MISC.' Defenders of the deal pointed out that foreign valuers were brought in to ensure transparency and that the price paid Mirzan was at the low end of the range of valuations.

Throughout the period of economic crisis, Dr Mahathir dismissed foreign criticism of such agreements that appeared to be bail-outs of favoured companies, saying the government could not let key corporations fail. He argued that failing companies had to be supported so they could prosper and pay taxes, and that foreigners wanted Malaysian companies to collapse so they could take them over. Responding to foreign analysts' complaints about Malaysian business practices, Dr Mahathir pointed out, with some validity, that fund managers and multinational corporations had invested vast sums of money in Malaysia before the regional crisis even though the same risk factors had then applied.

But times had changed and fund managers had taken a new look at the risk factors and found them suddenly unacceptable. And while Malaysia did not have the debt problems of Thailand or Indonesia, it was a victim of the regional thinking of the funds' controllers in the United States and Europe. Whereas their representatives in the field distinguished between the weak economies of Thailand and Indonesia and those in a better position to cope with the turbulence—like Malaysia—head office management saw a single region in which a fire was raging. Even Singapore, with its political stability and economic rectitude, was affected by the new perception of foreign investors.

In mid-1997, Thailand's economy attracted the attention of speculators because its growth was slowing amid signs of excessive expansion of loans to the property sector. Malaysia's central bank had taken measures to cool the Malaysian property market months earlier (causing a drop in property shares and the rest of the stock market as a result) but the ringgit soon came under attack together with the Philippine peso and Indonesian rupiah. Bank Negara, Malaysia's central bank, spent billions trying to defend the currency but finally let it float. The sinking ringgit proved disastrous for companies with offshore loans. The stock market decline reduced the worth of shares used as collateral and closed the door on executives trading their way out of the trouble they were in. By December 1997, the capitalisation of the Kuala Lumpur Stock Exchange had depreciated by 54 per cent. The market's Composite Index had fallen by 55 per cent from 1237.96 to 558.47. It had further to go, dropping below 300 before establishing a base from which it would eventually rise slowly.

It was a harrowing time for business and for the government. Dr Mahathir at first refused to concede the slightest fault on the part of Malaysia. He seized on George Soros, the Hungarian-born US financier, as a scapegoat, portraying him as the mastermind of a vast conspiracy of speculators determined to make billions at the expense of the countries and peoples of South-East Asia. Soros, who in 1992 had gained fame with his billion-dollar profit from speculating against sterling remaining in the European Exchange Rate mechanism, had publicly opposed Burma's admission to ASEAN because the ruling military junta was a 'totalitarian and repressive regime', which was a threat to the region's prosperity. Dr Mahathir accused him of taking revenge against Thailand and Malaysia for supporting Burma's entry in the organisation by driving down their currencies. Soros told the *New Straits Times*, Malaysia's leading English-language newspaper, that he would not dream of 'engaging in currency speculation for political purposes'. He also said that in mid-1997, his group had sold only US$10 million of Thai baht and had not traded any other regional currencies.

After Dr Mahathir attacked Soros at the ASEAN Ministerial Meeting in July, he was asked whether he considered the American a criminal. His response was that as much as people who produced and distributed drugs were criminals because they destroyed nations, so were people who undermined the economies of poor countries. In a commentary on the economy, published in *The Star* newspaper in September, Mohamed Ariff, executive director of the Malaysian Institute of Economic Research, said new realities called for 'vigilance and pragmatic policies, not rhetoric'. In a clear reference to Dr Mahathir's singling out of Soros as the malefactor, he stated: 'The fact remains that no single person can rock the boat so badly, unless there are enough speculators to follow suit.'

Unfortunately for Dr Mahathir, his perceived obsession with Soros obscured some telling points he also made about the regional economic crisis, the dangers of globalisation to developing countries, and the policies of the International Monetary Fund (IMF). In an interview with the *South China Morning Post* during a visit to Hong Kong, Dr Mahathir noted that while the intentions of the IMF were good, its methods were 'quite often not very helpful'. A year later, many people in South-East Asia were making similar comments about the IMF. But for the present the international and domestic scorn that poured on the Prime Minister for his wild attacks on Soros and his financial fumbles was a boon to Anwar and his supporters in their push for power. Publicly Anwar continued to speak supportively of the Prime Minister, declaring that his bold style had grabbed the attention of the world. But there was often an element of subtle censure in his remarks. In October, he said: 'If the Prime Minister were to take a soft approach and was too diplomatic, the impact would not be felt. Instead the financial community was jolted by his strong words, which angered some.' There was an underlying implication that Anwar would not have angered people whom Malaysia should probably be encouraging to re-invest in the country.

At the same time, members of the Anwar camp were privately belittling Dr Mahathir and saying it was time he was replaced, echoing the calls of some foreign commentators for the Prime Minister to step down. They accused him of damaging Malaysia's image, as well as his own, and of driving the stock market down with his remarks. Dr Mahathir's followers organised a campaign to rally the nation behind the Prime Minister, calling on people to unite to show their disdain for his foreign antagonists and their domestic lackeys. Cars throughout the country sported stickers proclaiming, 'We support Dr Mahathir'. Rumours spread that the Education Minister and UMNO vice president, Najib Tun Razak, and Tengku Razaleigh Hamzah were being considered as candidates to replace Anwar as Dr Mahathir's successor in another apparent attempt to scare the Deputy Prime Minister and his supporters.

More ominous for Anwar was the dissemination of what Malaysians call a surat terbang—literally 'flying letter', the Malaysian equivalent of a poison-pen epistle—accusing him of both heterosexual and homosexual affairs. But, like every other UMNO leader, he had been the target of a host of allegations in the past and the latest charges did not immediately appear to represent a danger to his political career. Dr Mahathir said at a press conference that the letter, which was addressed to him, was 'absurd' and an attempt to paint Anwar black to prevent his succession. A year later the allegations were no longer absurd but a reason for the Prime Minister to sack Anwar. After the letter was sent to the Prime Minister, in August, 1997, Anwar asked officers of the Special Branch to 'put a little fear' into the two people responsible for the letter and another document—Ummi Hafilda Ali, the sister of his private secretary, and Azizon Abu Bakar, a driver. His action, which led to the officers obtaining retractions of the allegations, provided the basis for five charges of corrupt practices brought against him in September 1998.

For a time, Dr Mahathir went along with the economic proposals of Bank Negara and Anwar's Finance Ministry, which included a tightmoney strategy. Their policies did not stop the rapid slowdown in the economy but Anwar's pronouncements found favour with the outside world and encouraged everyone to believe that he was steering the nation onto a responsible financial course. On 5 December, Anwar announced 'further strategic but painful measures', including a cutback in government spending and the postponement of a number of 'mega-projects'. He declared that corporate or individual borrowers 'should not be put on life support' if their loans were no longer viable. An approving editorial in Singapore's *Business Times* said Anwar's statement was 'exactly what investors needed to hear'. *Business Times'* sister publication, *The Straits Times*, said Anwar's measures were 'textbook-IMF', highlighting the direction Anwar and Bank Negara wanted to take despite Dr Mahathir's strong reservations.

Differences soon surfaced over how the cutbacks and shelving of mega-projects would be implemented. On a visit to the resort island of Langkawi, less than a week after Anwar's announcement, Dr Mahathir declared that a M$10 billion 'land-bridge', comprising a road, railway and gas pipeline, between Malaysia and Thailand would go ahead. Anwar told journalists he had called Dr Mahathir and obtained a 'clarification' that only the pipeline was still planned. During the period from the end of 1997 into the early part of 1998,

Anwar was relaxed and confident, saying privately to members of the media that they should listen to what he said rather than what the Prime Minister was saying. As public anxiety grew over the worsening state of the economy, people were looking for someone to blame. This provided opportunities for enemies of Dr Mahathir, who seemed less sure of himself and did not look well. Developments had clearly affected his health. But bolstered by close associates, especially chief confidant Daim, he gradually regained confidence and began to look for ways of reversing the economic decline that would reflect his personal views on the need to keep interest rates down and prevent the collapse of core businesses.

In his 60-page booklet *The Malaysian Currency Crisis*, published in August 2000, Dr Mahathir looked back at the battle he had with Anwar and the central bank over economic policy. As the financial crisis continued, he wrote, it 'became apparent that the Minister of Finance [Anwar], aided by the central bank was implementing policies which were making a bad situation worse'. They 'implemented a number of measures beginning in October, 1997, which appeared to reflect the views of the IMF', and the effect, according to Dr Mahathir, was that banks and businesses that were already suffering from the currency crisis were 'pushed into a situation of dire distress'. The Minister of Finance and the central bank, he said, had implemented a 'virtual IMF without the IMF loans', and as a result of these standard IMF prescriptions, Malaysia's economy plunged deeper into recession.

Dr Mahathir also caustically noted that 'everyone' was 'gleefully predicting' that the time was near for Malaysia to go to the IMF for help and to surrender economic control to it. It was felt that Malaysia had 'no choice but to open up its economy to foreigners without conditions' and then there would be 'rich pickings for foreign capitalists, including those who had invested in the hedge funds'. This latter remark suggests what was on the Prime Minister's mind throughout the crisis and explains his stubborn determination to find a different policy approach.

Dr Mahathir also acknowledged that he personally was under threat because of public worries over the country's financial future. He wrote that 'the 'recalcitrance' of the Malaysian leader (in possibly a wry recollection of former Australian prime minister Paul Keating's description of him) was also now coming under criticism by a segment of the local population, who 'wanted the leader to bow out and give the reins to his deputy'. Anwar's supporters, he claimed, accused the government, and by implication the Prime Minister, of cronyism, nepotism and corruption. 'The message for the Prime Minister was clear. The economy would not recover unless he stepped down and handed the reins of the government to his deputy. However, the Prime Minister did not seem to get the message.'

In his address to the nation on the eve of the new year of 1998, Dr Mahathir warned Malaysians that they would have to make sacrifices to defend the country's 'independence and dignity'. He said Malaysia would not borrow money from international institutions because they would force the government to increase taxes on an already impoverished people, increase lending rates and close down most of the banks and finance companies. Foreign conglomerates would take over Malaysian banks and businesses, and Malaysians would 'no longer be free'.

While Dr Mahathir was calling on Malaysians to stand united against growing pressure for the government to seek help from the IMF, *Berita Harian*, a leading Malay-language daily, was advancing an opposing argument—that Malaysia should bow to the inevitable and accept assistance from abroad. This was the Anwar doctrine, which other sections of the media were also promoting. In response Dr Mahathir set out to remove editors controlled by or sympathetic to Anwar. It took some time because he was not then ready to confront his deputy directly and had to move cautiously to avoid further spooking the markets. The principal Malaysian newspapers are directly owned by government parties or in thrall to the authorities by virtue of their publishing licences, which can be withdrawn without notice. The media conforms closely to parameters set by the government. Senior executives of the Malay-language newspapers meet regularly with top officials of UMNO for briefings. Anwar took advantage of his position as deputy prime minister and finance minister to develop close links with top people in the print and electronic media. One of those was Nazri Abdullah, group editor of *Berita Harian*.

Nazri's support for Anwar became increasingly obvious during the economic crisis. In his Sunday column, 'Komentar', he crossed pens with the *New Straits Times'* A. Kadir Jasin, who used his weekly half-page of commentary, 'Other Thots' (sic), to defend Dr Mahathir. The *Berita Harian* editor's most trenchant criticism of Dr Mahathir appeared in 'Komentar' on 7 December 1997, when he wrote of a 'crisis of confidence' in the country and said investors and the IMF were puzzled by conflicting statements made by the country's leadership. He said that 'even before the saliva had dried up' following the government's vow that all mega-projects would be deferred, 'we announce the [Malaysia–Thailand] land-bridge worth billions of ringgit', unnerving both Malaysian and foreign investors. Nazri continued that in a crisis it was important to speak with one voice. It was also better to show humility. People viewed the government's decision to cut spending with uncertainty, he said, because there were leaders who liked to make announcements on projects costing billions. Malaysia needed to restore confidence in the economy and would lose nothing if it gave in temporarily to restore its strength and energy. He stated in a bold—for Malaysia—reproach to the nation's leader: 'We cannot afford to go to war with anyone but ourselves. If we have a tendency to talk too much, then we should talk less so that people are not hurt by what we say. We only possess a gun without bullets, so why should we fire at the wind?'

Kadir responded to Nazri's column with an attack on 'attempts by some unscrupulous elements to blame the government' for the economic problems and 'drive a wedge between the country's top leaders'. He said that despite the fact that Dr Mahathir was condemned by 'the foreign media and their cohorts from the East and West' for his outspokenness and for being unconventional, he remained 'the country's most versatile and visionary Prime Minister'. At a meeting of the UMNO supreme council in January, Dr Mahathir, too, expressed his displeasure with the tone of commentaries in *Berita Harian*. The supreme council decided that Nazri should step down, but he managed to hold onto his job for another six months with the help of Anwar.

January was a grim month for the ringgit and other Asian currencies, which were pulled down by the free-falling Indonesian rupiah. In two days the ringgit slid from 4.05 against the US dollar to 4.62. Rumours proliferated, including one, following a visit by Dr Mahathir's businessman son Mokhzani to a hospital which he part-owned, that he had committed suicide due to a business failure. At a subsequent press conference, Dr Mahathir responded: 'Now there is a new rumour circulating that my son has committed suicide. I do not understand why people listen to such stories.'

Malaysians worried about the health of domestic banks shifted their money to foreign banks with offices in Malaysia. New accounts increased sharply at Citibank, Hongkong Bank, Standard Chartered Bank and Singapore-owned OCBC Bank. Many people transferred their savings to banks in Singapore and Hong Kong. An estimated total of more than M$20 billion was siphoned from local financial institutions in the three months ending 31 December 1997. Government pleas for Malaysians to be patriotic and keep their money in Malaysian banks went unheeded. Malaysia was markedly less afflicted by the regional economic crisis than Thailand and Indonesia. However, the paper wealth of the country had been halved, some companies, mainly in the service industries, were shedding staff, civil servants faced restrictions on overseas travel and bonus payments to workers were on hold. At the same time, because of a widespread fear that the situation would become worse, Dr Mahathir remained under pressure to treat the nation's economic sickness with medicine prescribed by the IMF rather than his home-made remedies.

On 18 January, Indonesia's President Suharto pledged sweeping economic reforms, including the removal of subsidies, the termination of business privileges enjoyed by members of his family, and the scrapping of costly projects, to secure aid from the IMF. The photograph of the Indonesian leader signing a letter of intent with Michel Camdessus, IMF managing director, gazing down upon him with an imperious mien became a symbol of Western oppression—Dr Mahathir's neo-colonialism—to South-East Asia's reform-minded younger generation. Ironically, in Malaysia the 'reformasi' cry originating with protesting Indonesian students was taken up by

Anwar, champion of the IMF, and his followers. Their target was a leader who, unlike Suharto, stood firm against the nefarious instrument of the West.

The picture appeared on the front page of the *New Straits Times* on 16 January. On page two, another photograph showed Camdessus, who flew from Jakarta to Kuala Lumpur after the signing ceremony, receiving an embrace from Anwar. In return, the IMF chief praised the measures that were announced by Anwar on 5 December, describing them as 'quite important and welcomed'. At a press conference with Camdessus, Anwar said Malaysia had always taken the opportunity 'to have adequate consultation and take the views of the IMF and explain our position'. Camdessus, for his part, advised that Malaysia needed to continue such 'preemptive steps' as those announced by Anwar. He recommended Malaysia consider raising interest rates because of the country's rapid credit growth and the international pressure resulting from the depreciating ringgit—a proposal running counter to Dr Mahathir's viewpoint. A month later, Anwar won another strong endorsement from Camdessus when he announced new measures to reduce credit and monetary growth. The IMF head said Anwar's package took 'a welcome comprehensive approach'.

But Dr Mahathir had already taken steps to reduce Anwar's influence. On 20 January, the government announced the establishment of a National Economic Action Council (NEAC) 'as a consultative body to the Cabinet in its efforts to deal with economic problems'. The NEAC comprised Dr Mahathir as chairman, Anwar as deputy chairman, and 22 other members. They included nine ministers, the government's chief secretary, and Tajudin Ramli, the MAS chairman, in his capacity as president of the National Chamber of Commerce and Industries Malaysia, as well as other businessmen, bankers, brokers, employers and trade union representatives. The membership was heavily weighted with friends of Dr Mahathir, but more significantly the key job of executive director was given to Daim Zainuddin.

Daim had developed his close relationship with Dr Mahathir while he was establishing himself as a highly successful businessman in the 1970s. In 1982 Dr Mahathir, who had become Prime Minister the previous year, persuaded Daim to stand for parliament in a constituency in Kedah, the home state of both men. Daim won the seat and in 1984, Dr Mahathir appointed him Finance Minister. The mid-1980s was the occasion of an earlier economic crisis for Malaysia and Daim is credited with playing a major role in pulling the country out of that recession. He had always been a reluctant minister and left government to concentrate on his business activities in 1991 (to be replaced as finance minister by Anwar), but he continued to be economic adviser to the government and treasurer of UMNO. Now Daim was roped in to help out in another economic emergency—and serve as a counterweight to Anwar and Bank Negara on the formulation of policy.

Seven days after the announcement of the NEAC, 27 January, Anwar was still pledging that the tight monetary policy would continue despite pressures for it to be reversed. He declared: 'There is no question of any reversal or change . . . We are fully committed.' But he was fighting a lost battle.

3 | Tensions rise between 'best of friends'

Two days after Anwar's promise to continue tight monetary policy Dr Mahathir delivered a speech to mark the end of the Muslim fasting month of Ramadan. He again called for patience and sacrifice from Malaysians to 'save the country from being colonised again'.

> We have seen how people in other countries who had to bow to international aid agencies are suffering. Their workers are unemployed, their companies and banks have closed, prices of goods have escalated, there are supply shortages and people have had to put up with other hardships. If we do not want these things to happen to us, then we should avoid putting the interests of self, race and associations above national unity.

But the economic downturn after years of growth caused an uneasiness among Malaysians which Anwar would later seek to exploit.

On the political front, Dr Mahathir brought in Tengku Razaleigh Hamzah from the cold, giving him his first appointment since he ceased trying to make his party, Semangat 46 (the Spirit of 1946, the year UMNO was founded), a credible alternative for Malays and rejoined UMNO. Tengku Razaleigh, uncle of the Sultan of

Kelantan, was Finance Minister before Daim and an UMNO vice president. He twice challenged Musa Hitam, in 1981 and 1984, for the position of UMNO deputy president and lost. In 1987 he challenged Dr Mahathir for the top post and Musa joined the bid to topple the Prime Minister as Tengku Razaleigh's running mate. Dr Mahathir survived by a mere 43 votes out of 1479 cast. Ghafar Baba defeated Musa for the post of deputy president.

Tengku Razaleigh's supporters launched a court action challenging the election outcome, which led to UMNO being declared illegal. Dr Mahathir and his followers had to register a new UMNO. It was a time of great stress for Dr Mahathir, who suffered a heart attack in January 1989, and had to undergo coronary by-pass surgery. But in 1996, Dr Mahathir and Tengku Razaleigh came to an agreement under which the prince and most members of his Semangat 46 were taken back into UMNO. In January 1998, Dr Mahathir appointed Tengku Razaleigh chief of an UMNO division in Kelantan state. The appointment was relatively minor but it provided an opportunity for Tengku Razaleigh to re-establish himself as a leading UMNO figure with the task of helping the party regain control of Kelantan from Parti Islam se-Malaysia (PAS), his one-time opposition ally. Dr Mahathir clearly saw Tengku Razaleigh as an important asset in the fight against PAS, but by giving the Kelantan prince a significant party role again he secured his political allegiance against any challenge from Anwar, who, for his part, would have to wonder whether his position as Number Two was under threat. Some months later, the return of another figure from the past—Ghafar Baba—who had every reason to want to get even with Anwar, worried the Deputy Prime Minister's followers even more than Tengku Razaleigh's come-back.

Throughout the early part of 1998, Dr Mahathir and Anwar acted publicly as the best of friends and as if in agreement on economic policy. But it became increasingly evident as the weeks passed that this was a charade. On 1 February, Anwar fired a test salvo in preparation for his planned campaign to force Dr Mahathir out of office, using ammunition that he had borrowed from the Indonesian student movement—allegations of corruption, cronyism and nepotism. In carefully phrased remarks, which did not directly target Dr Mahathir but made clear Anwar's own position, he set the stage for the battle ahead. he expressed support for calls by the IMF and World Bank for East Asian countries to resolve to combat corruption, cronyism, nepotism and excesses of power; and to show they believed in the principles of democracy and 'inculcate the spirit of a free civil society'. Anwar delivered a token rebuke to the Western detractors, but acknowledged faults in the Eastern system and by extension Malaysia. It was totally unacceptable, he said, speaking at his post-Ramadan Hari Raya open house in Penang, for Western powers to intimate that corruption, nepotism and excesses of power were the exclusive domain of the East and developing economies: 'The fact is these excesses are to be found both in the West and the East and there should, therefore, be a common global resolve for good governance irrespective whether it is in the East or the West.'

It was a remarkably open commitment by the Malaysian Finance Minister to do what the West and IMF wanted in direct contradiction to the position of his Prime Minister. The media treated his comments cautiously but three days later, when Anwar boldly expanded on his theme before a larger audience, his remarks were reported on the front pages of the establishment press. Addressing the Third Regional Ethics in Leadership Conference, Anwar said the current economic problems would prompt countries in the region to re-evaluate the position of ethics in every level of their social and government system. He said the source of the present 'malaise of turbulence' was partly ethical, since the uncontrolled attempt to generate wealth and profit had overshadowed moral and ethical considerations. Referring to shortcomings in the region's economic development, Anwar noted that the most damage had been caused by 'excesses, corruption, nepotism and cronyism'. The region's problems, he suggested, should be overcome with reforms and greater transparency in the government and business sectors, and it was fortunate that the economic crisis had forced many countries to undertake reforms. In some countries, he warned, changes such as the dismantling of 'flawed social and political systems' could only be achieved through a revolution.

Did Anwar at this early stage anticipate that he might lose his job and have to resort to 'revolution' to oust Dr Mahathir? In retrospect it sounds like a portent of the street violence that erupted between Anwar's followers and police after his arrest. But he could not have foreshadowed the startling end to his role in government and UMNO and was probably thinking in terms of a bloodless revolution within the party.

The conflict between the two leaders became openly obvious on 10 February, when newspapers carried their clashing viewpoints. In the *New Straits Times*, Dr Mahathir had his say on the front page while Anwar was featured on the first page of the business section. Speaking at a dinner for the visiting Lebanese Prime Minister, Rafic Hariri, Dr Mahathir attacked the 'self-righteousness and hypocrisy' of those who accused South-East Asian governments of indulging in corruption, cronyism and nepotism and not being transparent. Making a point that he was to return to repeatedly, he said: 'If we had cronies and practised nepotism, then we must consider all the people of Malaysia as cronies and family members, for all of them gained from the administration and policies of the Malaysian Government and, indeed, from [the policies of] the governments of the tiger economies of South-East Asia.' On the same day, Anwar addressed the Global Think-Net Tokyo conference. He said Asians need not be apologetic or defensive about the charges of corruption and lack of transparency levelled against them, declaring: 'Asians are not the only ones afflicted with this disease. And our struggle to eliminate them must not be seen as efforts to placate others. They are based on moral convictions that corruption and cronyism are moral diseases of great peril to society if we tolerate them.' The battle lines were plainly drawn.

February was a month of growing unrest in Indonesia where people were being hit hard by the collapsing economy and the soaring prices of basic necessities, such as rice, cooking oil and milk. Riots flared throughout the country, with mobs setting fire to shops and homes owned by ethnic Chinese. Calls mounted for President Suharto to step down. Dr Mahathir referred to the situation in Indonesia, saying that in other countries where people resorted to irresponsible actions like riots and looting when they faced problems, 'the situation worsened and threatened national unity and public security'. He contrasted this with Malaysia where the situation was under control because the people chose to be united. He followed up these remarks some days later by saying changes to the top leadership should be effected gently, like pulling out a strand of hair from a mound of flour so that the hair was not broken and the flour not scattered. Clearly aware of the parallels being drawn between himself and President Suharto, he asked: 'Of what good is a new leader, even if he is supposed to be better, if the party he is going to lead has been destroyed?'

In other remarks he expressed relief that Malaysians had 'not been forced to submit to the agencies' that desired to establish control over them. In an obvious allusion to the Anwar camp, he said only those who had 'certain political priorities', would not admit that the government's policies and approaches to develop the nation were good and effective. 'I hope no one in the Barisan Nasional [the ruling National Front coalition] would use the economic problems for their political ends.'

Meanwhile, the economy continued to slide. On 24 March, Anwar revised the growth rate for 1998 to between 2 and 3 per cent. The economy had grown by 7.8 per cent in 1997 and Anwar had projected a similar expansion in 1998. But he was forced to make downward adjustments as the economy worsened, eventually contracting by more than 7 per cent. By April, banks, finance houses and stockbrokers were showing the strain of the economic downturn. Sime Bank, once thought to have been a solid institution, was put up for sale by parent company Sime Darby, after it was found to have a crushing debt of M$1.8 billion. Other banks had heavy burdens of non-performing loans and needed cash injections. In March, Bank Negara admitted Sime Bank and three other financial institutions required capital injections but assured depositors their savings were protected. The government announced an inquiry into Sime Bank's losses.

Public discontent arising from the economic crisis was further aggravated by a growing water shortage in a number of states, caused by lower rainfall than usual and mismanagement of resources. The worst hit area was the Klang Valley, which takes in Kuala Lumpur, the capital, and a large part of Selangor state. Some 1.2 million people in the Klang Valley suffered severe water rationing over a period of three months. The perennial problem of haze, caused by burning-off of forest and bush on the Indonesian island of Sumatra, was worse than usual due to an El Niño-induced drought. March also saw a street battle between Muslims and Hindus in Penang over the construction of a temple, underlining the delicate religious fabric of Malaysia and adding to a public perception that 1998 was an ill-omened year.

In his 24 March speech, Anwar also gave a reassurance that public funds would not be used to bail out troubled corporations and that transparency requirements—that is, more openness—would be tightened both in the private and public sector. Four days later, on 28 March, in a seeming rejoinder, Dr Mahathir said foreigners did not want to see Malaysian banks and companies rescued. They wanted them to go bankrupt so they could go in and buy them at a low price. He said they accused Malaysia of bailing out troubled companies using public funds but the truth was they wanted to buy the firms cheaply. The next day, in one of his most direct references to foreign praise of Anwar, Dr Mahathir said foreigners were trying to determine who should become the leaders of other countries, those countries' policies, and how they should carry out their trade. He declared: 'This [would mean] we have lost our independence.' In Parliament on 8 April, in response to an opposition member's suggestion that there 'confusing signals' on financial issues, Anwar sought to dispel the notion that he was taking a different tack from the Prime Minister Referring to himself and Dr Mahathir, he said unconvincingly: 'We complement one another.'

As Anwar was preoccupied with the financial affairs of state as well as his personal ambitions, another politician was discovering the fearsome penalties that can be imposed under certain Malaysian laws. In their imperial wisdom, the British, who had extended their control over the Malayan peninsula from the 1820s onward, had introduced draconian legislation to keep the natives under control. UMNO and its coalition partners found it convenient to keep some of these laws in place. No leaders past or present, including Dr Mahathir and Anwar (while he was part of the establishment), showed any inclination to abolish or amend them. So it was that unwary citizens could find themselves falling foul of such legislation as the *Printing Presses and Publications Act*, the *Sedition Act*, the *Official Secrets Act* and the *Internal Security Act*.

Lim Guan Eng, deputy secretary-general of the opposition Democratic Action Party (DAP), which his father headed, had taken up the case of a 15-year-old girl who was detained at a rehabilitation centre after she allegedly had sexual relations with several men. Lim wrote about the alleged involvement of the Anwar Vision Team member, Rahim Thamby Chik, in a pamphlet entitled 'True Story'. Subsequently, at a public forum he criticised the Attorney-General's decision not to prosecute Rahim for alleged statutory rape of an under-aged girl due to insufficient evidence. In the Malacca High Court in April 1997 Lim was convicted of publishing false news in the pamphlet under the *Printing Presses and Publications Act*, and of inciting the public in his remarks at the forum under the *Sedition Act*. He was fined M$15 000. A year later, the Court of Appeal dismissed his appeal and increased his sentence from a fine to 18 months' imprisonment on each charge, the terms to be served concurrently.

The jail term, which was reduced to 12 months for good behaviour, deprived Lim, 37, of his parliamentary seat and the right to seek re-election for five years after his release. It interrupted the career of one of Malaysia's most promising opposition politicians and one of the stars of political debate in parliament. Like any standard Malaysian prisoner, Lim was put in a small unfurnished cell with only two blankets as bedding. After three months, in accordance with prison procedures, he was issued with a thin mattress. Although Anwar was brutally assaulted by the chief of police on the night of his arrest, once he was ensconced in Sungei Buloh Prison he was treated with the feudal respect Malays traditionally accord top leaders, in or out of power. He had been, after all, the second most powerful man in the land. He was given a larger cell than most prisoners and, unlike the unfortunate Lim, had a bed and other furniture. But that was still months away and only the opposition and Lim's friends took much interest in the DAP official's fate.

While Dr Mahathir was busy exploring possible measures for stabilising the economy with Daim and other people whom he felt he could trust, Anwar was pressing on with his IMF-oriented agenda. In an address to the Council on Foreign Relations in New York, he said that all that was old and bad in Asian economies must be done away with. He described the gale sweeping through Asia as an 'agent of creative destruction', saying: 'The pressure has been building up in recent months in the region itself and we are aware that unless we reform the system from within, changes will be imposed from without.' In Washington the following day, at a press conference in conjunction with a meeting of the IMF and World Bank, Anwar said that 'corruption and crony capitalism, the enemies from within for any economy' could be eradicated as nations affected by the Asian financial crisis began the process of rebuilding their economies. 'But before they can do so', he added 'they have to admit that the problems exist'.

On 29 April, Dr Mahathir was asked to comment on a suggestion by the IMF that Malaysia should further tighten its monetary policy. He replied: 'We have already tightened so much that the companies are complaining that they can't breathe.' Yet despite these obviously contrary approahces, Dr Mahathir and Anwar were still keeping up appearances of unity. Only six days later on 5 May, Dr Mahathir told journalists there was no rift between him and Anwar: 'Every morning, we sit down [and] he, Daim and I decide what we have to do together. But no matter how we do it, even if I were to kiss and hug him in public all the time, they will say there is a rift because that is what they want to see.' When Dr Mahathir flew off to Cairo in May for a meeting of the Group of 15 developing countries, the *New Straits Times* carried a photograph of Dr Mahathir and Anwar smiling happily at one another at the airport. The message for the public was manifest: See, our leaders are really good friends.

President Suharto cut short his attendance at the G15 summit because of rising unrest in Indonesia. He told members of the Indonesian community in the Egyptian capital that he was prepared to step down if people no longer wanted him. In Khartoum, at the end of a three-day visit to Sudan following the Cairo meeting,

Dr Mahathir defended President Suharto from his critics, saying Indonesia had become a very advanced developing country under him—but there were attempts to topple him by outsiders. 'As for Malaysia', he said, 'there are attempts to topple me by outsiders'.

In mid-May Dr Mahathir and Anwar made comments that showed how starkly they were at odds. Declaring that the IMF was not 'sensitive to the social cost of economic restructuring' in Indonesia, Dr Mahathir said by pulling back people's subsidies it seemed to be 'almost wanting them to react violently'. Anwar, on the other hand, warned that if Malaysia did not want the IMF to bail it out, it must implement the appropriate measures. In one of his boldest—if still indirect—stabs at the Prime Minister he said: 'Our problem is that some of us yell that we don't want the IMF to interfere but still take actions that leave us exposed.'

On 18 May, *Utusan Malaysia*, the UMNO-connected Malay-language newspaper, caused a stir when it published an editorial blaming President Suharto for the unrest in Indonesia. It went against the established practice of the media and officials to refrain from criticising fellow members of ASEAN. But this was not simply an attack on Suharto. The editorial, which was widely seen as a poison arrow loosed at Dr Mahathir, said Suharto 'could be at fault after more than three decades of practising favouritism, during which he enriched his sons and cronies while ignoring the plight of his citizens'. Suharto was certainly aware that he had 'been in power for too long'. It added: 'If Suharto is guilty let him be judged by his people.' *Utusan*'s editor-in-chief, Johan Jaaffar, like *Berita Harian*'s Nazri owed his position to Anwar. Both editors would soon be out of a job.

Malaysia and the rest of South-East Asia were anxiously watching Indonesia. A nation of 190 million in turmoil was a danger to its neighbours, and Indonesia was aflame. Under pressure from the IMF, the Indonesian government withdrew a petroleum subsidy, resulting in a 25 per cent hike in the price of kerosene, the people's basic fuel. The price of petrol rose by 71 per cent. The *New Straits Times'* A. Kadir Jasin wrote: 'This is yet another example that while the IMF may lend money to a troubled economy, its package of assistance may not necessarily reduce the suffering of the people of the affected country.' Within days Indonesia was racked by violent protests. But the worst violence was committed on 12 May by security forces who shot and killed six university students handing out flowers. Two days later mobs rampaged through Jakarta and other cities, looting, overturning cars and setting fire to buildings, in the worst riots for more than 30 years. Chinese homes and shops were targeted while male members of this ethnic minority were attacked and women raped. Foreigners and Chinese fled to Singapore.

In this atmosphere of intense anxiety among Malaysian Chinese and growing fears of a spillover of the violence into Malaysia, or at least an influx of refugees, Anwar delivered a highly provocative speech. It reflected either an extraordinary insensitivity to the inflammatory nature of his remarks or, more plausibly, a determination to use the situation to serve his own purposes. Addressing a National Youth Day gathering held to foster patriotism among young Malaysians as a means of strengthening national stability, he seemed instead to be encouraging them to revolt against the established order. Patriotism, he said, did not mean accepting that everything in one's country was good, including that which was not good. Patriotism must come from a desire for improvement and wanting 'to save the country, not oneself or the interests of a small group'. He went on to say that young people were often the movers of reform as they were more receptive to new ways of thinking and were idealistic. 'Reformasi', or reform, was the battle-cry of the students and other activists in Indonesia bent on ousting the government of President Suharto. Anwar declared: 'If we want reform in our community, it's the youth and youth leaders who should be in the front line. But reform cannot happen in a vacuum. It must spring from confidence and patriotism based on an enlightened spirit from within.'

On 21 May, Suharto stepped down after 30 years as president. His resignation came a day after US Secretary of State Madeleine Albright had urged him to go and to provide for a transition to democracy in a speech which no doubt reinforced Dr Mahathir's jaundiced impression of her. Suharto's successor, Bacharuddin Jusuf Habibie, promised constitutional reform and also said he would implement the agreed IMF programme. The sudden fall of a man who had been firmly in control of his country and a major influence in ASEAN since its foundation encouraged critics of Dr Mahathir at home and abroad to believe that he too could be pressured into retiring. Three weeks later the *Asian Wall Street Journal* ran a commentary by Barry Wain under the heading, 'Why Doesn't Mahathir Bow Out?'. Depicting President Suharto as an aging leader who overstayed his welcome and who, despite an economic crisis, continued to bestow business favours on his friends and family, the writer said the description also fitted Dr Mahathir. He said it was becoming apparent that Dr Mahathir was psychologically incapable of making the adjustments necessary to chart a recovery. Wain wrote that it was hard to escape the conclusion that he was 'an impediment to the process'. Dr Mahathir could best serve Malaysia by announcing immediately his intention to retire in the near future. Noting that Dr Mahathir had indicated that he intended to stick around and nurse Malaysia back to health, he wrote that this was 'almost certainly beyond his capacity'. The Prime Minister ultimately proved him wrong. Wain had nothing but praise for the 'urbane and skilful' Anwar. He declared that Anwar was known to feel a strong loyalty to Dr Mahathir and was 'reluctant to challenge him'. This was an inaccurate reading of the Deputy Prime Minister who had been working towards the ouster of his mentor since he became his heir.

Dr Mahathir, of course, had no intention of standing down. He and Daim were almost ready to put in place an economic strategy that would owe nothing to the proposals of the IMF. In a speech to the Malay Chamber of Commerce on 27 May, Daim outlined the position of the anti-IMF forces and gave a small hint of what was to come. He said that stabilising the ringgit remained 'the main objective of our recovery plan'. While many groups believed that a high interest rate was a prerequisite to exchange rate stability, their point of view could not be adopted entirely because 'punitive interest rates would certainly push more business enterprises into bankruptcy'. Two days later, Dr Mahathir said the government would continue to help big and small bumiputra (Malay and other indigenous people) companies to enable them to compete with other races in the business sector. If they were allowed to collapse, Malaysia would find itself in the situation existing before the New Economic Policy was introduced, 'where the poor were generally the Malays'. Certain foreign quarters, he sounded, wanted the Malays to remain stupid and the poorest race in the country.

His remarks were part of a continuing warning to Malays that unless Malaysia followed the economic policies he promoted they could lose the privileges granted to them under the NEP, which included quotas that secured them places in universities over more qualified Chinese and guaranteed employment. The NEP affirmative action process also included measures to give Malays a share of companies going public and priority in acquiring control of corporatised government entities. While the NEP was Dr Mahathir's carrot to keep Malays behind him, it was also a vital ingredient in reducing the chances of an explosion of the kind occurring next door in Indonesia. Malaysia had a tenth of Indonesia's population and a significantly smaller gap between the rich and poor. But, more importantly, it had addressed the resentment of Malays over Chinese financial power. As in Indonesia, the Chinese controlled a proportion of the nation's wealth far exceeding their percentage of the population. In the 1960s, when the Chinese accounted for about 30 per cent of the population and Malays more than 50 per cent, the latter had a mere 2.4 per cent of the economic pie with the rest held by the minority race and foreigners. This disparity was a major cause of the country's worst racial riots on 13 May 1969, which resulted in the deaths of nearly 200 people, more than 70 per cent of whom were Chinese. The riots led to the implementation of the NEP which aimed to raise Malay ownership of the economy to 30 per cent. The government also acquired major corporations held by British interests in raids on the London stock market. By 1997, before the economy's collapse, the Malay share of national wealth had risen to more than 20 per cent. This was less than the goal of 30 per cent but the growing number of rich Malay corporate chiefs and the emergence of a comfortable middle class had made Malays feel less deprived.

Dr Mahathir's comments on the NEP were made at a ceremony attended by the two prominent political figures of the past, Tengku Razaleigh Hamzah and Ghafar Baba, now Mahathir allies. Two weeks later, Dr Mahathir announced the establishment of the UMNO Veterans Club, a consultative body conceived and headed by Ghafar, the man Anwar had ousted from the number two job. Ghafar's first piece of advice was directed at cabinet ministers whom, he said, must be united. If anyone was unhappy with a decision he should leave. Anwar could have had no doubt that the message was intended for him.

In the last week of May, both Daim and Dr Mahathir advocated lower interest rates. Daim warned that high interest rates and the reluctance of banks to lend, even to productive sectors, would cripple the economy. Questioning the prescription of a regime of high interest rates and reduced credit, the Prime Minister repeated that such measures would bankrupt companies, throw workers out of jobs and lead to riots and political instability. On 30 May, Bank Negara announced that growth had contracted by 1.8 per cent in the first quarter of the year. Shortly after this announcement, Dr Mahathir said the government was working to find ways to reduce interest rates, adding: 'We are under pressure because the so-called market forces want us to raise interest rates.' In his *New Sunday Times* column on the same day that the newspaper reported the first quarter's negative growth, A. Kadir Jasin echoed Daim's comments, saying the 'damning reality' was that the high interest rate and tight liquidity policies were making it impossible for companies and individuals to borrow even for productive purposes.

> Saving the financial system is important. Being praised by International Monetary Fund managing director Michel Camdessus and the foreign media may also be important to some of us. But what good is an inflated ego when the economy is in imminent danger of contracting, confidence diminishing and the survival of businesses getting more precarious by the day.

Some two and a half years later, on 31 December 2000, Kadir identified the recipient of Camdessus' praise and reminded Malaysians 'how close the country came to surrendering its fate to the IMF and sovereignty to the agency's Western sponsors'. He asked: 'How many of us still remember how former deputy prime minister and finance minister Datuk Seri Anwar Ibrahim had steered us towards the IMF by virtue of his friendship with former IMF managing director Michel Camdessus?'

Amid the political and economic drama of 1998, Malaysia was also preparing to host the Commonwealth Games in September. Since the government was looking forward to a boost in annual tourism income from an expected 80 000 visitors, it was important that the country should not be seen to be in crisis. The authorities also had to counter foreign reports that the smoke haze still hanging over the country might endanger athletes' health. But as the political action came to a climax in June, there was little the government could do to conceal the fact that major events were in train. On 1 June, at the Third Asia Oil & Gas Conference in Kuala Lumpur, Anwar launched a new attack on corruption, cronyism and nepotism and hardened his stand on interest rates. On this issue he was allied with Bank Negara governor Ahmad Mohamad Don, which emboldened him to oppose the position of Dr Mahathir. In his speech to the conference, parts of which sounded more like a battle call to the masses than remarks intended for leading figures in the petroleum industry, Anwar noted the economic, political and social changes seen throughout the region in the last twelve months had made it patently clear that business as usual was impossible. He said: 'The people of the region will no longer tolerate the old ways. They reject corruption, cronyism and nepotism. They demand greater accountability, transparency and a real say in the decision-making process.'

At a press conference following his address, Anwar pursued his stand on monetary policy. The business community he said, must understand that domestic interest rates could not be much lower than offshore rates, which stood at about 20 per cent, as it could lead to an outflow of funds. In remarks which appeared to be directed at Dr Mahathir and Daim, he said: 'It's important that people who talk about interest rates know the offshore rates for ringgit. If you do not take this into consideration, you are putting the entire financial system at risk because what is stopping people from taking out our funds?' The question of the high rates for ringgit deposits in Singapore was, in fact, very much on the minds of Dr Mahathir, Daim and their advisers, who eventually found a way to deal with it so that interest rates could be relaxed. Returning from a visit to Japan, the Prime Minister reaffirmed his stand, stating that he did 'not necessarily endorse Bank Negara's tight monetary policy', adding: 'High interest rates have actually caused the economy to contract.'

Corruption remained on the agenda. In he weeks leading up to the party general assembly UMNO Youth chief and Anwar man Zahid Hamidi began speaking out more strongly against corruption and the other associated ills of governmental business that had become the identifying mantra of the Deputy Prime Minister's supporters. Speaking at a conference on Strengthening the National Economy, he said a new management code was needed to fight corruption, nepotism and abuse of power. In the same week, he said UMNO members had been 'bottling up their feelings' on the subject of these 'negative practices', which had to be curbed. Taking a fairly obvious potshot at the Prime Minister, he asserted: 'In the current economic situation, we should never condone nepotism whereby the interest of family members and certain groups are given priority.'

A week before the UMNO general assembly, with word spreading that Zahid would use the party meeting for a major assault on corruption, cronyism and nepotism, Dr Mahathir took a pre-emptive action by stepping up his countering arguments. On June 12, he urged Malaysians not to be influenced by the Malaysian media's dissemination of Western capitalist propaganda aimed at manipulating the people's minds to create disunity and weaken the country. He said the West had coined many words such as 'globalisation', 'deregulation' and 'crony capitalism', which were often used by Malaysians and the media. It sounded 'nice' and the Western capitalists were pleased when they knew that the poison they injected was working and they had 'succeeded in controlling minds'. Outsiders though, said Dr Mahathir, were not interested in helping the country but in controlling it by bringing down the value of the ringgit. In doing this, they wanted to colonise Malaysia. A day later, he said those making allegations of cronyism should realise that they were someone else's cronies. Overseas students denouncing

cronyism had received government scholarships which made them Dr Mahathir's cronies: 'So cronies shouldn't complain about other cronies.' Mahathir supporter Senator Zainuddin Maidin criticised Zahid for harping on the issue of nepotism and cronyism, saying this threatened party unity. He noted that Zahid 'got positions in several companies' due to so-called cronyism. The UMNO Youth chief was at that time chairman of the National Savings Bank, having been appointed to the job by the government.

It was apparently still not time to finger Anwar personally, although the indirect signals were intended to show him that the Mahathir camp knew what was going on. This led to the oddest denials of any rift by the Mahathir camp. Fauzi Abdul Rahman, who held the position of deputy minister in the Prime Minister's Department, conceded there were some people in the country who were 'unhappy with the political scene' and intended to 'make use of the cronyism and nepotism issue to create political instability', but added: 'I do not believe there is friction between our Prime Minister and his deputy because as a deputy minister at the Prime Minister's Department I see the close relationship between the two.' He said people trying to create tension between the two men should 'look for something better to do' because there were 'no ill-feelings between Dr Mahathir and Anwar'.

Dr Mahathir said UMNO was united but there were other people, especially certain sections of the foreign media, trying to find differences between him and Anwar. He said certain statements were analysed and used as evidence of a rift. The Prime Minister declared: 'But it is not true. We get along as well as can be. Of course, there are problems we are faced with, but we work closely together.' When a *Time* magazine interviewer suggested the differences between Dr Mahathir and Anwar seemed to have widened considerably over the past year, the Prime Minister responded forcefully: 'Do I have to kiss him on the street before people will stop saying there is a rift? We get on together, we manage the country together. I admit we have differences but in the end a common view prevails.'

As the UMNO general assembly approached, expectations grew that the Anwar camp would use it to argue the time had come for Dr Mahathir to go. With political tension mounting, the Prime

Minister let his anger show over the implementation of a tight monetary policy. On 16 June, he lashed out, saying banks that continued to impose a credit squeeze should close down, as they had no confidence in the Malaysian economy. He accused them again of tightening the screws to the point where people could not do business. The banks were 'more interested in themselves than in supporting businesses'. He also said he would discuss the matter with Anwar, but his outburst reflected a frustration that would soon push him to end the policy dominance of Bank Negara and his deputy.

4 | Protégé outfoxed by mentor

In the weeks preceding the UMNO general assembly, Anwar's men were actively promoting —both within the party and to local and foreign journalists—the contention that the winds of political change stirred up by the South-East Asian economic crisis, which had swept President Suharto from power, were now buffeting the last of the region's old-guard leaders. They said in private that support was growing within the party hierarchy for a change in the presidency. Malaysia, they asserted, needed a new leader with new ideas to meet the challenges of the next century at home and in the region. Like Suharto, Dr Mahathir had been in charge for too long. At an UMNO convention in Johor, Anwar warned Malaysia could go the way of Indonesia if reforms were not undertaken. His remarks were widely interpreted as inferring that like the 'reformasi' programme in Indonesia, which had focused on the ouster of President Suharto, reform in Malaysia should include getting rid of Dr Mahathir. As delegates set out from cities, towns and kampungs across Malaysia for Kuala Lumpur to attend the general assembly, there was an air of expectation among them that it would be a pivotal meeting.

As was customary, the youth and women's wings of the party were due to meet the day before the assembly's opening. Anwar was scheduled to address a joint session of UMNO Youth and Wanita UMNO, while Zahid Hamidi, as UMNO Youth chief, was the opening speaker at the meeting of the young male delegates. Since both he and Anwar had included attacks on nepotism, cronyism and corruption in remarks ahead of the assembly, the three ills were expected to be on the agenda. However, in a closed-door briefing for general assembly delegates a day before the UMNO Youth and Wanita UMNO meetings, Dr Mahathir issued a warning. He said delegates who raised issues that might destabilise the party must be accountable for their actions. Asked at a press conference whether this applied to delegates speaking about nepotism and cronyism, he said: 'If they cause a split within the party or other adverse effects, then they should be responsible.' He added: 'If you want to bring up such matters, you must have the facts.'

While Dr Mahathir insisted his remarks were not a form of blackmail, students of the Prime Minister did not doubt that if Zahid raised the nepotism and cronyism issue he would face retribution from the nation's leader. Zahid ignored the warning. He had pinned his hopes for political advancement on the party deputy, not the president. Dr Mahathir also had some cautionary advice for Anwar and his supporters at the press conference, where he was asked if the winds of change blowing in South-East Asia would bring political change to Malaysia. He replied: 'The winds can blow in any direction they like but whether there should be a change or not is the choice of the people.' He also noted that some people were fanning the wind to bring about an inflammatory result. But if the embers were weak and there was plenty of water they would not burn.

As people set up stalls peddling food, clothing and trinkets on the footpaths outside and in the lobby of the Putra World Trade Centre, venue of the general assembly, one item on sale raised more serious questions for Anwar than Dr Mahathir's remarks. It was a book entitled *50 Dalil Mengapa Anwar Tida Boleh Jadi PM*, or '50 Reasons Why Anwar Cannot Become Prime Minister', with the author given as Khalid Jafri, a former sports editor of *Utusan Malaysia*.

50 Dalil, as it came to be known, was not only on sale to members of the public visiting the Putra World Trade Centre but also inserted as a give-away into the souvenir bags of delegates. As soon as he learned about it, Anwar asked a law firm to seek an injunction to have publication and distribution of the book stopped. After the injunction was obtained, Anwar categorically stated through his lawyers that the book contained gross libel against him and he would not hesitate to take whatever legal action was necessary to 'protect the dignity of his office and his own self esteem'.

The book was one of the most severe denigrations of a national leader in a country where politics had spawned a virtual industry in character assassination by pamphlet. It comprised a miscellany of alleged misdeeds, sexual and otherwise, of Anwar, including the accusations made in 1997, which had been dismissed by Dr Mahathir and the police chief. But it went further than the original letter's allegation that Anwar was having an affair with the wife of his private secretary, suggesting that he was the father of their daughter. Deoxyribonucleic acid (DNA) testing subsequently showed that Azmin Ali, Anwar's private secretary, and Shamsidar Taharin, his wife, were parents of the child.

At a press conference in his office in the Finance Ministry, Anwar called on the authorities to take harsh action against the author and the publisher of the book and their agents. He said it would be a good lesson for those involved and prevent Malaysian politics from being manipulated by irresponsible writers: 'Although the book is not to be taken seriously and has no credibility, there is a writer and a publisher. I believe it is a conspiracy to smear my image and topple me.' He called it 'a very serious fabrication' against him his family and friends, and said it covered issues such as his 'alleged complicity in a murder' and sex, and named him as 'the most corrupt man in the country'. It also alleged that he was an agent of foreign powers and wanted to topple the country's leadership. Although Anwar portrayed himself as the victim of a conspiracy—a word that was to take on a larger meaning after his sacking—he did not then suggest any involvement by Dr Mahathir. The distribution of *50 Dalil* to delegates was obviously a move to damage Anwar's reputation, but he had been a target of surat terbang from the time Dr Mahathir took him under his wing and became a threat to other UMNO members with ambitions to be the nation's leader. And there was nothing immediately evident in the book's publication to suggest that it was the precursor to one of the most dramatic political events in Malaysia's history.

Despite his indignation, Anwar was at first less concerned with *50 Dalil* than his personal agenda of persuading the UMNO general assembly that Dr Mahathir had ceased to be an effective leader and should be replaced. But the man-who-would-be-king was strangely loath to directly lay his claim to the throne. Instead, like a feudal lord, he sent his champion, Zahid, to do battle on his behalf. Few UMNO members doubted that Zahid spoke for Anwar. A week before the assembly, they had made almost identical attacks on nepotism, cronyism and corruption. Yet, Anwar chose to affirm his loyalty to his mentor to the end.

In the light of Anwar's manifest collaboration with Zahid and his later public admission that he had prompted Zahid to lead the fight against nepotism, cronyism and corruption, the deputy president's speech to the UMNO Youth and Wanita UMNO delegates was awash with hypocrisy.

> UMNO must stand united with the leadership headed by Prime Minister Datuk Seri Dr Mahathir Mohamad in facing the currency crisis. Individual interests must be set aside and factional and tribal tendencies must be contained. We must learn from mistakes by those who have resorted before to factionalism.

But there were coded messages for his disciples. Anwar said the UMNO assembly was different because of the circumstances, which had influenced the delegates' thinking. He declared: 'I can feel it and you can feel it.' He also said that UMNO Youth had regained its position as the people's voice, 'calling for social justice and pointing out the weaknesses in society'. But apart from this small tribute to the party wing led by his point man, Zahid, Anwar seemed, as always in his political career, to be bent on self-preservation while leaving others to test the waters.

Zahid proved to be a staunch paladin, launching the vigorous attack his master wanted, despite Dr Mahathir's warning and scathing comments by the Prime Minister's supporters that he was the last person to denounce cronyism given his position as chairman of the National Savings Bank. In addition to making the expected call for political reform, the UMNO Youth chief also attacked the arguments of the party president. He said it was sad that views from the grassroots were said to be voices that could bring about disunity. More disappointing, according to Zahid, was the fact that attempts to bring about a more transparent government and more responsible leadership were viewed as playing into the hands of foreigners. Zahid said UMNO's political power would be eroded and its struggle for the Malays would come to an end if negative elements like nepotism and cronyism were allowed to prevail. Denouncing those who used their positions to favour family members, relatives and friends, he said that unless the practice was ended, the credibility of UMNO and its leaders would suffer. He then put his own credibility on the line by asserting that his attack on nepotism, cronyism and corruption should not be linked to the issue of the UMNO leadership or the pushing up or bringing down of any leader. Zahid stated: 'Certainly, we have no interest in causing any form of power struggle which can lead to the destruction of the party.'

Few people at the top believed his declaration that his remarks had nothing to do with promoting or bringing down any leader. His message was clear: the changes he called for could come only with a change in leadership. And for the Mahathir camp, the applause of the UMNO Youth delegates signalled Zahid had support among his peers. One of the delegates, Hamdan Taha, a chicken breeder from Perak, provided a relevant parable to complement Zahid's speech: there was a large ship called the *Titanic*, he said, on which the captain was always entertaining the rich passengers while the needs of the poor crew were neglected. When the ship crashed into a rock and started sinking, the captain allocated the limited number of lifeboats to the rich passengers, while the crew had to fend for themselves. Hamdan wondered whether the same fate would befall the small businessmen of Malaysia in the economic crisis affecting the nation. His audience roared in delighted approval.

Zahid's speech had plainly struck a chord with UMNO Youth delegates but among observers there was a sense of something missing. The lieutenant and the foot soldiers were ready to make their assault on the president's fortress but where was their leader? He had made a brief appearance on the battlefield, but had not unsheathed his sword. If Anwar thought that the mere threat of a challenge would cause Dr Mahathir to withdraw, he was badly mistaken. Once again it seemed he had misjudged the master politician and shown he was no match for him. Although Anwar seemed prepared to deceive both associates and enemies, to achieve power and to walk over anyone in his way to achieve power, he nevertheless lacked the political toughness of his mentor. Dr Mahathir did not accept defeat. He used his power brilliantly to isolate enemies and cultivate friends. And he put into practice the maxim he often recited—that there were no permanent friends or foes in politics. Anwar often seemed unwilling to commit himself to a risky venture either through fear of failure or plain irresolution. When Dr Mahathir was ready to act he moved decisively and fearlessly. Anwar would probably have been better advised to wait for the UMNO elections the following year and try to set the grassroots afire ahead of the voting, as he had done in his campaign against Ghafar Baba. But he no doubt worried that he might face the same kinds of obstacles raised to protect the president in 1996. He was also under pressure from followers eager to benefit from his rise to power.

Although Anwar's challenge lacked grit or determination, Dr Mahathir did not take it lightly. There was a strong possibility Anwar's supporters in the general assembly would push ahead with the nepotism–cronyism theme unless they were stopped in their tracks. So in his opening speech at the general assembly he went immediately on the offensive, demonstrating his understanding of what was important to Malays, especially those who had succeeded in business or politics, by raising the spectre of them losing the money and power they had gained. Dr Mahathir said Western allegations that crony capitalism, corruption and non-transparency existed in Asian countries were only excuses to attack their economies. It was no longer necessary to take control of a country by military strength because this could be achieved through currency trading. Wealthy countries could be colonised by making them poor. He said that when a country became poor, its politics became unstable and a fight for power ensued. The Western attack on the country's economy would continue until a leader was chosen who would submit to the wishes of the foreign powers and be prepared to have his country once again colonised. When this happened the economy would be open for foreign funds to acquire major local companies.

Dr Mahathir warned that if Malaysia had to resort to IMF assistance, it would be required to open up the Malaysian economy '100 per cent to foreigners'. Foreigners would then not only have 100 per cent equity in Malaysian companies and banks but also carry out business in Malaysia without Malaysian participation. He said Malaysians might be given 'lower-rung positions' but foreigners would forever hold senior positions because they would claim the nation's people were incompetent. There would no longer be any bumiputra quotas because the foreigners maintained the NEP was an injustice and unacceptable to their liberal democracy. There would no longer be any bumiputra billionaires or millionaires with their Mercedes, private jets and luxury yachts. The foreigners would get rid of 'all those who are accused of being political leaders' cronies' and the rest would be paid 'salaries commensurate with their limited abilities'. The millionaires and billionaires would all be foreigners and Malaysians would come under foreign rule. Dr Mahathir declared passionately that this was not something he was making up to frighten Malays but the scenario desired by the critics of the NEP and the Malaysian leadership. 'If we try to imagine the situation in Malaysia without the NEP, this is the scenario that we will get.'

Having put fear in the hearts of Malays that they might lose their economic, educational and employment privileges, Dr Mahathir then attacked those who echoed Western condemnation of cronyism and the NEP. He said it was strange that people who were taken in by the Western accusations were those who had benefited from the NEP: in education, high positions in government and share disbursements because they were bumiputras. If they had had to compete against the non-bumiputras, chances were they would not have gained scholarships, or high positions in government, or shares. In a remark with particular meaning for Zahid, he suggested critics should look at themselves before accusing others of being cronies. And in a summing up of the fate that could befall Malays, he declared: 'They are trying to destroy all that we have built, the developments we have achieved and the corporate figures we have nurtured. Their intention is to enslave the Malays and other bumiputras once again.'

In his speech, Dr Mahathir also reaffirmed his determination not to accept the West's prescriptions for the troubled economy. He said that hoping for market forces to create a stable currency exchange rate, stable economy and stable politics was the same as not doing anything and leaving everything to fate. While expressing confidence that the government could deflect the attacks against Malaysia and redevelop the country, he did not reveal the prescriptions that would be applied in another two months. The speech was warmly applauded and delegates unanimously adopted a motion supporting it.

The next day, Dr Mahathir launched a second offensive in his counterattack against Zahid and Anwar, using a weapon that took his opponents by surprise. Lists of the shareholders of companies awarded government projects under its privatisation scheme were distributed to delegates and posted on noticeboards in the corridors of the Putra World Trade Centre, venue of the general assembly. Dr Mahathir said the lists were released in response to allegations that the government had practised nepotism and cronyism in awarding contracts. With manifest satisfaction he observed: 'There have been accusations that privatisation has benefited only a few friends and cronies of the Prime Minister, maybe also the Deputy Prime Minister, so we provide these lists to show who got the privatisation projects. There are literally hundreds of them.' There was no way he could 'be very intimate with [all of] them', he remarked. He also pointed out that the name of his son Mokhzani was on the list, so people could see 'how many hundreds of times' he had been given projects. His son's name, linked to only one project, was included along with those of relatives and supporters of Anwar and other well-known personalities. Zahid was shown as the majority shareholder of a company awarded a government construction project. While some politicians and businessmen were unhappy to have their activities made public, Dr Mahathir had destroyed Zahid's arguments. Pro-Anwar delegates who had been expected to speak up in support of Zahid were wavering after Dr Mahathir's warnings about the threat to Malaysia's independence. They were routed when he released the lists showing the beneficiaries of privatisation.

Anwar himself did not have a word to say in support of his flag bearer, leaving him to 'swing in the wind', as one delegate put it. He was a model of rectitude at the general assembly, laughing at Dr Mahathir's jokes, congratulating him on his speech and dismissing speculation that he was planning to challenge the president. Dr Mahathir let him get away with his portrayal of innocence. At a press conference, he promised to support Anwar if he were challenged for the deputy president's post at the UMNO elections in 1999. Anwar was then asked whether he would support Dr Mahathir if the president were challenged. No one present, including the Prime Minister, could have failed to notice the deputy leader's careful language, which left open his future options. He said he had 'made specific reference to the matter' in his speech to the youth and women's wings of the party the previous day. In fact all he had said on that occasion was that UMNO 'must stand united with the leadership' headed by Dr Mahathir. Asked directly if he planned to challenge the president, Anwar did not reply with a simple 'yes' or 'no'. He said: 'At no time did I make any reference to the possibility of challenging the president. It is only the interpretation of some of you, especially the foreign media.'

Few delegates failed to conclude that Zahid's attack on cronyism and corruption was intended to set the stage for a challenge to the president's leadership and remarks by several speakers brought the matter further into the open. A supreme council member, Affifuddin Omar, likened developments to an invasion of the northern Malay state of Kedah several hundred years ago by Siam (Thailand). He recalled that a 'whispering brigade' was sent in ahead of the main group to soften up the Malays by giving extravagant accounts of the invincibility of the Siamese forces. The strategy brought 'fear and disintegration' to the Malay ranks. His implication was that Anwar's people had adopted a similar strategy to try to force the retirement of Dr Mahathir, who hails from Kedah. Sanusi Junid, Mahathir supporter and Anwar foe, put Affifuddin's allegorical reference to the Siamese whispering brigades into a contemporary context by asserting that two weeks before the general assembly an 'UMNO leader' had been spreading a false report that a majority of party divisions no longer supported Dr Mahathir; that 30 members of parliament would soon ask him to step down; and that university students would demonstrate and call for his resignation. Sanusi issued a warning, tempered with a jokey manner, to Anwar. He said he did not hate Anwar, as some people had alleged, because he was a childhood friend, 'But if he wants to bring down Dr Mahathir, he will have to see me first.'

At the closing session of the UMNO general assembly, Dr Mahathir said the lists of people who had benefited from the government's privatisation schemes and affirmative action programmes showed that cronyism and nepotism were not major problems in Malaysia. He said his children were 'treated like everyone else' and, ignoring the ASEAN convention of eschewing criticism of fellow members, referred disparagingly to the economic activities of the Indonesian First Family. While Dr Mahathir did not name President Suharto, who had stepped down a month earlier, or Indonesia, speaking only of a 'neighbouring country', it was apparent to which nation and leader he was alluding. He stated: 'National car, the clove monopoly, toll roads. Everything belongs to his children. That is surely nepotism or cronyism. But it is a different situation in Malaysia.'

This was Anwar's cue to make, once again, a grovelling commitment of loyalty to the party president. Denying any rift between them, he stressed the need for party unity and recited two poems. The first said his fidelity had not changed, it was 'only people spreading poison'. The second warned against any attempt to undermine his loyalty to, and support of, Dr Mahathir. However, if Anwar thought he could carry on as usual, he was soon to find out this was not the case. Three days after the conclusion of the general assembly, the Prime Minister's Department announced that Daim

Zainuddin had been appointed Special Functions Minister. He now had full ministerial rank in addition to his roles as economic adviser to the government and executive director of the National Economic Action Council (NEAC). Dr Mahathir rationalised the move by saying it would enable the new minister to explain NEAC decisions to the cabinet, adding that without ministerial rank Daim would find it difficult to deal with foreign ministers on trips abroad. But the appointment was widely seen to have significantly reduced Anwar's influence. Earlier in the year, brushing off suggestions by journalists that statements by the Prime Minister were contradicting his pronouncements, Anwar had declared: 'I'm in charge of economic matters.' That claim was now in doubt. Dr Mahathir confirmed that with Daim's support he was calling the shots on the economy. When journalists asked how the new appointment would affect decision making, he said: 'Domestically, I have full control.'

Just two days after nepotism was the hot topic at the general assembly, UMNO member Ismail Kassim was nominated as the ruling National Front's candidate in a by-election for the parliamentary seat of Arau, in Perlis State, which had never fallen to the opposition. Ismail was the brother of the Chief Minister of Perlis, Sahidan Kassim, who claimed he had had nothing to do with his sibling's selection. On polling day, voters showed the extent to which the UMNO leadership was out of touch with the public mood. Malaysians did not need Anwar or Zahid to highlight nepotism, cronyism and corruption. In Arau, former UMNO supporters rebelled against the arrogance of the hierarchy in not only failing to deal with these issues, but in thumbing their noses at people demanding change. The supposedly safe seat fell to Parti Islam se-Malaysia by 12 864 votes to 11 541. It was the first time PAS had won a parliamentary seat in Perlis. Dr Mahathir refused to concede that nepotism was a factor in the PAS victory, stating that it was 'just a coincidence' that the defeated candidate was the Chief Minister's brother. The Arau by-election outcome was a warning signal which the leaders of UMNO disregarded. It underlined a growing discontent among Malays over party failings, including the spreading disease of money politics and the increasing influence of corporate chiefs in place of the teachers and other respected members of rural communities who were its early core members. The Anwar affair intensified their feelings of disgust with UMNO and drove them into the arms of the opposition.

Meanwhile, Dr Mahathir still had some use for Anwar. Recognising the importance of his deputy's friendship with government and corporate leaders in the West, he announced that he would lead one of two road shows abroad to drum up investment support. The other was headed by Daim. But while Anwar was overseas, Dr Mahathir completed the purge of Anwar supporters in the media that he had begun some months earlier. Within days of each other, Nazri Abdullah, group editor of *Berita Harian*, who had been hanging onto his position by his fingernails since he earned Dr Mahathir's displeasure in January, and Johan Jaaffar, editor-in-chief of the Utusan Melayu Group, were forced to resign. Both owed their jobs to the Deputy Prime Minister. Johan Jaaffar had been hand-picked by Anwar in 1992 to take charge of the Utusan Melayu Group, one of the largest newspaper companies, which is controlled by UMNO. Jaaffar had replaced Zainuddin Maidin, who had been appointed a senator and became a strong defender of Dr Mahathir. Editorials in *Utusan Malaysia*, the group's flagship newspaper, had echoed the criticism of nepotism and cronyism raised by Zahid. With Jaaffar's departure, Zainuddin returned to *Utusan* as deputy executive chairman, while Khalid Mohamad, the deputy editor-in-chief, took over Johan's job as group editor-in-chief. In April 2001, Zainuddin gave substance to conjecture surrounding Anwar's media role, saying that from his experience, 'political influence in government [sic] newspapers before the former DPM's (deputy prime minister) dismissal in 1998 was very serious'. He stated: 'Newspapers were in fact controlled by the DPM's office.' Denying that anyone had been pressured to resign, Dr Mahathir said: 'Editors come and go.' However, he delivered a sharp attack on the Malaysian media and specified how he expected the newspapers to operate. He enjoined the Malaysian media not to imitate its counterpart in the West, where news reports were written 'without any consideration of morality and the implications on society' and aimed only at making the writers and newspapers popular. Dr Mahathir proposed that the future training of reporters should focus on their responsibility to society rather than on how they could make a name for themselves.

During the month of August, there was a growing sense of events mounting to a final political showdown between the Prime Minister and his deputy. At a press conference on 7 August, Anwar denied increasingly persistent rumours that he was about to resign. But he showed less confidence than usual when asked if he were firmly in charge of his finance portfolio. He answered: 'Yes, in a way. We are dealing with a difficult economic situation. You would expect the PM to be involved.' At the same time, police investigations of the *50 Dalil* book were going in a direction more fraught for Anwar than the author. A businessman and tennis partner of Anwar, Solaimalai Nallakaruppan, who was alleged in the book to have arranged sexual liaisons for the Deputy Prime Minister, was arrested and on 12 August charged in court under the *Internal Security Act* with unlawful possession of 125 rounds of live ammunition, an offence carrying a mandatory death sentence.

The 'Nalla case' was one of the most curious aspects of the entire Anwar affair. It was subsequently disclosed that police found the bullets while conducting a search of Nallakaruppan's house. He said he had forgotten he had the bullets, which were for the use of a licensed gun he had kept for the managing director of the company employing him. He had returned the gun but not the ammunition in 1991. Six months later Nallakaruppan pleaded guilty to an amended charge under the *Arms Act* of having 125 rounds of ammunition without a permit at his house and was sentenced to 42 months' imprisonment. On 8 October 1999, he was freed when the Court of Appeal allowed his appeal against his sentence. In September 1998, before Anwar was arrested, Nallakaruppan issued a statement through his lawyer denying that he was ever involved in any sexual impropriety or had taken Anwar to properties where the alleged sexual trysts had taken place. He said: 'My fault, if it can be described as one, is that I played tennis with a great man, a fact known to many and now exploited by a few.' When he walked out of a court a free man a year later, Nallakaruppan said to reporters: 'I thank God, my counsel and my wife. I will come back but I won't play tennis any more because of my health.'

A day before Nallakaruppan's first court appearance, Anwar praised Dr Mahathir effusively at a Penang function, which was also attended by the Prime Minister. It appeared to be a desperate attempt to hang onto his job, which was looking increasingly at risk. He called on people to stand firmly behind the Prime Minister and give him their support to overcome the nation's economic problems. He said he wanted to show his loyalty and love to Dr Mahathir, to whom he was indebted. Dr Mahathir had 'vast experience' and his style of politics was 'extraordinary'. Compared with him, Anwar was 'a mere student'. 'I know it is impossible to fight a teacher, what more a father. I wish to take this opportunity to quash any rumours. If these rumours continue, they must originate from people who have bad intentions, who want to cause a fight and weaken the party and the country.' When Anwar said eleven UMNO division leaders in Penang had agreed to nominate Dr Mahathir for the presidency at the party polls the following year, the Prime Minister joked that he hoped they would also give him their votes when the ballot was held. But behind the smiles, the tension was rising and Anwar's renewed pledge of loyalty was too late to save him.

Throughout the month of August, the plunging economy, the political uncertainty and the eruption of a new row with Singapore—with which Malaysia seemed always to be at odds—created an uneasy atmosphere and fuelled wild rumours. In July, at the annual meeting of ASEAN foreign ministers in Manila, Thai Foreign Minister Surin Pitsuwan proposed that the organisation's policy of non-intervention in the internal affairs of member states be replaced by 'flexible engagement'. He said there should be open and frank discussion when problems arose in one member state that affected others. It was a proposal in line with ideas advanced by Anwar and firmly rejected by Dr Mahathir. Indonesia, Malaysia and Singapore all rebuffed the Thai initiative. Singapore's Foreign Minister, S. Jayakumar, said the 'ASEAN way' was 'to mute differences' while his Malaysian counterpart, Abdullah Badawi, depicted it as not 'criticising loudly' or 'posturing adversarially'. But on the return of the Malaysian and Singaporean foreign ministers to their nations' capitals, ASEAN gentility was forsaken for sharp public exchanges at the official level and in the media.

The dispute was over a Malaysian-operated railway station in the island republic. Under a 999-year lease granted in 1918 to the Federation of Malaya, which became Malaysia, the Kuala Lumpur government held 200 hectares of land in Singapore for the purpose of operating a railway service. It comprised several pieces of prime Singapore real estate, including the downtown terminus at Tanjong Pagar. New heat in a long-running dispute over the future of these properties was generated when Singapore shifted its customs and immigrations operations from Tanjong Pagar to premises at the border between the two countries and indicated that Malaysia had agreed to the new arrangement. Denying this, Malaysian officials asserted that Singapore wanted to shut down operations at Tanjong Pagar and take back all the Malaysian properties on the grounds the land was no longer being used for railway purposes.

In Singapore, Mr Jayakumar warned in parliament of 'serious consequences' if Malaysia did not change its stand and a senior Malaysian Foreign Ministry official said Kuala Lumpur would 'view gravely' any disruption of the railway operations.

Blasting Malaysia's 'bristling nationalism', Singapore's *Straits Times* newspaper, which is seldom out of step with government policy, accused the Malaysians of breaking an agreement 'between sovereign states' and, in a comment very much at variance with the ASEAN way, suggested this could harm its neighbour's international standing. It said Malaysia's 'sovereign credit' could be 're-rated downwards with devastating effect by international credit agencies'. Soon after this ominous pronouncement, rating agencies Moody's and Standard & Poor's did just that. Dr Mahathir delivered a warning to Singapore: 'Do not take for granted our good-naturedness.' At the end of the month, Singaporeans were to find out that Kuala Lumpur's 'good-naturedness' had evaporated, resulting in a major blow to their stock market and the freezing of their Malaysian investments.

Meanwhile in mid-August, Dr Mahathir set out on a nationwide tour 'to inform the people about the economic problems' and prepare the ground for the unprecedented financial developments he and Daim were planning. In Kota Kinabalu, the capital of Sabah, he said the government needed the people's 'unwavering support and confidence' as it undertook to revive the economy. He warned that the government might be taking a number of measures that could shock Malaysians. 'We may feel frightened or doubtful as to whether they will benefit us and whether they will help overcome our economic problems. But believe me, every time we act, we think about it deeply and ensure the approach is only for the people's benefit.'

As Dr Mahathir was concluding his national tour, supporters of Anwar were reported to be holding special prayers for the Deputy Prime Minister. This may have been prompted by the sudden interest of some UMNO figures not known to be close friends of Anwar in the issue of morality. In a speech in his role as president of the Malaysian Association of Youth Clubs, Sanusi urged leaders who indulged in immoral activities to step down. The only leader then facing any questions relating to morality was Anwar, because of the allegations in *50 Dalil*. Sanusi said Malaysians should not allow themselves to be influenced by events in the United States where President Clinton, whose frolic with Monica Lewinsky had attracted disapproving attention in Malaysia, hoped Americans would allow him to remain in office 'as if his immoral character was not important'. Another old foe of Anwar, Abdullah Badawi, added to the growing perception that the deputy leader, at the very least, could no longer look forward to succeeding Dr Mahathir. He also referred to Clinton and said Malaysians would not accept such a leader 'as he does not have the credibility to be one'. Malaysians, he said, could not have a leader who had been implicated in such acts. When a Malaysian journalist asked him what such a leader should do, he said it would be 'best for him to resign'. Badawi also noted that while Malaysia was facing a battle to restore its economy, Malaysians must be united, adding: 'There can only be one general, not two.'

While these party leaders seemed to be telling Anwar to resign, a top government officer appeared to hint at another, grimmer prospect ahead for the Deputy Prime Minister. On 22 August, the Attorney-General, Mohtar Abdullah, who would later launch the prosecution of Anwar in his two trials, released a paper entitled 'The Prosecution Policy of the Attorney-General's Chambers', as 'parts of efforts to be more transparent within the limits permitted by the law'. At a press conference, he said there might be more arrests in connection with police investigations into *50 Dalil*, following the laying of charges against Khalid Jafri, the author, and Nallakaruppan. Mohtar said the decision to prosecute anyone was based on evidence, regardless of whether those involved were leaders of the ruling coalition, the opposition, senior government officials or top corporate figures. He said: 'There is no fear or favour. We act strictly on the facts and evidence.' On 30 August, Mohtar featured in press photographs with a judicial commissioner named Augustine Paul on the occasion of the latter's formal installation as a judge of the High Court. The new judge would later gain international exposure when he presided at Anwar's corruption trial.

Meanwhile, Anwar had more reason to feel beleaguered. As the economy showed a second quarter contraction of 6.8 per cent, the Prime Minister's preferred interest rate policy prevailed. Bank Negara cut its main rate from 10 per cent to 9.5 per cent. Within the central bank, the bankers who had encouraged Anwar to toe the IMF line found their views were no longer accepted in cabinet. And when Dr Mahathir and Daim presented to them their plan to stabilise the economy the central bankers argued against it in vain. Continuing to prepare the public for his audacious economic programme, Dr Mahathir said Malaysia did not need advice from foreigners, including the foreign media, on how to revive its economy. Certain parties outside the country, he suggested, were disappointed because Malaysia could still defend its economy without having to call on the IMF, but Malaysia would never 'surrender' to the agency. He said Malaysia would revive the economy in its own way.

On 28 August, the Finance Ministry issued a brief statement to the press announcing that Bank Negara governor Ahmad Mohamad Don and his deputy, Fong Wen Phak, had both tendered their resignations. The statement said Zeti Akhtar Aziz had been appointed as acting governor. It gave no explanation for the resignations. The *New Straits Times* said it was reliably learned that they resigned because they were unhappy with the government's decision to lower interest rates. But in his book, *The Malaysian Currency Crisis*, Dr Mahathir linked their resignations directly to the currency controls that were to follow. He wrote that a 'last minute bid was made by the Governor of the central bank and his deputy to stop the control measures . . . Both of them resigned. The government had to quickly authorise the Assistant Governor to act as head of the central bank and to implement the measures.' The resignations underlined the weakened status of Anwar, who had little to say except to tell people not to pay heed to foreign speculations and deny again that he was quitting.

Events signalling the final repudiation of IMF-favoured policies and Anwar's financial leadership followed in quick succession. As Malaysia celebrated its National Day on 31 August, the Kuala Lumpur Stock Exchange (KLSE) announced the introduction of 'incisive new measures'. Their main impact was to limit trading on KLSE-listed shares to the local bourse, which meant KLSE no longer recognised transactions on Singapore's Central Limit Order Book (CLOB). It was a devastating blow to more than 170 000 Singaporeans who had invested in Malaysian shares. CLOB was instituted following Malaysia's decision to break a long-standing alliance between the KLSE and the Stock Exchange of Singapore (SES), which resulted in the delisting of more than 180 Malaysian counters on the island republic's bourse in 1990. The split reduced the number of shares listed on the SES by half, the Singapore market's size by about a third and business volume by some 40 per cent. Singapore responded by setting up CLOB with 134 Malaysian stocks and six Hong Kong stocks, which were a token gesture to the supposedly 'regional' character of the new over-the-counter trading. From the outset, Malaysia said it did not recognise CLOB and considered it an illegal market. Kuala Lumpur repeatedly called on Singapore to close CLOB, but it continued to operate with the blessing of local authorities. Malaysians suggested that Singapore's inaction was due to the fact that CLOB accounted for 40 to 60 per cent of total trading in the island market.

With the onslaught of the regional economic crisis, official voices in Kuala Lumpur became more strident in their condemnation of CLOB, which they fingered as the centre of 'unbridled foreign shorting' of Malaysian shares. The National Economic Action Council, which was set up to tackle the collapsing Malaysian economy, announced that 'as a matter of national interest, the authorities must address the growing domination of CLOB'. They did so on 31 August. In February 2000, protracted negotiations involving the two exchanges and private Malaysian groups bidding to take over the frozen shares at a discount finally produced an arrangement which most of the Singaporean investors were prepared to accept. It called for the staggered release of the shares for trading or selling directly through the KLSE, with investors paying a transfer fee to Effective Capital, a company headed by Akbar Khan, a well-connected tycoon with interests in Singapore, Malaysia and other countries. The CLOB affair put new strains on the uneasy Singapore–Malaysia relationship and some Singaporeans complained about the deal. But CLOB investors benefited from the delay in the release of the shares. By early 2000, the stock market's recovery from the gloomy days of 1998 meant that their worth had doubled from about M\$10 billion to M\$20 billion.

A day after the deep-freezing of the CLOB shares, Malaysia slapped controls on the currency trading that Dr Mahathir had blamed for the collapse of the economy. Bank Negara announced that from 1 October the Malaysian ringgit would no longer be tradable overseas and that the central bank would soon introduce a fixed exchange rate for the currency. It was eventually pegged at 3.8 ringgit to the US dollar. Under new rules, holders of ringgit in overseas banks would have to bring their funds back within a month or see them lose their value. Foreigners would be required to obtain Bank Negara's permission to convert ringgit in external accounts into foreign currencies. Bank Negara explained that the measures were introduced 'to regain monetary independence and insulate the Malaysian economy from the prospects of further deterioration in the global economic and financial environment'. In another move, investors in the stock market were not permitted to cash in their share holdings for a year.

An important benefit of the government action was that it gave Malaysia freedom to implement a lower interest rate policy to reflate the economy. The *Singapore Business Times* called it a 'bold but high-risk gamble'. But many Western financial analysts decried it in commentaries disparaging towards Dr Mahathir. In The Malaysian Currency Crisis, Dr Mahathir said the primary objective of Malaysia's selective exchange control regime was for Malaysia to 'regain control of its economy from the currency speculators and manipulators' so that Malaysians could 'decide the destiny of Malaysia'.

In a speech to a 'Symposium of the First Anniversary of Currency Control' in Kuala Lumpur, Dr Mahathir said that before deciding on controls, Malaysia had 'tried practically everything . . . And everything we tried failed.' Dr Mahathir said that when the real economy began to collapse, they had 'made a horrible mistake'. The government had adopted what was called, 'The IMF package without the IMF'. He said that 'under the finest IMF advice' the government had cut fiscal spending when it should have introduced a deficit budget, something Malaysia could well afford after years of budgetary surpluses. The banks should have been left alone but, instead the six-month non-performing loan regime was reduced to three-months and after the institutions were told not to lend money for so-called non-productive activities they 'stopped lending altogether'. Dr Mahathir said the government was told that the markets would not see the return of confidence until they saw blood. 'We obliged but it was never enough. Blood, more blood must be spilt.' The currency fell in value from 2.5 ringgit to the US dollar to 4.8, while the collapse of the stock market resulted in market capitalisation diving from M$800 billion to M$300 billion.

Dr Mahathir took evident delight in recalling that following the introduction of currency controls, a senior White House official described the turn of events in Malaysia as a tragedy and predicted the measures would be a 'spectacular failure'. *Time* magazine quoted a Bangkok-based expert as saying: 'Mahathir is turning Malaysia into a Burma.' *Business Week* said the steps taken could run down foreign reserves, making devaluation likely and prompting trade restrictions'. Dr Mahathir said the 'great economist Milton Friedman' described Malaysia's move as 'the worst possible choice'. But Malaysia's 'unorthodox, bold and strong measures' stopped the economic rot. At the time of Dr Mahathir's speech, the stock market's capitalisation had risen to M$500 billion while foreign reserves, which amounted to US$20 billion in August 1998, stood at US$32 billion. Many financial analysts who at first criticised the measures taken by Malaysia subsequently agreed that they stabilised the economy. In February 2001, Michael Dee, Morgan Stanley Dean Witter's Singapore-based regional chief, said the capital controls introduced by Dr Mahathir had worked for Malaysia, 'And they never took a dime from the IMF.'

But at the time of their introduction, the measures sent shock waves through the region. A Reuter report said Asia was rocked by an earthquake when Malaysia 'imposed draconian foreign exchange controls and sent investors fleeing regional markets'. However, the impact of Dr Mahathir's economic recovery programme was a minor tremor compared with the stunning jolt of the extraordinary political developments which followed within days of the imposition of currency controls.

5 | The axing of an heir

Anwar's role as the number two leader came abruptly to an end on 2 September 1998. Rumours surrounding his future and the introduction of financial measures which ran counter to the policies he had championed had led people to anticipate some action against him. But Malaysians were nevertheless shocked to pick up their newspapers on 3 September and discover that the man who had been deputy prime minister and anointed successor to the Prime Minister had been removed from office. Greater shocks were to follow. On successive days, Anwar was sacked, then expelled from UMNO. He was no longer Deputy Prime Minister, Finance Minister or party deputy president. In a blink, the second most powerful man in the country had become merely a vulnerable citizen.

Anwar's sacking was announced on the night of 2 September in a brief statement issued by Bernama, the national news agency. No reasons were given for his dismissal. The *New Straits Times* said it was not immediately clear why he was removed but for a year he had been 'battling allegations of sexual improprieties following the release of a letter in August last year and the publication of a book entitled "50 Reasons Why Anwar Cannot Become PM"'.

Suddenly the sexual allegations were taking on a life they had not had a year earlier when they were dismissed by the Prime Minister and the chief of police. And yet nothing had changed on the face of it except for their restatement in *50 Dalil*.

One of the most riveting elements in the events of early September was the instant transformation of Anwar from suave, sophisticated, affable, senior member of the hierarchy, who had been publicly ingratiating and subservient towards his mentor, the Prime Minister, into a fierce anti-establishment rebel. He went quickly on the attack. Shortly before nine o'clock on the night of his dismissal, Anwar addressed a group of followers at his official residence. They were mainly members of UMNO Youth and from the Muslim youth movement, Abim, from which he had drawn his core support in the past. He said that he was a victim of a political conspiracy—a claim that was to become the refrain of his defence against his accusers. He also said he might be arrested under the *Internal Security Act* and called on his supporters to be calm.

Soon after Anwar's dismissal was announced, the police chief, Rahim Noor, was asked by journalists whether the former deputy prime minister was being investigated on the basis of the contents of *50 Dalil*. Rahim answered that several things were mentioned in the book relating to Anwar, so naturally investigations would cover him as well as the author. Whether the reports would lead to Anwar being charged in court would 'depend on the outcome of the investigations'. No one in a senior position spoke out on Anwar's behalf. Rather, newspapers featured statements from UMNO officials and state leaders urging the public to support the decision to sack Anwar. Most significant was the comment by Najib Tun Razak, the Education Minister, UMNO Vice President and member of Anwar's Vision Team, who said he believed Dr Mahathir had studied in detail all the facts before making the decision, and called on people to give the Prime Minister their 'full trust and remain solidly behind him'.

Abdul Razak Baginda, executive director of the Malaysian Strategic Research Centre, which was founded by Najib, believes Anwar had a 'false notion of his popularity', which led him to believe senior party people would support him. He told me Anwar 'never got key people on his side'. Razak recalled that when Tengku Razaleigh unsuccessfully challenged Dr Mahathir in 1987, he had a significant number of senior people supporting him, including his running mate, Musa Hitam, as well as Abdullah Badawi and Rais Yatim. Razak said: 'In 1998 when Anwar fell, when he was removed from office in September, he never got anyone. No one was willing to cross the line. Had Anwar been able to persuade five, six cabinet members to cross the line, things could have been dramatically changed. He never got the support.' Anwar made the mistake of not consulting anyone. If he had, he would have learned that 'everyone thought that what he did [in trying to oust Dr Mahathir] was wrong'. Razak said that while he personally came to the conclusion that 'what they did to Anwar was entirely wrong', he thought it was also 'wrong for Anwar to have taken that step against Mahathir' . . .

> I mean, if you think about it, Mahathir must have felt really hurt. It's like a father and a son. A father is in deep trouble and the son thought that it was the right time to kill the father.

Razak said that in the period leading towards the UMNO general assembly of 1998, Dr Mahathir was 'very vulnerable' as a result of the events in Indonesia and the failing economy. He said: 'And here you have his deputy, his loyal deputy, whom Dr Mahathir had nurtured and taken into the party despite protests from a lot of prominent UMNO members, starting to move against him. Now, I think this 73-year-old man was bitterly hurt by that and that was it.' Razak believes Dr Mahathir would not have reacted so strongly against Anwar if his deputy had not started the campaign against him. During the economic crisis of 1997–98, Anwar 'should have remained loyal and steadfast to Mahathir'.

Razak said even people who thought it might be time for Dr Mahathir to go were opposed to the action taken by Anwar, adding: 'In UMNO, you do not kill a prime minister—at least not so blatantly.' He said that while some UMNO elders were uncomfortable with Anwar's liberal policies and style, his succession was ensured before he made his grab for power. The job was his. Everyone knew that he was going to be prime minister. But Anwar was impatient. Razak said: 'At some point, he had this self-aggrandisement. He thought he was a great person. Americans were urging him on. The international media was playing him up. Obviously he thought he was there. He thought it was the right time to seize the moment. But he thought wrong.'

Anwar was expelled from UMNO at a four-and-a-half hour meeting of the supreme council on the night of 3 September. Again no one spoke up for him. While the disquiet of Anwar's peers over his push for power was part of the cause of his isolation, as Razak observed, there was another factor that deterred any supreme council member from taking his side. That was Dr Mahathir's authority as UMNO president and his clear determination to rid the party of his offending one-time heir. Anyone who stood in his way was likely to find himself bereft of any influence or standing in the party. The only backing for Anwar came from outside the senior party ranks. After Dr Mahathir announced the supreme council action, several hundred of Anwar's supporters from UMNO Youth and Abim demonstrated at the entrance to the party headquarters. They shouted, 'Long live Anwar', jeered Mahathir supporters on the supreme council and threw crumpled pieces of paper, plastic water bottles and cups in the direction of the Prime Minister and other officials as they entered their cars under the protection of riot police.

That day also there were developments in the Nallakaruppan case. A police officer from the Criminal Investigation Department, Musa Hassan, filed an affidavit in the High Court in relation to the case involving Anwar's former tennis partner. Although no charges had been laid against Anwar as yet, the details of the affidavit were spread over the front pages of the nation's newspapers, together with reports on Anwar's expulsion from UMNO. Under the heading, 'Ex-DPM implicated in sexual misconduct', the *New Straits Times* said Anwar's impropriety included 'sodomy with a man, illicit sex and seducing a businessman's wife'. Some of the encounters, it reported, were alleged to have been facilitated by Nallakarappun. The affidavit outlined statements by seven witnesses, 'including a man who claimed he was sodomised 15 times by Anwar and a woman who alleged she was paid M$350 by Nallakaruppan after having sex with Anwar'. According to the newspaper the affidavit also stated that Anwar had 'attempted to seduce the wife of a businessman who were both in his delegation on a trip to Washington'. Anwar was subsequently charged with a single count of sodomy. No charges were ever laid against him in relation to the other allegations in the lengthy affidavit, which also referred to a driver who had been asked to 'fetch Chinese, Mexican and Eurasian women and women of other races for illicit sexual activities', two women who rejected his advances and a third who reportedly said she discussed matters of national politics after having sex with Anwar. After the allegations were printed in the press and implanted in the minds of the reading public, they were never mentioned again.

In a second affidavit, Attorney-General Mohtar Abdullah said the police investigations involved national security. If there was prima facie evidence, 'Nallakaruppan and/or the national leader concerned could be charged in court under the country's laws'. These laws, according to Mohtar, included the *Internal Security Act*, *Official Secrets Act*, *Penal Code*, *Women and Girls Protection Act* and *Prevention of Corruption Act*. The full text of the police officer's affidavit, which the *New Straits Times* published, made reference to an 'apartment, Tivoli Villa in Bangsar', to which Nallakaruppan had access as a director of the company owning it. The apartment was later to feature in bizarre testimony given and then wiped from the record at Anwar's first trial. But before there had been any public move by the authorities to bring Anwar to court, the media had put him in the dock and presented the case for the prosecution. The issue of sexual misconduct was no longer a mere allegation but a charge which he was being required to disprove. Whatever the outcome of any future court case involving Anwar, he had been smeared with enough dirt to severely damage his reputation outside his support group.

From this point on, there appeared to be close collaboration between the establishment press and members of the administration on coverage of the Anwar affair, which intensified long-standing public distrust of the media. The Bar Council said in a statement that it was dismayed at the lack of responsibility by the media in publishing the affidavit and other documents in relation to the Nallakaruppan case. Their publication was 'a breach of the rule of natural justice and fair play'. As the saga progressed, the main newspapers steadily lost credibility with Malaysians. While they continued to hold readers for a time because they reported extensively on Anwar's public statements before his arrest and later published detailed accounts of his trials, their circulations eventually suffered after Malaysians discovered alternative information sources on the Internet and in foreign media.

At the supreme council meeting, Anwar was invited to resign from the party. In view of the potential threat to his liberty contained in the affidavit presented in court that day, his smartest move would seem to have been to quit UMNO and take the first flight out to a foreign country. He would have been welcomed in the United States, where he would have had no problem in obtaining a comfortable college appointment. UMNO officials said later he would have been allowed to leave the country. But Anwar chose to fight the system. It was an ill-fated choice.

At a press conference after the supreme council meeting, Dr Mahathir announced that he would act as Finance Minister until he found a replacement for Anwar. Asked why Anwar had been sacked from his jobs as deputy prime minister and finance minister, Dr Mahathir said only that he found him 'unsuitable' for the two positions. The details would come later. Anwar also held a press conference at his house, where he said Dr Mahathir had given him an ultimatum to either resign or be sacked, with the possibility of charges being brought against him. In a convoluted remark, he seemed to concede that his loyalty to Dr Mahathir had been feigned, although he also said he regarded the Prime Minister as a father. He asked how it was that only when he was alleged to be preparing to challenge the party president he had suddenly 'become a threat to the country, a foreign agent, the most corrupt person'. He added: 'If I had continued to show my total loyalty, none of this would arise.'

Newspapers continued to report that the removal of Anwar from the cabinet and party was supported by UMNO leaders and members of parliament. Asked to comment on Anwar's allegations of a political conspiracy, Najib said: 'One should not attack the very system which one upheld when in government service. The system has worked well.' At a press conference on 4 September, Anwar announced his intention to make a nationwide tour to meet the people and counter the charges against him. He also announced that a reform movement was now under way in Malaysia. With this declaration, the reform theme that he had borrowed from Indonesia was formally installed as a political platform. He was now prepared to draw more clearly a parallel between the ouster of Indonesia's President Suharto and the current situation in Malaysia, declaring: 'The fall of Suharto has precipitated this crisis.' Asked whether he would join PAS, Anwar said he had not made up his mind, but he added that PAS president Fadzil Noor and other opposition leaders had called at his house or telephoned him.

Earlier in the day, Anwar had attended Friday prayers at the national mosque dressed in a plain white tunic, sarong and sandals, like the Pak Sheikh of yore. Anwar, who was displaying a new spirit of combativeness after several weeks of treading softly in an attempt to save his job, was every day looking more like the student activist of his youth than the former finance minister. At his press conference he said that at the mosque one could 'sense the spontaneous support for the struggle towards reform'. From the time of his sacking, there was a theatrical quality to Anwar's pronouncements, as if a simple unadorned statement could not convey the awful injustice he had suffered. His oratorical bent assured him a receptive audience when he spoke publicly. But his remarks at press conferences sometimes sounded more designed to impress than to inform the journalists. He had only been sacked, after all. Later, of course, he would win widespread sympathy for the worse fate that befell him.

Anwar's wife, Azizah, who was seated beside him at the press conference was asked whether she believed the sexual allegations against her husband. She said they were baseless and added that she believed totally in her husband's innocence. 'This is not a politically correct statement, because I really believe it. It is not just the I-stand-by-my-man stuff. I really believe him. I married him for the man he is and for what he stands for.' Throughout the period of Anwar's arrest and the two trials ahead, Azizah would be the most credible and admired person in the Anwar camp, calm (most of the time), steadfast and courageous in the face of the dramatic events that snatched her from her stable and secure life as wife of a senior leader and plunged her into a bleak and nightmarish existence.

The sacking of Anwar came as a shock to foreign governments and observers as well as to Malaysians. Together with Dr Mahathir's earlier imposition of currency controls, it shattered the image of Malaysia as the most politically and economically stable nation among the troubled Asian economies. In 1997, Malaysia had stood out as the country that seemed better equipped than most other ASEAN members, by virtue of its political tranquillity and succession arrangements, to weather the regional financial storm. Anwar was not only in line to succeed Dr Mahathir as UMNO president but had also been publicly anointed as heir apparent by the Prime Minister himself. The remarkable events surrounding Anwar, however, reinforced the shift in international perceptions of the country, which persisted even when the economy recovered and relative calm returned to the political scene. Anwar's friends abroad have continued to present a jaundiced view of Malaysia, which has coloured many overseas evaluations of the situation.

In the immediate wake of Anwar's dismissal, foreign analysts said it had created a political vacuum by removing the man widely considered as the most capable person among possible candidates to succeed Dr Mahathir. The nation's international standing was also undermined by the revelation that the picture of a harmonious relationship between Dr Mahathir and Anwar was a charade, promoted by the government and supported by much of the Malaysian media. And, if there was any truth in the sexual allegations against Anwar, the portrayal of Malaysia's leaders as models of morality was open to question. Indeed, the uncertainty now seen to be surrounding Malaysia's future was bad for ASEAN, strengthening the outside impression that the region was in deep trouble, from which it would not soon recover. Now, only tiny Singapore, among the members of ASEAN, was free from the serious tribulations of its neighbours.

The first shots were fired in what was to become a major cyber offensive by Anwar supporters with the publication on the website *www.anwar.com* of two letters which Anwar had written to the Prime

Minister towards the end of August. They showed that up to the last minute Anwar was endeavouring desperately to persuade the man whom he had tried to depose to save him from the growing threat to his political career. He did not then link Dr Mahathir to the conspirators he held responsible for the allegations against him, although he was later to brand the Prime Minister as its mastermind. In the first letter, dated 25 August—most of which is reproduced below—he denied leaking government secrets and implored Dr Mahathir 'not to let the lies of the envious cause you to doubt it'. The second letter, dated 28 August, ended suppliantly: 'I submit this for your wise consideration. And may God give you peace and blessings.' Before long the words of esteem would be replaced by excoriation of his mentor.

On 25 August he wrote:

The Honourable Dato' Seri Dr Mahathir Mohamad,

Dear Dato' Seri,

I would like to enlighten you regarding the calumnious campaign against me as a person and a politician. Considering the method by which the slander was spread and the timing of its release, I cannot but conclude that it was politically motivated. Only the two of us can clarify the muddied waters and untangle the knots.

The conspiracy to bring me down through calumny began more than a year ago with a poison-pen letter circulated so widely that it reached even the small UMNO branches. Normally, I would ignore accusations contained in unsigned circulars, but this time they were too offensive to be left unchallenged. I therefore lodged a police report on August 15 last year. I hoped then that the smear campaign would stop.

Imagine my consternation when I learned, a few days before the UMNO general assembly, that a person by the name of Khalid Jafri had written a book which in part repeated all the poison-pen lies and that the book would be distributed by the tens of thousands at the venue of the assembly. To prevent it, I had no choice but to get a court injunction. Unlike the poison-pen letter, the book carries the names of an author and a publisher, as if daring anyone to challenge the truth of its contents. I had to go to court to make that challenge; otherwise some readers would suspect that there was truth in the book.

My confidential secretary, Mohammed Azmin Ali, made a police report over the distribution of the book, the contents of which are clearly criminally libellous, and I have appointed a lawyer to handle a civil defamation suit against the author and publisher. I have since won an interlocutory injunction, effective until the case is settled. The named suspects are the ones who should be subject to police investigation. According to the *Information Act*, the onus is on them to prove their accusations, to show admissible evidence in court—not rumour, hearsay or fabrications. But a week after my report was lodged, it became obvious that the police were instead looking into my personal affairs. It was as if I had become the suspect. Their current behaviour indicates some malice towards me. Instead of concentrating on the libellous book, they are now listening to stories churned out by the rumour mill, which is operated by politicians and millionaires who are intent on driving a wedge between the two of us and cutting me down.

I see a picture of contradictions emerging, one that is unsettling. I do not object to the raid on the house of Datuk Nalla and his arrest on the justification that these would help the police in their investigation. But I have since received information that the idea was to extract a confession from him that would incriminate me in activities that are immoral and disgraceful.

I am certain that the author of the book would not have made up such wild and fantastic accusations if he were not sponsored by influential personalities willing to pay him huge sums of money. I have indicated above that there is a factory churning out these lies. And there is no lie more hurtful to me—and the others who are implicated—than the one that says I have fathered an illegitimate child. It shocked me to hear the police suggest that I undergo a DNA test. Eventually, my lawyers agreed to the test but proposed that it would be sufficient to carry out the test on Azmin, his wife and the affected child to confirm that the child issued from them. Praise be to God, it was thus confirmed. The Minister of Science,

Technology and the Environment, Datuk Law Hieng Ding, himself telephoned me to give the good news.

But now, telephone conversations from my home, which are recorded by the police, have become an issue. I am accused of being a foreign agent. Many stories have been woven regarding the role of Datuk Nalla, indeed about all the friends I play tennis with and several of my officers. I play tennis once or twice a week at the Tropicana, Kiara or Bangsar. There are stories that have been concocted about activities besides tennis during my tennis hours, complete with the name of a woman, a car registration number and an apartment number at Tivoli Villa. They are all lies.

I play tennis openly, not in secret, beginning around 6.15 pm and stopping before the maghrib prayers, although I would sometimes stop for maghrib and continue with a game afterwards. Every time I play, there are policemen posted outside the court. My tennis games are never played in secret and they are always under police watch. I have also been accused of meeting a woman at the Flamingo Hotel, a place I have never set foot on. And I have been to the Tivoli Villa only twice—accompanied by Azizah to visit my adopted brother, Sukma.

I have been told that I may be charged under the *Official Secrets Act*. What a baffling thought! To charge under this act a person who holds the second-most important position in government is nothing short of insulting. If it were true that government secrets had leaked, this would be the first time in history that the immediate suspect was the DPM.

Please do not let the lies of the envious cause you to doubt it. They are but a political conspiracy.

Yours truly,

Anwar Ibrahim

The letter implied that the Minister of Domestic Trade and Consumer Affairs, Megat Junid Ayob, as well as Daim and Dr Mahathir's political secretary, Abdul Aziz Shamsuddin, were involved in the political conspiracy. All three denied involvement. Megat Junid's glamorous, actress wife, Norzielah Jalil, was a friend of Ummi Hafilda, who had sought her help in having the surat terbang—the letter containing sexual allegations against Anwar—delivered to Dr Mahathir. The letter found its way to Abdul Aziz, who disclosed to reporters a year later that he had passed it on to the Prime Minister. He said Dr Mahathir gave it to Anwar, telling him to 'read and destroy it'.

Abdul Aziz's relationship with the Prime Minister went back to 1975, when Dr Mahathir, who was then Education Minister, recruited him fresh out of university as a special officer. In 1981, when Dr Mahathir became Prime Minister, he made Abdul Aziz his political secretary. At the time of their first meeting, Abdul Aziz was president of the University of Malaya's Malay Language Association. As Education Minister, Dr Mahathir wanted him to counter the growing anti-government agitation fostered by another student, Anwar Ibrahim. Recalling his introduction to Dr Mahathir in a newspaper interview, Abdul Aziz said he was asked by the Education Minister to 'find a way to make students understand the importance of being responsible'. Some 23 years later, Anwar was an anti-government agitator again, having soared to heights of political power above Abdul Aziz, while his former fellow student was still working for Dr Mahathir. By the time Abdul Aziz, then 62, was sworn in as a senator in November 1999 ahead of his appointment as Deputy Education Minister, Anwar had accused him of being the mastermind behind the conspiracy. Speaking to reporters, the new senator said the allegation was baseless, adding that he was 'not as clever as that'. He said it was Dr Mahathir's prerogative to remove anyone working under him.

Early in 2000, Megat Junid was involved in an apparent gambit by Anwar to have the former Minister of Domestic Trade and Consumer Affairs, who had lost his parliamentary seat in the November 1999 election, help his defence. In April 2000, Megat Junid said that he had met Anwar at the latter's request during a recess in his sodomy trial. He said that they had chatted, joked and laughed together. On 27 March, Megat Junid signed a statutory declaration which said that he did not believe the allegations of sexual misconduct against Anwar 'up to today'. Megat Junid said that when he signed the statutory declaration he thought it was the same as the draft to which he had agreed with Anwar's lawyers. But when he received a copy of the declaration he spotted a difference. He said he 'could not sleep for two nights' so he went back to the same Commissioner of Oaths and made a change. The amended declaration said he did not believe the allegations of sexual misconduct against Anwar up until 2 September 1998. Megat Junid said Anwar's lawyers were unhappy with the amendment. Only the first statutory declaration was released to the media and posted on a pro-Anwar website. Megat Junid said his conscience was clear. With the second declaration, he was doing justice to himself and the court. He added: 'I have to tell the truth.' Megat Junid also said he still considered Anwar his friend, stating: 'What he did is a different question. Whether he did it or not, that is his responsibility.'

On 28 August Anwar wrote again to Dr Mahathir:

The Honourable Dato' Seri Dr Mahathir Mohamad
Dear Dato' Seri,

I would like to add to the letter I wrote on August 25, 1998. For more than a year, the police have known of a plot to drive a wedge between the two of us by raising doubts in the public mind regarding my character. (The [police] report is hereby submitted by hand.)

I attach here also Dato' Nalla's affidavit and clippings of press reports on them. It is clear that his detention and interrogation have nothing to do with national security. Instead he has been promised his freedom provided he signs a statement prepared by the police to disgrace his friends.

I would also like to inform you that a police officer has telephoned a former Universiti Kebangsaan Malaysia lecturer to extort a statement from him to the effect that he once had a homosexual relationship with me. He was threatened with prosecution on charges related to his past activities.

These are additional pieces of information that support my conviction that all those lies about me were concocted as part of a political conspiracy.

I submit this for your wise consideration.
And may God give you peace and blessings.
Anwar Ibrahim.

There was more bad news for Anwar on 5 September. Police chief Rahim Noor announced the police had evidence that he had used his position as deputy prime minister to interfere with investigations into the book *50 Dalil*. The police chief said information had been received from members of the public that Anwar had intimidated witnesses to prevent them from cooperating with police investigations and had tried to tamper with evidence. Anwar then provoked Rahim into an angry response by stating at a press conference that the police chief should be more professional and not allow the police to be used by the government for political reasons. Rahim responded angrily: 'It is not true that we are not professional, it is not true that we are biased and it is not true that we are part of what is thought by him and others to be a conspiracy.' Anwar was to become even more critical of Rahim and the police, building up a store of animosity in Rahim which found its release in his brutal attack on Anwar on the night of his arrest.

At times Anwar seemed bewildered by the swiftness with which he had been stripped of power and accorded criminal status. However, Malaysian political analysts to whom I spoke commented on his political naivetey. In an interview with Cable News Network, Anwar said, referring to his sacking by Dr Mahathir: 'I thought he would have done it in a more refined way.' Anyone who thought the hard man of Malaysian politics, a survivor of many savage power struggles, would deal with a foe in a refined way was defeated before the battle began.

On 6 September, the law enforcers closed in further on Anwar with the arrest of Sukma Darmawan, the son of an Indonesian friend of his family, who had been adopted by the former deputy prime minister's father when Sukma had come to Malaysia as a teenager to study. No reason for the arrest was immediately given. Anwar attacked the authorities over the arrest in an address at his home to a group of supporters, among whom were none of the senior UMNO politicians or corporate leaders who had been his intimates. He said his erstwhile friends were 'shaken and lacking in courage'. The evaporation of his support at the senior levels of UMNO was reflected in the fact that his only staunch followers with party positions at the time were Ruslan Kassim and Abdul Rahim Ghouse, UMNO

Youth chiefs of Negri Sembilan and Penang. A veteran Malaysian journalist, echoing the comparison made by the Malaysian Strategic Research Centre's Razak, recalled that Tengku Razaleigh took 'a number of other heavyweights with him' when he left UMNO to form his opposition party and asked: 'Who does Anwar have in the heavy-weight class? No one.'

Anwar's public support came from a motley band with limited political influence. They included such strange bedfellows as the non-government organisation Burma Solidarity Movement, the two main opposition parties—DAP and PAS—and student movements. The groups had little in common apart from an antipathy towards Dr Mahathir and the government. Anwar was also supported by ulama (religious officials), who had clashed with Dr Mahathir over his moderate approach to Islamic issues, and other conservative elements such as Islamic students and language nationalists opposed to greater use of English. They clearly did not regard Anwar as a modern liberal Islamic moderate. On 7 September, Badawi accused Anwar of a deliberate attempt to 'get his supporters to rise up against the government' and of focusing public attention away from the 'real issue', which was his sexual behaviour.

At a meeting with UMNO leaders and at a later press conference on 8 September, the Prime Minister finally gave more concrete reasons for Anwar's dismissal: he had been sacked for 'moral misconduct'. The Prime Minister said he had carried out his own investigations into the sexual allegations against Anwar and he was 'convinced' they were true. He had concluded that his deputy was 'not qualified to lead the country'. The dismissal, he said, was not due to differences over political or economic matters but because Anwar's character did 'not qualify him to be a leader of a country like Malaysia'. His investigations were not triggered by the possibility of Anwar challenging him as UMNO president in the next year's party elections. He could defend himself against any such challenge. Dr Mahathir said that when the allegations surfaced the previous year, he did not believe them, thinking this was a plot to oust his deputy. However, he had now concluded that Anwar was not suited to succeed him because the evidence implicating him was very clear. Dr Mahathir said his decision to sack Anwar was the 'most unpleasant experience' in his 17 years as Prime Minister. He was thinking of retiring in 1998 and even gave Anwar a chance to lead the country while he took a vacation. If it had not been for the economic problems he would have stepped down.

Dr Mahathir said that what was unacceptable was the fact that Anwar had not only indulged in immoral activities but at the same time portrayed himself as a very religious person and one who held strongly to the teachings of Islam. What he did was 'against the image that he portrayed'. He believed that people would understand that what he said about Anwar was true; after all, why would he make such accusations against a person whom he had brought in to succeed him and was a friend. He had 'lots of enemies', he said, against whom he would prefer to make the allegations. Asked whether there was any possibility of Anwar being reinstated, the Prime Minister said: 'No, not a hope.' However, his expectation that people would believe his accusations against Anwar was not fulfilled.

From 11 September, the government and establishment media did its best to turn the public's attention away from the Anwar affair to a more wholesome form of entertainment—the Sixteenth Commonwealth Games. The event was opened by the Malaysian monarch, Yang di-Pertuan Agong Tuanku Ja'afar, in the presence of Dr Mahathir and Commonwealth Games Federation president Prince Edward, whose mother was scheduled to officiate at the closing ceremony. While the Games were a sporting success, they did not stir as much interest in Malaysians as the unfolding political drama. Taking his case to the people, Anwar became increasingly more populist in speech, more rumpled in dress—with uncombed hair and untucked shirts—and more fierce in criticism of his former establishment associates. The ex-deputy prime minister repeatedly portrayed himself as the protector of the poor while he was in government. He said he was 'a thorn in the flesh' of the people who framed him because he stressed the need for low-cost houses and for wealth to be more evenly distributed.

Critics of the new Anwar questioned his credibility, asking what he had done for farmers, fishermen and the working class when he was agriculture minister and finance minister. Supporters said he had been more liberal-minded than other members of the government.

Chandra Muzaffar, a prominent social and political commentator who later became deputy president of the National Justice Party formed by Anwar followers and headed by his wife, Azizah, issued a statement saying the former deputy prime minister had 'spearheaded the government's programme to identify and assist the hardcore poor'. But Chandra acknowledged that it would be naive to expect Anwar to 'translate these and other attributes of good governance into reality in a situation where preserving the awesome power of authority is the primary purpose of the state'. Other social activists, like Rustam Sani, as mentioned earlier thought nothing would have changed significantly [in the status quo] if there had been a smooth transition of power from Dr Mahathir to Anwar.

Meanwhile, in his Penang constituency, Anwar unveiled his Permatang Pauh Declaration, in which he promised to work towards justice for all, equality in the distribution of wealth and the eradication of corruption, among other goals. In speeches, he depicted Dr Mahathir as another President Suharto. Addressing himself to the absent Prime Minister before a gathering of thousands of people, he said: 'You have power. You monopolise everything. You give things to your children and you make people poor.' In Alor Star, at a meeting organised by the Kedah Ulama Association, he said he would go after the people who conspired against him, including newspaper editors. Back in Kuala Lumpur, he declared that he was the leader of the people, representing their conscience. He said he had never received 'such love and affection' from the public as he had since his sacking, adding: 'I will fight and ensure their struggles are not in vain.'

On 15 September, police chief Rahim Noor announced the arrest under the *Internal Security Act* of Munawar Anees, a Pakistani with permanent resident status in Malaysia and the United States, and of one of Anwar's former political secretaries. He also said a second political secretary would be detained if he did not turn himself into police. Anwar told visitors to his house about the arrest of his 'friend' Munawar, who had written speeches for him and was the former editor of an Islamic publication published in Malaysia. He also said the family of his former secretary Muhamad Ahmad were warned not to inform anyone of his arrest, declaring: 'I don't know what kind of system [it is]—the Shabak or Mossad?' Shabak or Shin Bet is Israel's internal security agency while Mossad deals with espionage. He did himself no favours with Rahim Noor by comparing the police with the intelligence agencies of Israel, a pariah state in the eyes of predominantly Muslim Malaysia. Anwar said the police should use the rule of law and not the law of the jungle. Rahim Noor, ominously advised Anwar not to 'step beyond the limit' in criticising the police. The police, he said to reporters, took offence at him comparing them with Shabak and Mossad. Rahim Noor said Israel was a 'very sensitive word in the country', adding: 'We could understand if he were to accuse us of acting like pirates but comparing us with the Israelis is unacceptable.'

Anwar gradually dropped the pretence that he had not planned to challenge Dr Mahathir in 1999 and that Zahid had acted on his own, admitting publicly for the first time that he had prompted the UMNO Youth chief to raise the issues of cronyism and nepotism which had been directed against Dr Mahathir. Speaking in Kuantan, the capital of Pahang state, he said he would have challenged the president at the UMNO elections the following year, declaring: 'That was why they sacked me from the party.' In Kuala Terengganu, capital of Terengganu, he disputed Dr Mahathir's contention that had planned to retire in 1998. He said: 'As his former deputy, I know that the only way to remove Dr Mahathir as Prime Minister is by the people ousting him.'

Dr Mahathir would 'have to bear the consequences' if he did not resign. Anwar stated: 'A prime minister who is fair will be supported but a prime minister who is cruel will be opposed.' In Kota Baru, capital of Kelantan, he said that Dr Mahathir had lost the support of the people and should step down honourably. His attacks on the Prime Minister became steadily harsher, and in Kuala Lumpur he told a press conference that Dr Mahathir was 'now orchestrating the entire mission' against him using Gestapo tactics. But the party leadership continued to stand publicly behind the president. Responding to Anwar's call for Dr Mahathir to resign, Najib said at issue was the former deputy prime minister's moral and personal problems; it had 'nothing to do with the position of the Prime Minister'. He said the National Front members of parliament were solid in their support of Dr Mahathir, who also had the unanimous backing of the UMNO supreme council.

As Anwar moved around the country, attracting tens of thousands of people to hear him denounce the Prime Minister and his government, the authorities said he was breaking the law by speaking in public without a permit but took no steps to stop him. However, it soon became clear they had not been idle. There had been many indications that events were moving towards a climax but when it came in the weekend of 19–20 September, Malaysians were left stunned and disbelieving.

6 | Sexual shocks for a prudish people

On Saturday 19 September, Anwar's adopted brother Sukma, then 37, and Anwar's friend Munawar, 51, who had been arrested earlier in the month, made brief appearances in separate Sessions Court hearings. Each man pleaded guilty to a charge of committing an act of gross indecency by allowing Anwar to sodomise him and was sentenced to six months' imprisonment. Malaysia's usually staid Sunday newspapers took on the appearance of Western tabloids, plastering reports on the court cases across their front pages under provocative banner headlines. 'We were sodomised', blared the *New Straits Times* over its lead story. The *Star's* article appeared under the words: 'Two jailed for sodomy, They implicate Anwar in unnatural sexual acts.' Some newspapers gave every detail of the charges, publishing for the first time in Malaysia explicit descriptions of an act both illegal under Malaysian law and forbidden by Islam. The *New Straits Times* did not merely say that Anwar had engaged in a homosexual act with the two men. It printed in full the charges, which in each case stated that the defendant had committed the alleged act of gross indecency 'by allowing him [Anwar] to introduce his penis into your anus'. The publication of these words—taboo under normal circumstances—was an astonishing departure for the establishment media and was widely believed to have been officially encouraged to counter Anwar's attacks on the government by destroying his Islamic credentials. Side by side with photographs of Sukma and Munawar on newspaper front pages was a picture of yellow track-suited members of Malaysia's rhythmic gymnastic team beaming for the camera after winning the Commonwealth Games gold medal. It was a grotesque juxtaposition, which underlined the peculiar nature of what was occurring in Malaysia.

The court-appointed lawyer for Munawar said that the defendant was 'all the while under the influence and pressure of Anwar Ibrahim and therefore in a hopeless predicament'. By pleading guilty, the 'heavy burden of the guilt of these immoral activities, which he has been keeping in his chest for so long has been finally lifted'. Sukma's lawyer, also court-appointed, said his client was a 'passive participant' who felt indebted to Anwar for help given to him and was 'under his influence'. Munawar was in an agitated state and when he was approached by Zainur Zakaria, a lawyer friend of Anwar, who had been sent to the court by the defendant's wife, he shouted at him: 'Who the hell are you? Who the hell asked you to come here? Who the hell gave you the right to call my wife?' But he later said Mohamad Yacob Karim, who appeared for him, was never his lawyer of choice.

At a press conference after the two men appeared in court, Anwar denied that he had 'been involved in these despicable activities'. He said the prosecution of Sukma and Munawar further confirmed his claim that there was 'a political conspiracy of the highest level to destroy my political career by means of character assassination of the most virulent nature'. Later, both Sukma and Munawar alleged that they had been coerced into confessing to the sodomy charges, although their allegations were denied by the authorities. In a 55-page statutory declaration, dated 7 November, 1998, which reads in parts like the memoirs of a Soviet-era East European political prisoner, Munawar vividly described his arrest under the *Internal Security Act*, incarceration in a window-less cell, and interrogation as 'Number 26' with shouts, screams and threats.

I was interrogated over long and continuous sessions. I was always removed from my cell as Number 26, always blindfolded and hand-cuffed. I was systematically humiliated by my captors, who always remained unidentified. They stripped me of all self-respect; they degraded me and broke down my will and resistance; they threatened me and my family; they frightened me; they brainwashed me to the extent that I ended up in court on September 19, 1998, a shivering shell of a man willing to do anything to stop the destruction of my being.

He said he did no wrong and God knew he was innocent.

The interrogation techniques described by Munawar had much in common with the methods used by the Special Branch to obtain retractions from Ummi Hafilda Ali and Azizan Abu Bakar of their allegations, via the poison-pen letter, of sexual impropriety against Anwar a year earlier. In the course of presenting its case in Anwar's first trial to demonstrate that he had corruptly abused his power, the prosecution drew testimony from police officers which disclosed the illegal procedures used by the Special Branch to 'turn around' or 'neutralise' people in custody—in this case Ummi Hafilda and Azizan Abu Bakar. The published trial evidence delivered another blow to the public image of the guardians of the law. But even before the allegations of police coercion of Sukma and Munawar were aired, Malaysians were remarkably sceptical about the reports they read in their newspapers. It was all too pat, creating widespread suspicion of an orchestrated process. Two men pleading guilty to identical charges and receiving identical jail sentences in identical court proceedings on the same day was stretching plausibility too far in the view of many people.

If the authorities thought that after the court disclosures, Malaysians would stay away in disgust from Anwar's public appearances, they must have been surprised by the turnout at the National Mosque in Kuala Lumpur on the day after Sukma and Munawar pleaded guilty to sodomy. During his travels across Malaysia, thousands of people from all walks of life—predominantly Malays—attended Anwar's rallies, many saying they wanted to see and hear Anwar and decide for themselves if there could be any truth in the charges levelled against him in Kuala Lumpur. The overwhelming judgment appeared to be that there was none. The number of people thronging to hear Anwar had been steadily increasing as he moved around the country, but the size of the crowd that gathered to listen to him on Sunday 20 September, was the largest attracted by any leader in recent years. About 40 000 men and women of all ages stood in a crush around the mosque and spilled out into nearby streets blocking traffic as Anwar addressed them from a balcony, accompanied by his wife. While many people came out of curiosity, a large number of enthusiastic supporters demonstrated that Anwar had become a political phenomenon. They applauded, cheered and laughed at the jokes he made at the expense of Dr Mahathir and the government. They simply did not believe that he could be involved in any of the illegal sexual activities linked to him. He was too good a man: a pillar of Islam and a man of the people. The background of the mosque served to underline his claim to unswerving piety, and in his address, Anwar reminded the people of his radical student youth when he had used the mosque as a refuge from the authorities.

In the grounds of the mosque, hawkers sold badges bearing pictures of Anwar and the word, 'Reformasi'. People chanted: 'Long live Anwar', 'Reformasi, reformasi' and 'Mahathir resign'. Many carried posters attacking the Prime Minister. The balcony where the former deputy prime minister spoke, with his wife standing beside him, was decked with banners proclaiming 'Justice for Anwar' and 'Power to the people'. The crowd roared when Anwar and Azizah raised their clasped hands aloft to show they were united against the authorities. They erupted again when she wiped sweat from his brow. A man who described himself as a retired public servant told me he did not believe Anwar had engaged in homosexual acts. He asked: 'Why are the two men who are supposed to have been sodomised in court and not the person alleged to have sodomised them?' A young woman said he could not be guilty of any of the sexual allegations because his wife was still at his side.

Anwar's populist message tapped a deep vein of discontent within the community, especially its Malay members, who had grown increasingly disillusioned with the money-hungry politicians in UMNO and their apparent preference for the company of their corporate tycoon friends over the people who had voted them into office. His attacks on corruption and cronyism were especially greeted with enthusiasm. Although corruption was not as pervasive in Malaysia as Indonesia, the Philippines or Thailand, many Malaysians had experienced it in their daily lives. At the highest level, it could affect people's livelihood and health when pay-offs allowed contractors to raze forests that had been home to tribes living off the land, demolish villages to make way for highways and undertake projects that blocked or polluted rivers. At a lower level it caused resentment among members of the public forced to pay 'tea money' to public servants for services that every citizen had a right to expect. Anwar's claim to be a victim of the system found sympathy with Malaysians who had spent their lives being fearfully careful not to infringe controls on freedom of expression or breach the harsh laws allowing detention without trial, which might have had a reason for existence in the early years of independence when the country faced a communist insurgency and regional uncertainties but were now inexcusable. With his vague call for 'reformasi', the slogan he borrowed from Indonesia to signal that Malaysia too should dump its leader, Anwar provided disillusioned Malaysians with a cause.

On what was to be his last day of freedom for many years, Anwar was the passionate revolutionary, whipping up the crowd with taunts directed at Dr Mahathir, the establishment media and the police. He was also the consummate orator-cum-agitator, creating a rebellious mood among listeners, which manifested itself in vandalism and a street protest of a kind not seen for decades in Malaysia but soon to become, for a time, a daily occurrence. Anwar clearly revelled in the reaction he stirred with his stinging criticism of the government, punctuated with stabbing motions of his right arm. At times he looked fierce and wrathful, his voice hoarse and near hysterical. Then he would relax and smile as he ridiculed his enemies, charming and enthralling his audience.

The mosque rally coincided with the visit of Queen Elizabeth to St Mary's Anglican Church on the other side of Dataran Merdeka (Freedom Square) from the mosque. Around the time the Queen, who was due to close the Commonwealth Games the following day, was waving gracefully to a small group of onlookers as she entered the church, Anwar was shaking a clenched fist as he denounced Dr Mahathir. The crowd's disrespect for the authority of the Prime Minister or the police force, whose officers watching the mosque proceedings were jeered and insulted, alarmed the authorities. Police chief Rahim Noor later told the Royal Commission at which he admitted beating Anwar that in view of the events that day he had considered seeking assistance from the armed forces. After Anwar finished speaking, people spilled out from the mosque grounds and swept along Jalan Raja Laut to Dataran Merdeka, the site where Malaysia's independence was proclaimed, with Anwar in their midst. After he had been carried on the shoulders of supporters around the cricket pitch in front of the Selangor Club, he mounted the back seat of a motorcycle and returned to his home. Having stirred up the crowd, he removed himself from the scene before he could be associated with any violence. Azizah stayed behind to read out a 24-point declaration, which included calls for reforms and Dr Mahathir's resignation. After the crowd dispersed, one group of Anwar's supporters broke into UMNO headquarters and defaced pictures of Dr Mahathir and other party leaders. Others numbering several thousand marched on the official residence of the Prime Minister, some among them vowing to set it on fire. Riot police stopped the second group and dispersed them with tear gas and water cannon. It was an unusual outbreak of turmoil in a city that had been relatively placid since the race riots of 1969. But the sacking of Anwar had brought about a sea change in Malaysia.

That night, the new paradigm of the political environment in Malaysia was even more sharply defined by an extraordinary assault by security forces on Anwar's home in an upmarket section of Kuala Lumpur, as supporters and journalists watched in amazement. Anwar would have been arrested in due course under a criminal charge but the events of Sunday prompted the police to take him into custody sooner than planned. They could no longer leave him free to stir up more opposition to the Prime Minister. Members of the police Special Action Unit, a section trained for anti-terrorist operations, wearing ski masks and brandishing weapons, smashed their way through the front door of the house as Anwar was holding a press conference. He was arrested in the glare of the television lights of foreign and local camera operators, as supporters chanted 'Reformasi'. Malaysians were staggered by photographs in newspapers showing armed masked men confronting the occupants of Anwar's house as he was escorted out to an unmarked police van and driven away.

Dr Mahathir said Anwar was a man in desperation who was breaking the law. He stated: 'I do not enjoy this. I wish he had not done this and succeeded me and everything would have been fine. But here I have this thing thrown into my face. I have economic problems to deal with. Sukom [the Commonwealth Games]. APEC [Asia Pacific Economic Cooperation forum] is coming. But it happened.' On the Monday night following Anwar's arrest, the Sixteenth Commonwealth Games ended with a ceremony at the National Stadium attended by the Malaysian King, his consort, Queen Elizabeth, Prince Philip, Dr Mahathir and his wife. It was a surreal counterpoint to the political drama gripping the nation, marking 'the end of 11 heady days of sports which saw records smashed and new champions bursting onto the scene', as the *New Straits Times* put it. It said the closing ceremony 'rode high on an exuberant spirit of celebration tempered with a touch of thankfulness for a successful games'. The Prime Minister was no doubt thankful that the event was not disrupted by any pro-Anwar protests.

With Anwar's arrest, Azizah took centre stage. The slight, softly-spoken woman, who had been mostly a silent partner of the government's deputy chief and finance minister, was suddenly forced to become a revolutionary like her husband. Although Azizah looks gentle and reserved in repose, she soon showed that she had a tough spirit, averring that the struggle started by Anwar would continue. A doctor of ophthalmology, who had given up her practice to take care of her six children, Azizah was seen as the epitome of a dutiful Islamic wife, perfectly complementing the young religious activist she had married. Anwar might not be a hero to all men but as his wife was forced to take on more responsibilities there seemed to be few men or women in Malaysia who do not regard her as a heroine. In the weeks after Anwar was sacked and came under increasing threat of imprisonment or detention under the *Internal Security Act*, she gradually raised her public profile, standing by her husband's side at press conferences and meetings held around the country to drum up support for him. At the Sunday rally before Anwar's arrest, she not only stood beside him but led the crowd in chanting Islamic phrases before her husband spoke.

But she was sometimes uneasy about the new image she was projecting. Half-jokingly she once told me (in a dig at the establishment press): 'The newspapers like to use photographs of me taken that day [at the mosque]. I look very fierce.' Her public support was crucial to Anwar's success in winning public acceptance of his denials that he had been involved in homosexual activities, or affairs with women, as alleged in the court affidavits. It promoted the image of a strong, untroubled union instead of a shaky match as suggested by the supposed infidelity of the husband. She remained cool despite having police twice raid her home, first to arrest Anwar and some hours later to seize documents and video cassettes. Azizah complained mildly that there had been no need for the police to break down the door when they came for her husband as he had said he would not resist them.

The police, who also pulled in key associates of Anwar, at first gave contradictory reports on the former deputy prime minister's arrest. The Kuala Lumpur police chief, Kamarudin Ali, said on national television on Sunday night after the deputy prime minister's arrest that he would be charged the next day with public order offences, holding illegal gatherings and vandalism. But on Monday the national police chief, Rahim Noor, said Anwar was being detained under the *Internal Security Act*, which allows indefinite detention without trial, and would not appear in court that day. On Sunday night Rahim had assaulted Anwar and on Monday his face was showing the effects of the beating, with one eye almost closed and the left side of his face severely bruised. This was not known to his family, lawyers or the public at the time. His injuries were recorded in photographs taken for police files and later released at the inquiry into his beating. The *Internal Security Act* detention delayed Anwar's appearance in court but pressure from the government, which was facing strong criticism from abroad over the manner of the former deputy prime minister's arrest, forced the police to produce him nine days after the beating. By then, the area around the eye had healed slightly but was still discoloured, exposing to the world the ill treatment he had received.

On Monday, Anwar supporters who turned up at court for his expected appearance clashed with riot police in the first of a series of confrontations, over several weeks in the centre of Kuala Lumpur. They were generally one-sided battles with the protesters confining themselves to shouting slogans and waving banners before they were forced to retreat from the water cannon and tear gas of the anti-riot Federal Reserve Unit. The establishment press launched blistering attacks on Anwar, which appeared to be aimed at countering the support he clearly still had. Calling him a 'rebel without a cause', the *New Straits Times* said that his encouragement and incitement of supporters to march to Dr Mahathir's residence on the Sunday was 'definitely a treacherous act'. It said Malaysians could not accept as their leader such an individual, who would 'definitely lead them down the path of destruction, lawlessness and irresponsibility'.

On 22 September, Dr Mahathir held an hour-long press conference in which he said he had concluded that the sexual allegations against Anwar were true after personally interviewing 'the people he sodomised, the women he had sex with'. Television cameras recorded most of what he said for transmission to viewers that evening. It was another astonishing episode in the Anwar saga. Here was the Prime Minister of a deeply conservative nation speaking explicitly about matters that had never previously been referred to, even obliquely, in print, far less on prime-time television.

Dr Mahathir prefaced remarks about the incidents on Sunday and Anwar's arrest by saying they might 'not be believed by certain members of the press' who assumed that he was a dictator who wanted to arrest his potential rival. He said it was clear that Anwar was 'working up emotions in order to develop the situation that was found in Indonesia', where people rioted daily and tried to obstruct normal life, with the hope of overthrowing the government and, in particular, the Prime Minister. Anwar had decided to become a rabble-rouser who wanted to instigate violence.

Dr Mahathir said that 'because of his incitement to violence' the police had had to take Anwar in before they were ready to prefer charges and had arrested him under the *Internal Security Act*.

Anwar's greatest fear, Dr Mahathir claimed, was that he would be charged in court because then all the things that he had done would be revealed. He said his deputy's greatest hope was that witnesses would not tell their stories because to do so would bring them shame. But he had not expected that his own adopted brother and his friend would come out in the open and make their statements. They did this, Dr Mahathir said, because the police, who were Muslims, pointed out to them that they had committed a great sin, which was punishable in the afterlife. They had told 'the absolute truth' even at the risk of being jailed for abetting in an act of sodomy and shaming their families by their confessions. At the time Dr Mahathir was talking to the media, the two men had not retracted their confessions but if they had it seems doubtful that this would have diminished the fierceness of his condemnation of Anwar. He dismissed his former deputy's readiness to swear to his innocence in a mosque, saying Anwar had for years been masquerading as a religious person and 'yet had been committing these things, not today, not yesterday but for years'. A man like that, who appeared to be religious but in fact was not, was 'quite capable of swearing in a mosque, knowing full well that what he was swearing was not the absolute truth'.

Then, in an emotional outpouring of words, Dr Mahathir bared his anguish over the collapse of his plans to turn the leadership over to Anwar: 'I had taken him [into UMNO] in 1982, brought him up and helped him along until he overtook many people who are veterans in the party. He overtook them and went ahead of them and was all set to become the Prime Minister after me. And yet, when I discovered he was guilty of something that I cannot forgive, something that the Malaysian society cannot accept, whether Muslims or non-Muslims, action has to be taken.' He had to act against the person he regarded as a friend, a colleague and his protégé because he could 'not be allowed to be a leader in a country like this'. In answer to a question, he said it was true that a lot of people still believed Anwar. It had taken years for the Prime Minister to believe the allegations against him. He had dismissed them as accusations made 'out of sheer jealousy for the man who was going to be the leader of the party'. Dr Mahathir also acknowledged for the first time the pretence to which he and his deputy had resorted for so long a period to obscure the real state of their relations. He said that although Anwar was very nice to him and smiling, 'at the same time he was plotting', and he added: 'I knew about it but I chose to ignore it because to me it is quite irrelevant. If he is chosen by the party as a leader, okay, he is welcome to it. I can contest against him. I have contested against others and I have a reasonable chance to win.' Returning again to his reason for sacking Anwar, he said: 'I cannot accept a man who is a sodomist to become a leader in this country.'

Dr Mahathir said he had carried out his investigation after police looking into the *50 Dalil* book had informed him the allegations made a year earlier were true. He could not believe the police just like that, he said, so he asked the people involved to see him with no officers present. As a result of what he was told he was forced to believe that there was truth to the allegations. Asked why he did not investigate the allegations when they were made a year earlier, he said the police had given him the retractions of Ummi Hafilda Ali and Azizan Abu Bakar and he thought the case was closed.

The most remarkable moment in the press conference came when Dr Mahathir sought to persuade the sceptical media of, as he saw it, Anwar's depravity. He said: 'Let me tell what Dr Munawar Ahmad Anees told the police.' Almost choking on the words, Dr Mahathir graphically described what Anwar was alleged to have done while engaged in a sexual act with Munawar. He said he could 'not understand how a man would invent a story like that'. In his statutory declaration retracting his confession, however, Munawar said that in his original statement recorded by a magistrate, he had narrated all that he 'had been asked to state' by his 'captors' (the police), adding: 'I state categorically that I have never had a homosexual relationship with Anwar Ibrahim or anyone else.' He declared that the details of the alleged homosexual relationship contained in his statement to a magistrate and given to the court by the prosecuting agencies and Yacob Karim [his appointed lawyer] on 19 September

1998, 'were untrue and were fabricated by the police'. But it was not until some weeks after the Prime Minister's press conference that Munawar made his statutory declaration. Dr Mahathir said: 'The act was despicable. And this [Anwar] is a man who talks about other people being despicable.'

He said that once the truth was known people would reject Anwar. But convincing people of the truth of the allegations against his former deputy proved more difficult than Dr Mahathir envisaged, even without the later declarations of Sukma and Munawar that their confessions had been forced from them. Despite Dr Mahathir's persuasive presentation of the facts at the press conference and on national television, many Malaysians remained unconvinced. They believed the sexual allegations were fabricated to remove Anwar as a rival for the party leadership. A leading Malaysian political analyst interviewed at the time said it was a 'sad, sad situation' that the institutions that Malaysians should hold in high regard—the government, police and justice system—were now widely seen as 'totally lacking credibility'. He said that Anwar's image as a man of impressive intellect, with strong religious convictions, who had risen to become the second most powerful man in the country, was so strong in the minds of many people that telling them he was flawed was 'almost like saying God doesn't exist'. Many people spoke of their sense of overkill in the plethora of accusations made against Anwar, causing them to feel that the authorities had no real case against him.

Malaysians also expressed their bewilderment over events of the past year: first, the nation's economy collapsing after a decade of dynamic growth, and then its political stability shaken by the arrest, amid unprecedented civil unrest, of the man they had expected to become their leader. A woman lawyer commented to me: 'My mind hasn't yet caught up with what my eyes see and my ears hear. It seems like it was just yesterday we were living in harmony and prosperity without a real worry in the world.' People were struggling to come to terms with what was happening while also unbelieving of what they were being told.

Many Malaysians said the government had only itself to blame for the credibility gap. For years, people had been fed a diet of bland domestic news comprising items indistinguishable from government press releases by radio and television stations. Newspapers were less obviously propaganda sheets but seldom strayed from the official line on political matters. The English-language and Malay-language newspapers were either directly or indirectly controlled by government parties. The independent Chinese-language newspapers were livelier but had to be careful not to seriously upset the government, which had the power under newspaper licensing regulations to close them down at any time. Malaysians complained that the government provided them only with the information it thought they should have. As a result, a large proportion of the population presumed the evidence against Anwar had been trumped up, as he claimed.

Hanif Omar, who was police chief from June 1974 to October 1993, and was regarded as a good and honest cop in his day, said in a press conference on 23 September that he had informed the Prime Minister shortly before his retirement, five years earlier, that Anwar had homosexual tendencies. Speaking to journalists, he said his report to the Prime Minister was based on 'convincing evidence gathered by his officers'. Hanif said: 'I registered a point but the Prime Minister did not register interest.' Hanif said that the police were worried that Anwar's activities would expose him to possible blackmail. Police evidence, according to Hanif, was that Anwar was involved in homosexual relations with two men, one of whom was a foreigner. Hanif said Anwar's nature, charisma and networking skills made it difficult for people to believe that he was involved in homosexual relations, adding: 'But I have no doubt in my own mind that as far as the old case is concerned it was true. We could not convict him on that basis but the evidence was strong.'

A few days after Hanif had informed Dr Mahathir about the police evidence, Anwar, through an intermediary, sought a meeting with Hanif. Hanif said Anwar asked him whether police officers would use the information to blackmail him. He told Anwar his officers were 'not in the blackmailing business' and advised him to stop his homosexual activities. In the existing climate of public scepticism, Hanif's remarks had little impact.

On 24 September police chief Rahim Noor told a press conference that Anwar was 'safe and sound', a remark that was soon proved to be false. On the same day, Anwar hit back at Dr Mahathir and other members of the government through a videocassette which he had recorded before his arrest and which was telecast in Asia by CNBC on 24 September. In it, Anwar claimed that members of his family had interests in the new Kuala Lumpur International Airport (KLIA). He also accused the Prime Minister of building himself a lavish '200 million ringgit' palace for himself. Dr Mahathir angrily accused the US-owned television network of spreading lies to turn the whole world against Malaysia. Three days later, the *New Straits Times* published an unsigned rebuttal, listing major projects awarded during Anwar's tenure as Finance Minister to 'his close friends, allies and relatives'. They included several contracts at the KLIA, independent power-generating projects, hospital and medical facilities, highways and the dedicated rail link to the airport. The article said that as chairman of the Cabinet Committee on Infrastructure and chairman of the Cabinet Committee on the KLIA, he 'had a direct say in the contracts'. It said a company linked to Kamaruddin Jaafar, 'Anwar's close aide and chairman of his think tank' was given six KLIA main contract packages. Malaysian Resources Corporation Berhad, which until recently had been under Anwar's control, was also given a number of airport-related contracts.

The *New Straits Times* went on to discuss the Prime Minister's official residence at Putrajaya, the new administrative centre south of Kuala Lumpur, which had been approved by cabinet, 'of which he [Anwar] was a senior member' before his dismissal. Its estimated cost was M$16.7 million, not M$200 million. Later, Dr Mahathir also noted that Anwar had been involved in planning the Prime Minister's residence, which he was next in line to occupy. He said the final design had six bedrooms, in addition to the master bedroom. This was to provide a bedroom for each of Anwar's six children, Dr Mahathir suggested. He himself had only two children still living with him.

Some of Anwar's accusations against his new-found enemies strained credulity and left him open to ridicule. In his allegations of government corruption, he repeatedly asserted that Daim Zainuddin carried M$1 billion in cash on board a Zurich-bound MAS aircraft. Responding to the charge, which was also aired in the CNBC telecast of the Anwar videocassette, Dr Mahathir said if people like Daim wanted to take a lot of money out of Malaysia they could do so just by 'writing [on] a few pieces of paper to transfer it', and if Daim had wanted to take a lot of cash out of the country he could have used his private jet instead of a commercial aircraft. Daim himself commented on the charge and his relationship with Anwar in his address at the UMNO general assembly in June, 1999. He said: 'I trusted him and he stabbed me in the back.' Daim, a former lawyer and highly successful businessman, whose personal wealth made him one of Malaysia's richest men, said he had never seen 'such a huge amount' as M$1 billion in cash. He noted with some validity: 'A briefcase can fit perhaps only M$1 million, so you would need 10 briefcases for 10 million and 100 briefcases for 100 million. Just imagine how many briefcases you would need for M$1 billion. I have only two hands.'

But all the rebuttals by the government did nothing to change the minds of Malaysians who believed Anwar was being victimised and people in the West who were championing his cause. The reaction of foreign government officials and the Western media reflected the success of Anwar and his image-makers had had cultivating contacts abroad during his years as Deputy Prime Minister and Finance Minister. His family's accumulation of wealth through the system of share allocations for Malays and government-assigned contracts, which were on a par with other leaders, and his sudden reversion to the radical anti-establishment persona of his youth were ignored by those in the West who took his side. *New Straits Times* columnist A. Kadir Jasin wondered: 'Is it because Anwar said the things they like to hear? Or is because they dislike Dr Mahathir so intensely that anybody who is willing to challenge him gets their support?'

Then, on 29 September, Anwar appeared in court with a black eye and the government's shaky credibility was totally destroyed.

7 | Black eye provokes outrage

The highest ranking Malaysian ever to face criminal charges was spirited into the century-old complex of buildings housing Kuala Lumpur's main courts shortly after 7 a.m. on Tuesday, 29 September, more than two hours ahead of the normal starting time for hearings. The traffic was still light as most of the capital city's working residents had not yet set out from home for their first day on the job after a long holiday weekend. After being kept in one of the basement cells routinely used to hold prisoners until their cases were called, Anwar was ushered up a back staircase into Sessions Court Four about 10.20 a.m., where he was charged before Judge Hasnah Mohamed Hashim with five counts of corruption and four counts of sodomy. He was alleged to have 'committed carnal intercourse against the order of nature' against his family's former driver, Azizan, his adopted brother, Sukma, his friend Munawar and a fourth person who did not feature in any of the two trials. The former deputy prime minister pleaded not guilty and claimed trial to each of the nine charges.

An official statement tied the most politically sensational prosecution in Malaysia's history to a sleazy denigration of Anwar compiled by his enemies to destroy his career which, having already been shown to include untruthful allegations, was a strange starting point for the judicial proceedings that followed. The Attorney-General's Chambers said it had 'studied and scrutinised all the latest evidence adduced by the Royal Malaysian Police following their investigations on Datuk Seri Anwar bin Ibrahim, former deputy prime minister of Malaysia', in the wake of a report lodged at the Dang Wangi police station on 19 June 1998, 'in connection with a book entitled *50 Dalil Mengapa Anwar Tidak Boleh Jadi PM* ('50 Reasons Why Anwar Cannot Be PM')'. The statement said the Attorney-General, as the Public Prosecutor, was satisfied there was 'adequate "prima facie" evidence to charge Datuk Seri Anwar bin Ibrahim' with five counts of corrupt practices and five counts of sodomy. He was formally charged in court with only four sodomy counts.

The only sign that anything unusual was taking place at the courts on Jalan Raja, facing Merdeka Square, which had been the scene of pro-Anwar demonstrations since his arrest, was the large number of photographers and television cameramen at the entrance and a heavy police presence in surrounding streets. The timing of the smooth, incident-free police operation was clearly aimed at fore-stalling any protest action of the kind which had led to clashes between the anti-riot Federal Reserve Unit and Anwar supporters a week earlier, when he had been expected to appear in court. Before the hearing began, Anwar's wife, Azizah, arrived, together with a nine-member legal team led by Raja Aziz Addruse, one of Malaysia's most respected lawyers and a former president of the Bar Council. One of the lawyers said later they had all offered their services to Anwar for a nominal fee.

Anwar's court appearance, a historic national event made even more dramatic by his accusation that the black eye was a result of a beating in custody while he was blindfolded and handcuffed, had a traumatic effect on Malaysians. Just four weeks earlier the pris-oner in the dock had been the deputy prime minister. Now he was being treated as a common criminal—or worse, given the evidence of his injured eye. Anwar told the court he was punched 'very hard' on the head, forehead and neck in the lockup at police headquar-ters at Bukit Aman (Hill of Peace), which had been the central base for law enforcement forces since British colonial days. He said the blows were so strong that his eyes and lips bled and he lost consciousness until the following morning when a police officer helped him and wiped away the blood. Anwar was only allowed to see a doctor five days later.

The impact of the black eye was devastating for the Malaysian government both at home and abroad. Any hope the authorities had of convincing sceptics that Anwar was guilty of sodomy or corruption was dashed when people learned through the media of his statement in court that he had been beaten while in police custody. A Malaysian company executive exclaimed in a conversation with me: 'Was the case against him so weak that police tried to beat a confession out of him? Or were they just frustrated by the fact that he was getting so much public support?' A comment by Dr Mahathir that it was not impossible that Anwar's injuries were self-inflicted only increased many people's sense of disbelief towards any government statements related to the former deputy prime minister. As a woman with a senior position in a government office asked rhetorically: 'How can anyone believe that?'

Malaysians' outrage over the incident intensified when it became public knowledge that Sukma and Munawar were now saying they were coerced into pleading guilty to sodomy with Anwar and were appealing against their convictions. The black eye brought new condemnation from countries that had earlier questioned Anwar's arrest. The United States and Australia expressed serious concern over the reports that Anwar had been beaten, and other governments were quick to condemn his apparent ill treatment. In a break with ASEAN solidarity, Philippine President Joseph Estrada called on his people to love and support Anwar, and Indonesian President J. B. Habibie, an old friend of the former deputy prime minister, said he was likely to call off a trip to Malaysia. Indonesian State Secretary Akbar Tanjung deplored the beating.

The authorities tried to show they were responding to public dismay over the injury by appointing Mat Zain, chief of the Malacca state Criminal Investigation Department, to conduct an investigation into Anwar's allegation he had been assaulted. But Malaysians were sceptical that the inquiry would disclose the truth and their cynicism was to prove well founded. It took a Royal Commission of Inquiry, belatedly appointed by the government to look into the matter in 1999, to find Anwar had been beaten and to expose the perpetrator. Meanwhile, as public anger mounted, Dr Mahathir declared that the government would not tolerate any unlawful police action, but he had already undermined this manifestation of rectitude with his suggestion that Anwar's wounds could have been self-inflicted. At the same time, there was an apparent move by the authorities to distance Dr Mahathir from any illegal deed that might later be ascribed to police. The *New Straits Times* reported that under a section of the *Internal Security Act*, the police did not need to inform the Home Minister—in this case Dr Mahathir—of every stage of investigations and actions taken against detainees.

As it became clear that no one doubted that Anwar had been assaulted, Dr Mahathir publicly dissociated himself from the beating, while also berating the press for dwelling on the incident. In a speech to the Commonwealth Press Union's conference in Kuala Lumpur on 26 October 1998, Dr Mahathir complained that Malaysia never had good press and the impression given to people all over the world was that Malaysia was in a state of perpetual turmoil; that it was a police state where police brutality was 'a daily, or even an hourly occurrence'. He said a full investigation was being made into the black eye, which he regretted; there would 'be no cover-up' and the guilty party would be punished. 'I must be crazy if I wanted the black eye, which the police then paraded before the world through the media—print and electronic. Yet the media implied that the Malaysian dictator is presiding over a police state where giving black eyes to prisoners is a common practice.'

Dr Mahathir repeated this assertion on several occasions to try to dispel public suspicion that he had countenanced the attack on Anwar. But the damage to the standing of the Prime Minister and his government had been done. The publication of reports and pictures of Anwar's injured eye was too obvious to be overlooked by the media, and nothing he could say could change the public perception of his involvement.

Singapore's Senior Minister Lee Kuan Yew, whose total control of events in his own country while he had been prime minister was never questioned or undermined, was astounded by the whole affair. At a press conference in Kuala Lumpur in August 2000, he described it as 'an unmitigated disaster'. Lee said he felt sorry for Dr Mahathir, who made 'several errors of judgment' and had 'paid a very heavy price'. When he met Dr Mahathir at a conference in Davos, Switzerland, in the early part of 1999, he had asked him why Anwar had been arrested under the *Internal Security Act* as 'a national security threat' when only four weeks ago he had been the Prime Minister's deputy. The Singapore leader was 'flabbergasted' to learn that Dr Mahathir did not know Anwar was going to be arrested under the Act. Lee said:

> That was the beginning of a series of blunders that cost him dearly. It should never have been done that way. It should have been a straightforward criminal charge under the penal code for corruption, for sodomy, whatever. Produced in court the day after his arrest. You can contest bail on the grounds that he would have interfered with witnesses or allowed him bail. But [they] arrested him under the ISA, then the next disaster, the blue eye.

Lee said he felt more sorry for Dr Mahathir than he did for Anwar, adding: 'I am sorry for Anwar too, because he had so many things going for him. He was set as deputy to take over. All these things now happen, damaging both of them. And it's just sad.'

The unfolding saga was worrying UMNO politicians. An article by a political writer in the *New Straits Times* unusually aired concerns in UMNO over the Anwar case. It quoted an unnamed UMNO politician who said people did not 'have to be pro this or that to feel very, very uncomfortable about how the whole thing has been handled—the way the police broke into his house and, now, those injuries'.

In the weeks that followed, the enormity of the dislocation the Anwar affair had caused in Malaysian society became increasingly apparent. There were growing signs of disillusionment among politically conscious Malaysians with both the Prime Minister and the man who had been expected to be his successor. While Anwar had won broad sympathy for the brutish manner of his arrest and detention under the *Internal Security Act*, and his virtual conviction of sodomy in the media before his case came to trial, many Malaysians said they no longer saw him as a credible potential leader. Reasons given by former supporters for their disenchantment were the ease with which Anwar shed his image of establishment respectability and returned to his Islamist and activist roots after being sacked from cabinet and expelled from the UMNO, and his allegations of corruption within an administration in which he had been a key figure. They were also turned off by his opportunistic flirtation with the opposition Democratic Action Party and Parti Islam se-Malaysia, both of which he had strongly attacked when he was an UMNO member.

For Dr Mahathir's part, although he was still esteemed for his leadership during the period of growth, prosperity and stability that had preceded the economic recession, many Malaysians said their confidence in his political acumen had been shaken. One leading corporate lawyer I spoke to put the situation starkly:

> First, he stripped Anwar of political power without any face-saving gesture, leaving him with no alternative but to fight back. Then he let his deputy dictate the course of events by holding ever bigger rallies to deliver his reformasi message and whip up popular support. This brought a heavy-handed response from the police, which is ultimately under Dr Mahathir's Home Ministry. Now we see in Anwar's allegation of police brutality a lack of control from the top or a disregard for human decencies and the nation's image.

On the application of the prosecution, Judge Hasnah transferred Anwar's case to the High Court where he appeared on 5 October. He seemed in a depressed mood and shouted angrily that he was being treated 'like a dog'. The High Court judge before whom he appeared was little known to the public or even to Anwar's lawyers. But he was soon to become an international celebrity, whose pronouncements aroused more controversy and attracted more obloquy (from Anwar supporters) than those of any previous judicial figure before him. With his balding head, bushy white eyebrows, and military mustache featuring in newspapers regularly during the course of the trial, he made a swift transition from obscurity to being one of Malaysia's most easily recognisable faces. Justice

Augustine Paul, 53, had been a judicial commissioner in Malacca, the city south of Kuala Lumpur where Europeans first traded with the Malay sultanates, before his elevation to the High Court and transfer to the capital four months before Anwar's arrest. Prior to that he had been a federal counsel, magistrate and Sessions Court judge. He was admitted as a barrister-at-law of the Inner Temple in England in 1971. Justice Paul fixed 2 November as the date to begin hearing four of the five charges of corrupt practices against Anwar and denied him bail. He announced, without explanation, that there would be a break in proceedings from 14 November to 23 November. This ensured that the trial was not in progress during the Asia Pacific Economic Cooperation summit in Kuala Lumpur, but the attempt to prevent the Anwar affair from overshadowing Dr Mahathir's hosting of this major conference was unsuccessful. The Americans made sure of that.

Although the High Court did nothing more than set dates for Anwar's trial, the session lasted from 9 a.m. to mid-afternoon. Legal argument and an application for bail, which was refused, prolonged the hearing. The dry, painstaking judicial process in the elegant colonial-era courthouse in the centre of Kuala Lumpur highlighted the bleak future immediatly facing Anwar. If found guilty of the charges of corruption and sodomy preferred against him, he could be sentenced to up to 34 years in jail. Even if he was eventually acquitted of all charges, his prosecution under British-based criminal law, following procedures established over centuries of legal practice, was going to tie him up in the courts for a long time. And as long as he was denied bail, he would be returned each day to a prison cell.

Just how effectively Anwar's arrest and prosecution had removed him from the political scene was demonstrated by a meeting of the UMNO supreme council the day following his first appearance before Justice Paul. The absence of the former deputy president was starkly underlined by the unoccupied brown leather chair next to Dr Mahathir as he briefed journalists on the meeting. It would be another three months before the Prime Minister appointed Abdullah Badawi Deputy Prime Minister as a prelude to his installation as deputy party president. The supreme council expelled from UMNO ten supporters of the former party deputy president, as members of the Anwar camp launched a propaganda campaign from abroad. Among those cast out of the party were Ruslan Kassim and Abdul Rahim Ghouse, former UMNO Youth chiefs of Negri Sembilan and Penang; Saifudin Nasution Ismail, the former assistant secretary of UMNO Youth; and Ezam Mohamad Noor, Anwar's former political secretary. Abdul Rahim, Ezam and Saifudin issued press statements attacking the government in facsimile messages to Malaysian newspapers from Manila and Bangkok. In a joint message from the Philippines capital, Abdul Rahim and Ezam accused Dr Mahathir of being power crazy and said UMNO was on the verge of splitting and heading towards destruction. Anwar's people, who flew to Jakarta as well as Manila and Bangkok, found sympathetic listeners in all three capitals, which created new tensions between Malaysia and its ASEAN partners. At a meeting on Indonesia's Batam Island, Philippines President Estrada and Indonesia's President Habibie increased Malaysians' anger by expressing concern about the situation in Malaysia.

The overseas response to the events in Malaysia highlighted again the remarkable success of Anwar in making friends in foreign governments during his years as Deputy Prime Minister—in contrast with Western and regional leaders' low regard for the blunt, uncompromising Dr Mahathir, to whom the concept of networking was alien. With the trial date set, foreign attacks mounted on the Malaysian government. The reaction in the United States was fiercest. Robert Rubin, US Treasury Secretary, said that what had happened to Anwar was 'deeply, deeply, deeply troubling'. Democrat Senator Sam Nunn and two officials who had served under the Reagan and Bush administrations, Douglas Paal and Paul Wolfowitz, called for a fair trial and Anwar's release on bail. Senator Nunn urged the Malaysian government to allow its people 'to conduct orderly demonstrations' without being 'chased through the streets and arrested'. Holding out a hint of retaliation, he said that to protect Malaysia's good name and to attract foreign investments, the authorities should allow Anwar and his associates to voice their opinions and be given due process. And in a forewarning of trouble at APEC, he said it would be sad if leaders attending the summit did not 'seek to ease Anwar's plight'. Later that month, a US government official announced that President Clinton would not meet Dr Mahathir outside the formal APEC discussions. Referring to the jailing of Anwar, he said the administration had been 'very concerned about the repression of political expression and the extra-judicial acts in Malaysia'. As it turned out, Al Gore represented the US with an arrogant and crude display of US imperiousness.

Justice Paul reported to police that he had received a call from a man claiming to be a US senator who said he would be 'closely monitoring the case'. The caller allegedly told the judge that justice must be seen to be done. In his role as Foreign Minister, Abdullah Badawi, said this was an example of interference which Malaysia could not accept. Separately, he also accused the Philippines and Indonesian leaders of interfering in Malaysia's internal affairs. The Malaysian government was further annoyed by the publication of a letter from Corazon Aquino, the former Philippines president, expressing sympathy for Anwar's wife, Azizah, and drawing parallels with the loss of her husband to an assassin. Officials in Kuala Lumpur were additionally upset by the visits of Nurul Izzah, Anwar's 18-year-old daughter, to Indonesia and the Philippines, where she met the president of each country. The sombre-looking young woman who had accompanied her mother to court on the day Anwar was charged with corruption and sodomy was pictured in the media around three weeks later with President Estrada in Manila, smiling as he told her to urge her father to 'remain unwavering' and expressed the hope that there would be a 'happy ending for his friend'. His remarks brought a diplomatic protest from Malaysia. When Anwar had argued two years earlier that ASEAN's policy of non-intervention in the internal affairs of member countries was no longer suitable in an era of growing regional crises, he could not have foreseen that he was to become the catalyst for a crisis that would not only provoke—at least for a time—the virtual abandonment of the organisation's 'fundamental principle' but also threaten future cooperation among Malaysia and its partners.

The widespread foreign criticism of Malaysia arising out of the Anwar affair generated a siege mentality within the establishment, manifesting in an increasingly paranoid reaction to the Western media. Dr Mahathir had never been a fan of the foreign press but Malaysia had eschewed the kind of measures used by Singapore, such as banning or restricting circulations of news magazines to register its objection to their reports. Just two years earlier, wire services, television networks and foreign correspondents had been encouraged to look to Kuala Lumpur as a regional headquarters, with Ministry of Information officials suggesting that it would be more attractive than Hong Kong after the territory returned to China. But the Malaysian attitude towards the Western media hardened significantly in the wake of articles about Anwar's treatment, leading to a steadily worsening working climate for foreign correspondents. From then up to the present they have been increasingly excluded from press conferences held by the Prime Minister and his cabinet colleagues. At the same time, government officials, local newspaper editors and columnists have been sniping away at Kuala Lumpur-based journalists writing for overseas publications with growing acerbity. In 2001, several foreign correspondents, including this writer, were threatened with prosecution for sedition as part of a growing campaign of intimidation, which has made conditions for the West's media representatives highly uncomfortable, if not unacceptable.

In 1998, Dr Mahathir led the assault on the Western media by accusing foreign journalists of spreading lies to influence the world against Malaysia, exaggerating pro-Anwar demonstrations to paint the Malaysian government as ugly and oppressive, and taking a view that was clearly racist. His comments were followed by a fierce attack in an article in the *New Straits Times*, which called for 'errant' foreign journalists who were not fair to the Prime Minister to be detained under the *Internal Security Act*. The newspaper, which often reflects official thinking, ran the article in two parts on consecutive days on its editorial page, under headlines declaring that the foreign media was 'peddling mass disinformation' and 'should be punished if disregard for fair play continues'. The article said it was time Malaysia took a 'hard stand on irresponsible foreign media', which had 'long adopted an adversarial attitude towards Dr Mahathir' and taken Anwar as their champion. Without a hint of irony, it added that Dr Mahathir had 'practised a gracious attitude towards the foreign media' but instead of appreciating his tolerance they had 'taken advantage of his liberal attitude and become bold in their attacks on him'.

Within a short space of time, Ruslan Kassim and Abdul Rahim Ghouse were the only senior UMNO officials maintaining public support for Anwar. Of 18 people arrested under the *Internal Security Act* as associates of the former deputy prime minister, twelve had been released by the first week of October and most of them had made public recantations. Dr Mahathir said only 'one or two people' were 'not with the party' and described UMNO as 'solid'. He demonstrated his confidence that the situation was under control, despite continuing street demonstrations by thousands of Anwar supporters, by making a five-day visit to Japan. Blasting Malaysians who were 'using mob rule and street justice' to show their dissatisfaction with the government, he said the *Internal Security Act* would continue to be used against those who wanted to 'create chaos'. He left the country without a deputy prime minister, remarking sardonically that anyone who 'wanted to make a coup attempt' could try while he was away.

In an early sign that the opposition PAS was benefiting from the Anwar affair, the Islamic party's leaders attracted a crowd of 10 000 people to a rally in Kepala Batas, Penang, at which they and other opposition figures denounced the *Internal Security Act* and expressed support for the former deputy prime minister. But it was becoming increasingly clear that Anwar's active supporters did not have the numbers or propensity for violence—with the exception of a small hard core of protesters—to create serious chaos in Malaysia, far less the kind of upheaval that had taken place in Indonesia. The worst disorder occurred on the night of 23 October when running battles between police and demonstrators armed with petrol bombs caused chaos in parts of the capital. However, there was no property damage, although tyres and rubbish were set alight in a main thoroughfare. Two hundred and forty-one people were arrested. The only significant destruction arising from all the pro-Anwar protests was the burning of two police motorcycles on the Saturday before the mid-November APEC summit. The motorcycles were abandoned by their riders on a main city thoroughfare when they were confronted by a small mob that broke away from a gathering of a few hundred demonstrators.

Although a minor incident compared with the serious riots in Indonesia, it had a disproportionate impact on some APEC delegates who saw the blazing motorcycles as they returned to their hotels that night and concluded the nation was facing growing turmoil. In fact, many young pro-Anwar supporters were dismayed by the violent confrontation between protesters and police on 23 October and by the bike burning. Several students told me they only favoured peaceful protests and would not copy the riotous behaviour of their counterparts in Indonesia. 'Saturday Night Fever' was the term applied by the media to a series of weekend street demonstrations in the last quarter of 1998, which each attracted several thousand people and were broken up by riot police using water cannon and tear gas. The ringleaders were invariably arrested and roughed up. However, throughout 1999, the number of people taking part in the protests fell steadily, with only a few hundred staunch Anwar supporters maintaining the rage, apart from a large turnout on the anniversary of his arrest. Opposition parties, including PAS, in combination were able to organise large anti-government rallies with an Anwar element, provoking a tough police response, but they were set-piece political challenges rather than spontaneous popular uprisings. In a statement from his cell, Anwar commented upon the continuing silence of people who might have been expected to speak out in support of him. His message was principally an attack on Dr Mahathir, whom he described as a desperate man and dictator who would 'resort to any means to cling to power'. But it was also an almost plaintive entreaty for an encouraging word from erstwhile comrades. Anwar said he was 'aware of the fear and reluctance of many in the leadership to express their views, so as to protect their own vested interests and to avoid retribution from the dictator' but called on them to 'take heed of the people's wishes' before it was too late.

Direct support for Anwar may have been limited but a large segment of the community was deeply concerned about the ugly developments that followed his sacking and their reflection on Malaysian society. An emergency meeting of about 2500 members of the Malaysian Bar Council, which represented some 8000 lawyers, expressed grave concern over the use of the *Internal Security Act* to arrest Anwar and his associates. The council said the Act was 'an obnoxious piece of legislation undermining fundamental human rights, basic democratic principles and the rule of law', and that all detainees should be released or charged in court as soon as possible. It went on to say all laws providing for arrest and detention without trial and for the imposing of restrictions and conditions without trial were 'contrary to the rule of law, international human rights standards and established religious values and norms'. Denouncing the 'unnecessary and excessive' use of police force, the council also expressed concern over the alleged beating of Anwar and reports of assaults against his supporters who had been arrested during street protests.

Some journalists went beyond their normal unquestioning approach to government matters with the intention of apprising the nation's leaders of the public mood. Wong Chun Wai, editor of *The Star*, wrote in his *Sunday Star* column that among some sections of Malaysians 'the cry for freedom, justice, democracy and greater transparency had never been louder'. He said those in power must realise that it came from many Malaysians who were 'not necessarily supporters of the [Anwar] reform movement', adding that it would be an insult to their intelligence if this was not understood. The columnist said no one could disagree that Malaysia needed to do more, including improving political institutions 'in our own way', and that it would be a shame if Malaysia had to do it the way of Indonesia which had no history of parliamentary democracy.

Malaysians who had been living normal, uncomplicated lives were unsettled by events over which they had no control. A retired school teacher related to me how she had been coincidentally at a public hospital when four young men and a girl who had been arrested during pro-Anwar demonstrations were brought in for treatment of injuries. They were handcuffed and had been ill-treated. She said that she felt insecure, and asked: 'What is happening to my country?' The growing discontent was not confined to the public at large. The solidity that Dr Mahathir ascribed to UMNO was largely superficial. Below the surface appearance of unity, the party was fracturing. At the grassroots there was deep discontent over the treatment of Anwar, which was eventually to result in large-scale defections to PAS.

The strains within the nation grew as the trial of Anwar on the four of his corruption charges began and the police, judiciary and government came under the bright glare of domestic and international media attention, which exposed deep flaws in the entire administrative system. A leading lawyer, who was not involved in the case, said it would be 'the most important trial ever held in Malaysia'. It was not just a trial of the man who was the former deputy prime minister, but also the justice and political systems. Dr Mahathir told journalists that it was a trial the government could not win, whatever its outcome: 'If Anwar is found not guilty, then we lose and if he is convicted we also lose because we will be accused [of rigging the trial].' Many people saw the trial not as a criminal prosecution but the product of a political power struggle within UMNO, which had a long history of machiavellian machinations. Amir Muhammad, a social critic and writer on the arts with a satirical bent, made the imminent opening of the proceedings against Anwar the occasion for a purported reappraisal of Franz Kafka's *The Trial*, the harrowing story of the persecution of a citizen of an authoritarian state. Writing for the literary section of the *New Straits Times*, where a little anti-establishmentarianism could sometimes slip through, Amir drew upon elements of the Kafka masterpiece to point up the concerns and confusion of Malaysians over the pending case (which many people were calling simply 'The Trial') without making a single reference to the Anwar hearing. Advising people to rush out and buy the book, Amir said 'a very good place to start' was the opening sentence: 'Someone must have been telling lies about Joseph K, for without having done anything wrong he was arrested one fine morning.' The book, he said, presented the reader with a challenge:

> Are we willing to accept this man for what he is or do we get
> bogged down by questions like, 'Who is the real K?' Do we believe

in him and want him to win? I think we do. I've never done a formal survey but I would think that only a few blockheads will finish *The Trial* thinking that K met his rightful fate.

8 | A citizen and a government on trial

The trial, which began on 2 November, lasted 77 days and became the longest in Malaysian history, soon eclipsed in impact the dramatic events preceding it. Almost daily, it produced a new sensation or startling disclosure that made the daily press coverage addictive reading for the public. Malaysians were transfixed by the epic production playing daily on the High Court stage, co-starring, in the dock, the people's hero and self-proclaimed victim of state tyranny and, in the public gallery, his loyal wife, whose devoted manner and tudung-covered head reinforced the public perception that since such a pious woman continued to stand by her husband he must be innocent. A supporting cast of colourful characters, either standing in the wings or listed for a later appearance, included the Prime Minister, two of his cabinet ministers, the head of the secretive Special Branch of the police force, an actress married to another cabinet minister and, with prominent billing, the driver of the hero's wife and the sister of his private secretary.

Ummi Hafilda Ali's letter to the Prime Minister accusing Anwar of sexual involvement with both her brother's wife, Shamsidar Taharin, and the driver, Azizan, was at the heart of the prosecution case. She was besieged by press photographers as she arrived at the court each day in a succession of fashionable outfits. Ummi was a member of a clique of glamorous women with well-connected companions or husbands. They did not conform to conservative Malay practice in what they wore, favouring Western-style clothing and looking as groomed as if they had come directly from their personal hairdressers. Among Ummi's friends was Normala Mohamad Yusof, a businessman's wife, who was listed as a witness and was also a favourite of press photographers. Ummi had borrowed Normala's car sticker to enable her to enter Tivoli Villas, the apartment complex featured in the trial, on an occasion when she had been tailing her sister-in-law to what she believed was a tryst with Anwar.

The cameras also focused on other photogenic figures, such as actress Norzielah Jalil—known as Zielah—the wife of the Minister of Domestic Trade and Consumer Affairs, Megat Junid Ayob. Another close friend of Ummi, Zielah was said to have handed over Ummi's letter to her husband. Megat Junid and his wife were among the 52 persons on the prosecution witness list, together with Dr Mahathir and Daim Zainuddin, but they were not called. Ummi's brother Mohamed Azwan Ali, compere of a popular television programme, was photographed playing the role of supportive sibling, escorting his sister to court. Trial testimony revealed that she had fallen out with her other brother, Mohamed Azmin Ali, Anwar's private secretary, over her allegations of an affair between his wife and his boss.

In response to defence questions aimed at showing she had taken revenge on Anwar as a woman scorned, Ummi denied that she had been in love with the former deputy prime minister. The *Sunday Star* said some people saw 'an uncanny resemblance to Monica Lewinsky, the woman involved in a sex scandal with US President Bill Clinton'. But the main spotlight throughout the trial was on the leading player. From the moment Anwar appeared at the top of a stairway rising from a tunnel connecting the courtroom to basement cells, he was the centre of attention from the media and members of the public—in the few seats set aside for them in the small courtroom. They stood up to watch as he kissed his wife and embraced other members of his family, greeted friends and tossed a quip or comment to the media.

Anyone poking their head into Court Number Three, in the Sultan Abdul Samad building, might think at first sight that nothing much had changed in Kuala Lumpur since the colonnaded structure was opened on 6 October 1894, by the Sultan in the presence of Sir Charles Mitchell, Governor of the Straits Settlements and W. H. Treacher, British Resident. Forty-three years after Britain extended self-government to its former colony Malaya, the court procedures of the Federation of Malaysia are still very British in nature. Judges and lawyers wear black robes and use the polite language of British courts. At Anwar's trial, lawyers addressed Justice Paul as 'M'Lord', or its Malay equivalent, Yang Arif (learned one). Judgments by courts in Britain and other territories following the British judicial tradition, including Hong Kong, were quoted in legal argument. Justice Paul followed the outdated practice of taking his own notes, which is common in courts in Malaysia and Singapore, another former British colony, and slows procedures to a crawl. But there were marked contrasts with Britain itself. A sign on the front of the judge's bench directly below him read, 'Gunakan Bahasa Kebangasaan', which means 'Use the national language'. However, legal judgments and research material are mainly written in English and many judges and lawyers are more at home with the tongue of the colonists than Malay. Although Justice Paul had been instructed by the Chief Justice, Eusoff Chin, to conduct the trial in Malay, the national language was soon getting little use.

The atmosphere in the courtroom ranged from relaxed to tense, as formal politeness gave way periodically to acerbic exchanges between the barristers for the defence and the prosecution. The prosecution team was headed by Abdul Gani Patail, Commissioner of Law Review in the Attorney-General's office when he was not handling a case. Most of the time, Anwar looked relaxed and in good spirits, but his control snapped periodically and he raged against the government and the prosecution. Addressing either the court or the media representatives, he repeatedly attacked the Attorney-General, Mohtar Abdullah, and denounced Dr Mahathir. Speaking from the dock to journalists at the end of the first day's proceedings, he accused Mohtar of being biased, unprofessional and failing to respect procedures, and asked: 'How do you expect me to get a fair trial in these circumstances?' It was a question that many other people were to ask as the proceedings took some strange twists.

From the start, the prosecution set out to weave a tale of alleged sexual misconduct over several years by a man whose presence in the dock would have been unimaginable just months earlier. The first witness, Mohamad Said Awang, 54-year-old Director of the Special Branch, who like the judge had an impressive, army-officer-style mustache, said that in 1992 he had been briefed on an operation code-named Solid Grip relating to sexual misbehaviour by Anwar but gave no other details. It was presumed to bear some relationship to the information former police chief Hanif had said he had given in 1993 to Dr Mahathir.

Later, the prosecution spent days eliciting evidence from witnesses intended to show that Anwar had cavorted with men and women on a semen-stained mattress, which was exhibited in court. But the testimony was wiped from the record towards the end of the trial when the judged ruled that it was 'not relevant' to the charge against the defendant. By then it had been blazoned across newspaper front pages and featured in television news broadcasts, bolstering the government's earlier assault on Anwar's moral character—and further breaching the conservative code, which had until now proscribed publication of anything of such a salacious nature.

In their devotion to the cause of crushing Anwar, the authorities were not only prepared to sacrifice national mores but also disclose damaging information about the operations of the Special Branch. Said testified that he and two other officers had been directed by Anwar to look into Ummi's letter to the Prime Minister—headed 'The Matter of the Deputy Prime Minister's Misconduct'—and find out why it was written. He said Anwar had wanted them to find Ummi and the driver, Azizan Abu Bakar, quickly and frighten the pair. According to Said, the former deputy prime minister used the Malay word 'gempar', which means to threaten or 'put a little fear in them'. Anwar later conceded that he had spoken the word but his intended meaning was to have them scolded like children. This was not the interpretation that Said gave to it. After the arrest of Ummi and Azizan, the Special Branch chief told his officers they had less than 24 hours to 'turn over' the pair. He explained that the expression 'to turn over' people meant having them 'change their stand'.

In subsequent evidence, Deputy Superintendent Abdul Aziz Hussin, the Special Branch officer assigned to get Ummi's retraction said she had been difficult to turn over because she 'was very firm in her original stand'. Ummi believed wholeheartedly that everything contained in her letter to the Prime Minister was true. Aziz said that in order to turn over Ummi Hafilda, the interrogation team used a 'psychological' approach. She was threatened with detention under the *Internal Security Act* and possible 'retaliation' from Anwar. He said she was subjected to a night-long non-stop interrogation to 'create an atmosphere in which physical threat is imminent'. The team also used persuasion and advice to 'confuse' her. According to Aziz, the Special Branch procedures placed Ummi Hafilda under 'intense mental pressure' until she 'lost her will to resist' and 'surrendered' to the interrogation team. The first letter in which she retracted the allegations was not committed enough so she was persuaded to write a second, which was accepted after some changes. Aziz said he considered the turn-over operation against Ummi Hafilda incomplete because she had not changed her stand, although she had retracted the allegations and apologised for making them.

Special Branch chief Said was also asked about the term 'neutralise'. He said if a person who was a security threat was 'neutralised' he was 'no longer a security threat'. Asked why he felt he had to neutralise both Ummi and Azizan, he said it was because the direction came from the Deputy Prime Minister. Said then caused a stir in court by saying in cross-examination that he might lie under oath if he was instructed to do so by 'someone higher than the Deputy Prime Minister'. He acknowledged that a situation might arise where he might have to do something illegal if it was requested by the police chief or Dr Mahathir.

The trial highlighted a complete turnabout in the position of the police and the Prime Minister on allegations of sexual misbehaviour against Anwar. At the time Ummi's letter to Dr Mahathir was first investigated by police, Said reported to the Prime Minister that there was no proof of her allegations. He said there were indications of the existence of a 'certain group that might have their own agenda and played a role behind the scenes' to urge Ummi and the driver Azizan to 'smear' Anwar. Further, Azizan made his accusations because he 'was influenced by the persuasion of Ummi Hafilda Ali' and 'did not like the arrogance of Shamsidar Taharin'. In a statement to the media on 2 September 1997, Police Chief Rahim Noor said investigations into two letters alleging a sexual scandal involving Anwar had found the charges were untrue. He said the police considered the case 'solved as far as the contents of the letters are concerned'. The writers of the letters had 'admitted their wrongdoings and that what they had written was untrue'. After receiving the police report, in August 1997, Dr Mahathir told the media that the accusations of a sex scandal involving Anwar were slanderous and the work of a group out to prevent the former deputy prime minister from succeeding him. But in September 1998, after sacking Anwar he said he believed the reports he had received of sexual misbehaviour by Anwar. Against this background, the defence said the charges against Anwar were 'trumped up' to remove him and 'destroy him politically'. Anwar testified that he had 'political foes who would stop at nothing to achieve their agenda' and that there was a 'major difference' between him and Dr Mahathir. But Justice Paul ruled as irrelevant the key defence argument that Anwar was the victim of a high-level political conspiracy.

In just a few days, developments in Anwar's corruption trial shattered the hopes of Malaysian officials that it would restore some of the government's lost credibility. The admission by the head of the police Special Branch that he might lie under oath at the direction of someone ranking higher than a deputy prime minister, his disclosure that in his 1997 report to the Prime Minister he said there could be a plot to 'smear' Anwar and his vacillation about a second document allegedly naming two ministers and other top officials left many Malaysians dumbfounded and drew further criticism of Malaysia from abroad. Aziz's revelations of the harsh interrogation techniques used against Ummi intensified public disrespect and distrust of the police. A lawyer with close government contacts described the trial as 'a real mess', saying to me Malaysians who supported Dr Mahathir were shocked by what was happening in court. Others who had accepted that Anwar must have engaged in homosexual activity were now less convinced. And many people standing on the sidelines had become Anwar supporters. Developments at the trial strengthened foreign opinion that Anwar was a victim of political persecution. Dr Mahathir looked increasingly isolated internationally as he prepared to receive the leaders of the eighteen governments represented in the APEC forum at its annual summit in Kuala Lumpur. Canada announced that its Prime Minister, Jean Chretien, would not hold one-to-one talks with Dr Mahathir, despite the fact that a formal meeting was requested by Malaysia. The reason given was concern over Anwar's arrest and trial. Philippines President Estrada also ruled out bilateral talks.

After complaints in newspapers that Anwar was 'receiving special treatment' and breaching the rules on speaking to family and the press, court police and his Special Branch minders made token gestures to keep him from talking to the media but allowed him considerable leeway to chat with his family and greet friends in the public gallery before each day's session and during court adjournments. And he still managed to toss remarks to journalists covering the trial, including scathing comments about the Prime Minister and other cabinet ministers. He also had the largest and most comfortable cell in Sungei Buloh prison. His privileged position, compared with other prisoners, prompted speculation that Dr Mahathir was appeasing his conscience by ensuring Anwar's incarceration was not as harsh as it might have been. But a veteran Malaysian journalist told me this was just the Malay way: Malays tended to remain respectful towards very powerful people even when they had fallen from power.

As Malaysia prepared to receive APEC delegates, the government tried to turn off the international spotlight on Anwar by taking him out of the courtroom and confining him to his cell in Sungei Buloh prison for a week-long trial recess, which conveniently coincided with the meeting of world and regional leaders. But many of the participants were determined to raise the Anwar issue, and the burning motorcycles on Jalan Sultan Ismail three days before the summit made it hard for Malaysian officials to pretend that nothing untoward was occurring in the capital. Additionally, the high visibility of the Federal Reserve Unit and their water cannons in the area adjacent to the court complex and the increased number of security personnel on the streets for the APEC meeting, including a paramilitary unit armed with automatic weapons, had given Kuala Lumpur the look of a city under a state of emergency. US Secretary of State Madeleine Albright, who had long demonstrated openly her dislike of Dr Mahathir, fired the first shot in support of Anwar by saying he had 'made very clear his own dedication to democracy and a market economy'. Later, at an APEC press conference chaired by Rafidah Aziz, the Malaysian Minister of International Trade and Industry, Albright said that the United States had made clear a number of times that Anwar was 'a highly respectable leader'. She also said the United States believed Anwar was 'entitled to due process and a fair trial', prompting an angry response from Rafidah, who described the American official's remarks as 'very unfair, unbecoming and uncalled for'.

Dr Mahathir tried to head off expressions of foreign support for Anwar by stating in an interview with Bernama, the national newsagency, that attempts to politicise APEC by introducing non-economic matters was 'unfortunate'. He said everyone had political problems so there was no one who was 'not guilty of some political abuse'. If Australian Prime Minister John Howard raised the Anwar issue, he could 'also raise issues about [Pauline] Hanson, about the treatment of Aborigines and all that'. He added: 'But, that doesn't get us anywhere.'

His appeal for delegates to confine themselves to the APEC agenda was ignored. Canadian Foreign Minister Lloyd Axworthy went ahead with a meeting with Anwar's wife, Azizah, despite Malaysian government objections. Axworthy told a press conference he had expressed concerns to Malaysian officials about the treatment of Anwar and other people who had been politically detained. But the Canadian's undiplomatic behaviour caused only a minor frisson within the Malaysian government compared with the shock wave resulting from the arrogance and rudeness of

American Vice President Al Gore. In a speech at a business dinner held in conjunction with the APEC summit, and attended by Dr Mahathir, delegates and leading corporate figures, Gore had been delegated to represent the United States after President Clinton decided the arms inspection issue with Iraq demanded his presence in Washington. With an insouciance bordering on contempt for the APEC host, who was seated at a table in front of him, the Vice President implied that Malaysia was a nation where freedom was suppressed and declared that people had 'power to determine their future'. He then went on to say, as Dr Mahathir listened stony-faced: 'And so, among nations suffering economic crises, we continue to hear calls for democracy, calls for "reformasi". We hear them today—right here, right now—among the brave people of Malaysia.'

It was a stinging slap in the face of Dr Mahathir. He had been a principal target of the reformasi protesters, who had called for his overthrow and burned his portrait. Adding visual insult to the verbal injury, Mr Gore walked out at the conclusion of his speech surrounded by a phalanx of secret service heavies, like an emperor who had delivered an edict. An economic analyst and former Finance Ministry official, Ramon Navaratnam, commented that Gore not only gave a bad speech but conducted himself disgrace-fully by 'leaving the dining room even before having his soup'. If Gore hoped to encourage wider support for Anwar, he miscal-culated. Even Malaysians sympathetic to Anwar's plight were appalled by his remarks. Giving comfort to people demonstrating in the streets was unwelcome at a time when many members of the public feared that the protests could escalate into Indonesian-style riots. The government was furious. A statement by the Foreign Minister, Abdullah Badawi, blasted the United States for inciting 'lawlessness' and said it would be held accountable for any resulting unrest. Describing Gore's remarks as 'most unwarranted' and 'provocative', Badawi complained they were a 'gross interference' in Malaysia's internal affairs. Malaysia found 'most abhorrent' the action of the US in inciting certain elements within Malaysia to use undemocratic means 'in order to overthrow constitutionally elected elements'.

The APEC summit should have been a high point in Dr Mahathir's seventeen years in office, allowing him to bask in the international spotlight on an equal footing with the leaders of the major Pacific powers. But for the second year running, he was host of a major conference in Kuala Lumpur that suffered from an outside distraction. In the case of the 1997 ASEAN heads of government meeting, it was the political unrest in Cambodia and the eruption of regional financial turmoil. At the 1998 APEC summit it was the Anwar affair. Dr Mahathir's failure to persuade visiting leaders from within and outside the region to stick to economic matters and avoid political issues demonstrated his diminished standing globally and in his own backyard. Never before had any Malaysian leader been subjected to such a barrage of foreign criticism or suffered the mortification of having a world leader publicly support his enemies on his home ground. But there was wide agreement among Malaysians that Al Gore had done more harm than good to Anwar's cause.

At the same time, many people continued to say that as a result of events of the past few months they had lost confidence in the system and wanted change. They wanted a Malaysia in which they could have more faith in their government, their police and their judiciary. This message was finally getting through to the nation's politicians and an increasing number of senior UMNO figures were remarking privately that the time had come for Dr Mahathir to retire. While he deserved high praise for his achievements, they said he represented the old guard, who could no longer command the respect and support that an UMNO leader must have to bind the party and the country together. Discussing the challenges ahead for UMNO, Harun Hashim, a columnist and former judge, said the 'era of the personality cult and strong one-man leadership of a country' was coming to an end. 'In the new millennium, collective leadership and consensus will be the order of governments.' But Dr Mahathir was not about to retire. And since no one in the UMNO hierarchy was prepared to suggest openly it was time for him to go, he was able to consolidate his authority as Prime Minister and UMNO president to the point where his decisions increasingly went unchallenged.

A week after Anwar's trial resumed, the relatively civil relationship between the bench and the defence ended abruptly. In a move that plunged relations between Malaysian lawyers and the judiciary to their lowest level in many years, Justice Paul sentenced Zainur Zakaria, a member of Anwar's legal team to three months' jail for contempt of court over an affidavit he had filed in his client's name. The judge's contempt finding against Zainur, followed by the imposition of a jail sentence, brought a gasp from members of the public and left the defence lawyers momentarily incredulous. Justice Paul's courteous manner, meticulous, case-law-based approach to issues, and attempts to be seen to be even-handed in considering defence and prosecution arguments had prompted some hope that the trial might, perhaps, be conducted in a straightforward way. But the contempt episode showed there was another side to the judge. He displayed a steely will that brooked no deviation from the path he had chosen. Declaring that the affidavit contained 'scandalous and contemptuous matters', Justice Paul accused Zainur of attempting to undermine the integrity of the Anwar trial.

The sensational development in the High Court arose out of an application by Zainur to have the chief prosecutor, Abdul Gani Patail, and his deputy, Azahar Mohamad, removed from the case. The affidavit filed in Anwar's name said that the two prosecutors had offered a plea bargain arrangement to a business friend of the former deputy prime minister in exchange for false evidence against him. The friend was his former tennis partner, Nallakaruppan. According to the affidavit, Nallakaruppan's lawyer, Manjeet Singh, had alleged in a statutory declaration that Gani had said he would consider a request for a lesser charge against his client if he was prepared to cooperate with the Attorney-General's department by 'falsely implicating' Anwar 'in the commission of sexual offences with various married and unmarried women'. The affidavit said the two prosecutors had abused their positions by going out of their way to get the friend to fabricate evidence in order to prefer more charges against Anwar.

Taking Zainur through the statutory declaration and a letter written by Manjeet Singh to the Attorney-General, Justice Paul said the two documents made no reference to fabricated evidence.

He asked where it said 'fabricated evidence'. Zainur said that he came to the conclusion from the two documents that there was a request to fabricate evidence. Justice Paul said there was absolutely no basis for this. He would show mercy by stopping further proceedings against Zainur if he tendered an unconditional apology to the court, the Attorney-General, Gani and Azahar for filing the application, which was 'baseless and an abuse of the process of this court'. Zainur said he would be unable to tender his apologies. Justice Paul announced that in order to preserve the dignity of the court and the integrity of the trial evidence, while also taking into account public interest and an element of deterrence, he was imposing a sentence of three months' imprisonment. He rejected an application by the Anwar team for time to prepare a defence for Zainur and call witnesses. Justice Paul said he had to act with all urgency to preserve the integrity of the trial, declaring: 'I will not hesitate to flex every inch of my judicial muscle to ensure the trial proceeds smoothly.'

Justice Paul's action against Zainur was seen by many lawyers as a reflection of the harshness of many court judgments in the late 1990s. They complained that judges were resorting to contempt of court actions too freely. Contempt of court was even the basis of a private action against a foreign journalist, Canadian Murray Hiebert, over an article he wrote for the *Far Eastern Economic Review* concerning a civil case. He was sentenced to three months' imprisonment, which was reduced to six weeks on appeal. But other offences were also incurring stiff penalties. The opposition DAP's Lim Guan Eng had discovered this when his sentence of a fine for publishing false news and seditious remarks was increased to eighteen months' imprisonment on each charge on appeal.

In these circumstances, the outlook was not encouraging for the High Court defendant who no longer had friends in high places and was appearing before a judge prepared to send his lawyer to jail for three months for contempt of court. For many Malaysians the actions of the police and the judiciary instilled fear. They had seen what could happen to the second most powerful man in the country and worried what might happen to them—as powerless, ordinary citizens—for minor breaches of the law or for supporting the opposition. It was also a time when the police appeared to have adopted a take-no-prisoners policy, with scores of suspected criminals shot dead over a period of a few years. It was rare for anyone to be merely wounded when officers of the law opened fire. These police killings prompted Raja Aziz Addruse to call attention to the dramatic increase in the fatal shooting of suspects in a letter to the media in 1998 (before he became the leader of the team of lawyers defending Anwar). He said that police could 'not assume the roles of judge, jury and executioner, all rolled into one'.

The jail sentence imposed on Zainur reinforced concern among members of the public that the system under which they lived was flawed and caused further damage to Malaysia's image abroad. Two years later Rais Yatim, the de facto law minister, whose official title was Minister in the Prime Minister's Department, was instrumental in bringing change to the judiciary. A former minister who supported Tengku Razaleigh's 1987 bid to replace Dr Mahathir, he was brought back into the cabinet by the Prime Minister as a gesture of goodwill to old foes in December 1990. In the middle of 2000 Rais clashed with the Chief Justice, Eusoff Chin, who had recently featured in pictures posted on the Internet showing him with a prominent lawyer, V. K. Lingam, while they and their families were on vacation in New Zealand in 1994. In an interview with the Australian Broadcasting Corporation, Rais was asked to comment on allegations that Eusoff, Lingam and their families had holidayed together. The minister said that the Chief Justice had been told in no uncertain terms that such an action was improper behaviour for a judge. Eusoff then called a press conference at which he denied being reprimanded by the government for improper behaviour and threatened to sue anyone who alleged that his family's holiday in New Zealand had been sponsored by Lingam. He said that he had been cleared of any impropriety by investigations conducted by the Anti-Corruption Agency and the Attorney-General and had allowed investigators to examine his bank account to verify if large amounts of money had been deposited in it.

On Rais's recommendation, Mohamed Dzaiddin Abdullah, 63, was chosen as Chief Justice to replace Eusoff Chin on his retirement at the end of 2000. Dzaiddin was refreshingly frank about what needed to be done. He said that his first priority would be restoring public confidence in the judiciary and 'put our house in order'. He said he realised there was 'plenty of work to be done to repair the damage' which had been caused by 'lack of leadership and direction'. According to Dzaiddin, public perceptions about the judiciary were also due to 'so many things that happened in the past', which he would not mention because it was 'history'. Noting that international organisations had questioned the independence of the Malaysian judiciary, Dzaiddin said transparency would be a mark of his style of leadership.

Some six months after Dzaiddin took over as Chief Justice, the Federal Court quashed Zainur's contempt of court conviction and prison sentence and savaged Justice Paul. One of the Federal Court judges on the three-member panel reviewing the case said the filing of the application for the removal of the prosecutors was justified. Another noted that Zainur was merely performing his role as Anwar's lawyer. Ruling that Justice Paul had acted wrongly in finding Zainur guilty of contempt of court, panel member Justice Abdul Malek Ahmad said he found the High Court judge to have acted in the matter 'as though he was arguing on behalf of the two prosecutors'.

This was the third judgment to go against the government in the wake of Dzaiddin's assumption of the post of chief justice. A month earlier a judge had released two men held under the controversial *Internal Security Act*, ruling their detention was unlawful. Then another judge annulled the by-election of a government candidate after finding there were phantom voters on the electoral role.

Lim Kit Siang, chairman of the opposition Democratic Action Party, said the Federal Court ruling was 'another welcome development on the long and hard road to restore confidence in the judiciary'. But the Prime Minister showed his displeasure with the new judicial independence and some analysts speculated that the change might not last. Eleven months earlier, the opposition and lawyers had welcomed the appointment of Ainum Mohamad Saaid as Attorney-General as warmly as they had greeted the installation of Dzaiddin as the new Chief Justice. The first woman to hold the position, she replaced Mohtar Abdullah, a controversial personality, who had directed the Anwar trials and at times taken over as chief of the prosecution team and on retirement was made a judge. But less than a year into Ainum's two-year contract, the government announced her resignation for health reasons. Her replacement was Abdul Gani Patail, the chief prosecutor in Anwar's trials—except when his superior was in the court—whom Zainur had applied to have removed from the first hearing. Lim said Malaysians had hoped for a new era of the Malaysian judiciary and administration of the law, but Abdul Gani's appointment seemed to have brought back the past. Abdul Gani had been 'fully associated with the dark age of the system and cause of justice in Malaysia', which all Malaysians, including the present chief justice and the judiciary, wanted to put to rest permanently.

9 | The semen-stained mattress

The shock waves from Zainur's contempt of court conviction were still reverberating across the nation when the public was subjected to another assault on its moral values from Justice Paul's courtroom with the published testimony of the man who had been the Anwar family driver. *The Star* newspaper summed up the first day's evidence of Azizan Abu Bakar in a banner headline dominating the front page: 'I was a sex slave', in capital letters, followed by the words, 'Azizan: I was sodomised by Anwar several times.' The bold type that again shattered Malaysia's conservative newspaper conventions while simultaneously stripping the former deputy prime minister of all dignity and stature.

Azizan, a boyish-looking 38-year-old, appeared timid in contrast with his co-accuser, the hard-edged, self-confident Ummi Hafilda Ali. He was not the official chauffeur of the former deputy prime minister but a driver employed to ferry Anwar's wife and children about. He was said to have volunteered to Ummi the information that he had been sodomised by Anwar and at her request provided a sworn statement to this effect for inclusion with her letter to the Prime Minister. Like Ummi, he had undergone Special Branch interrogation until he retracted his story. In court Azizan renewed his allegations against Anwar. Reading from his sworn statement as part of his evidence for the prosecution, he said that he had 'been a victim of homosexual acts by Anwar Ibrahim'. The sworn statement had the histrionic ring of a document that has been crafted to achieve the strongest dramatic effect, and Azizan later disclosed that it had been drawn up by Ummi. In his statement he said: 'This heinous act was committed several times in 1992 against my will.' It 'regularly took place in luxurious hotels' without the knowledge of the public or Anwar's wife. Azizan said that as long as he was employed as the family driver he was 'often called upon to commit this heinous act' although on several occasions he had 'tried to resist'. A feeling of guilt eventually overcame him as he always had to look at Anwar's wife, 'who had such high moral character'. He said: 'Finally, I decided to stop being a continuous homosexual victim of this man whom I regard as an animal.' According to Azizan, Anwar's behaviour 'could be categorised as chronic' and had caused the driver 'great mental stress'.

Azizan told the court that when he was interrogated by Special Branch officers at police headquarters in Kuala Lumpur, he swore in the name of God that everything in his statement was true. But his interrogator demanded proof. He told the police officer that a woman who was a virgin could prove that she had been assaulted but not a man. He said his interrogator was 'very fierce' and frightened him, threatening to have him held for two years under the *Internal Security Act*. He finally agreed to retract the allegations.

Azizan read his dramatic accusations in a low voice without looking at the man in the dock. Anwar was expressionless. Despite his feeling of guilt, Azizan apparently did not tell anyone about Anwar's 'heinous acts' until, five years on, he confided in Ummi. At that time, he was the driver of Shamsidar, the wife of Anwar's private secretary, Azmin Ali. He testified that in June 1997, Ummi told him at a meeting she arranged by telephone that Anwar was having an affair with Shamsidar. Why Ummi would disclose this fact to the driver of the woman who had allegedly cuckolded her brother was never made clear. Azizan said he then told Ummi that he had been sodomised by Anwar in 1992.

Defence lawyer Christopher Fernando asked him why he had 'suddenly decided after five years to come out with these kind of allegations'. Azizan said Ummi stirred his awareness of the 'despicable act' that had taken place. Under questioning by Fernando, Azizan said he could not remember any dates of the occasions when he had been sodomised by Anwar. It was usually 'in the evening' around 7.30 or 8 p.m. Azizan said it would be a sin for him, as a Muslim, to fabricate the allegations that he had been sodomised by Anwar. He made his disclosure five years after the acts were committed because he did not want to allow a sodomist to become prime minister. Under questioning by Fernando, he denied that Ummi made promises so tempting that he was prepared to sell his honour and his pride. He also rejected a suggestion that he had been promised a big sum of money and directorships in companies where he would not be required to perform any functions in return for making the allegations against Anwar.

Under re-examination by the prosecution, Azizan said: 'One of the acts I cannot forget is the incident that happened at Sukma's house at Tivoli Villas . . . The accused sodomised me first followed by . . .' A defence objection interrupted him but he was allowed to continue by the judge. Azizan said Anwar's adopted brother then sodomised him. The judge rejected a defence objection that the prosecution was adducing fresh evidence which was making the witness's allegations 'more sordid'.

Despite Azizan's declaration that he could not forget the act, there was a major discrepancy in his evidence, which was exposed at Anwar's later trial for sodomy. In the first mention of the sodomy charge in the Sessions Court, the date of the alleged offence was May 1994. Then, at the preliminary hearing, it had been changed to May 1992. Finally, when the trial got under way the prosecution successfully moved to have the charge amended to stipulate that the offence was committed some time 'between January and March 1993'. The apparent reason for the prosecution's amendment in the sodomy trial was Anwar's advance notice of alibi, which had shown that the apartment in which the offences were alleged to have been committed was not completed in May 1992. The apartment was the one referred to by Azizan as Sukma's 'house' in Tivoli

Villas but actually owned by a company for which Nallakaruppan worked. Azizan's evidence in the first trial consistently referred to 1992 as the year in which he had been subjected to Anwar's 'heinous acts'. And under cross-examination by Fernando, Azizan said he had 'no problems' with Anwar after 1992, when he maintained a 'cordial relationship' with Azizah and the children.

The trial took its most bizarre turn as the prosecution pursued its apparent aim of portraying the defendant as a man with a ravenous bisexual appetite by hauling into court a mattress allegedly stained with semen. The introduction of the exhibit ultimately served no purpose, other than to publicly besmirch Anwar, due to the judge's later ruling that evidence related to it was irrelevant. Musa Hassan, a senior officer with the police criminal investigation department, told the court the mattress was seized in a police raid on a Tivoli Villas apartment as part of a police investigation into the allegations in the book *50 Dalil*. The book included the claim that Shamsidar was taken there by Anwar's tennis partner, Nallakaruppan, for a liaison with Anwar. The police officer said Shamsidar was alleged to have had sexual relations with the accused at the apartment. Musa, who featured in other aspects of the Anwar case, said that in his examination of the mattress he 'found stains suspected to be seminal fluid'.

After unwrapping a grey king-size mattress and identifying it as the one his officers seized, together with a pillow, from the Tivoli Villas flat on 10 August 1998, Musa said cuts in the cloth cover had been made by an official of the police chemistry department in order to subject spots of suspected seminal fluid to DNA analysis. Lim Kong Boon, a chemist with the police chemistry department, testified that DNA profiles of semen stains on the mattress matched those of blood samples taken from Anwar and Shamsidar. He sourced other stains to another male and two other women. In each of two cases where the composition of a stain was 'mixed', he identified the sources as Anwar, the second male and a woman. The defence objected to the admission of the chemist's findings because the blood was taken from Anwar for the DNA tests without his consent but was overruled by the judge. Anwar had agreed to give blood for tests other than DNA. One of Anwar's lawyers,

Gurbachan Singh, said the defence was 'not conceding that [the specimen container] contains the blood of the accused'.

Lim said his findings showed there had been 'some sexual activity such as sexual intercourse' on the mattress. He said he compared a DNA profile developed from the blood sample taken from Anwar with the DNA profile of one of the male sources detected in the seminal stains. The sources of the stains and blood were the same and the probability of any other Malaysian Malay having the same DNA profile was one in 59 billion. The defence responded by seeking to discredit Lim, using information provided by DNA specialists from Australia and Britain, who sat in the courtroom taking notes and passing them to Anwar's lawyers. The government chemist showed unfamiliarity with some 'well-known' DNA analysis terms put to him by Aziz Addruse but stood by his findings. Subsequently, during cross-examination of a police officer, Fernando told the judge the defence alleged that the semen stains on the mattress were planted there. He suggested to the witness that the planted semen was extracted from Anwar while he was unconscious after his beating at police headquarters. Assistant Superintendent Mohamad Rodwan said he did not know if this could have happened or if body fluids from Shamsidar could also have been planted on the mattress. But he agreed that his investigations did not eliminate the possibility of such an occurrence.

The 31-year-old woman whose allegations against Anwar set in motion the events that brought him to trial finally appeared in the witness stand three weeks after the first hearing began. Ummi told the High Court that she had raised the issue of the former deputy prime minister's alleged sexual misconduct because she believed he was cuckolding her brother. She said she also made her allegations for the sake of truth, for UMNO and the nation. Ummi, it seemed, was a member of the dominant government party. Ummi made her first appearance on the witness stand, which had been eagerly awaited by the press and public, fashionably attired in a canary-yellow, full-length dress, and black white-trimmed jacket, set off with a single-strand pearl necklace. Speaking firmly in response to questions from the prosecution, she confirmed earlier evidence from police officers that she had written a letter to the Prime Minister alleging that Anwar was having an affair with her sister-in-law Shamsidar and had sodomised his driver, Azizan. She said that she was subjected to 'very rough' police interrogation and threats that she could be locked up for two years under the *Internal Security Act*, in order to get her to retract her allegations. She was sure her letter had 'a strong foundation for a police investigation' but the police 'continued their mental torture' and she finally agreed to sign a retraction. Ummi said she wanted to save her brother from 'continuing to work for a person who had betrayed him and was a hypocrite'. She wrote to Dr Mahathir to seek his help in investigating her allegations and providing protection for herself and her family. Ummi said she also requested appropriate punishment for Anwar if her allegations were found to be true, 'as a reminder to other leaders not to abuse their power and position'.

Under cross-examination by Fernando, she denied his suggestion that she had been in love with Anwar and was jealous of her sister-in-law Shamsidar. But she admitted she carried his photograph around in her handbag. She rejected Fernando's contention that she had confessed to people that she was 'crazy' about the former deputy prime minister. She said: 'I did say that I looked up to him as a leader before I knew the real person.' If there was a time when Ummi admired or even loved Anwar, her feelings subsequently changed dramatically. She acknowledged that on 20 September, after Anwar was sacked and arrested, she had written him a letter, which Fernando said was 'filled with hatred and venom'. In it she prayed that the 'dog Anwar' would be 'destroyed by Aids soon'. Ummi told the court Anwar deserved the letter because he had cheated the nation. Fernando's questions disclosed that Ummi's allegations against Anwar had caused a deep rift in her family and prompted her father to make a sworn statement saying he disowned her. She accused her brother Azmin Ali of bribing her father to make the sworn statement, which the defence submitted to the court. She said Azmin presented her father with a bungalow costing about M$300 000 and a car 'paid for in cash'.

When another Anwar lawyer, Gurbachan Singh, rose to continue the defence's examination of Ummi, she was at first unruffled. But her composure deserted her and she began to look uneasy as he put to her a series of questions about a conversation she had allegedly had with a Malaysian politician and businessman, Sng Chee Hua, a member of parliament from Sarawak state and a vice president of a small government party. As Gurbachan proceeded, quoting in detail what had been said between Ummi and Sng, the possibility that the alleged remarks may have been recorded dawned on the hushed courtroom. Ummi was noticeably rattled by the realisation that he was reciting word for word what she had discussed with Sng when they were both in London three months before Anwar was sacked. Ummi at first answered with denials when the lawyer began reading a series of statements and asking her if she had made them. But as he proceeded through what appeared to be a transcript of her conversation with Sng, she changed her response, saying she could not remember if the words were hers.

When he had finished asking his questions, Gurbachan unsuccessfully sought the court's leave 'to play a cassette tape of this conversation'. The defence believed the taped conversation, which had been secretly recorded by an employee of Sng, would support its contention that Anwar was the victim of a political conspiracy aimed at preventing him from becoming Malaysia's next prime minister. But the impact of the cassette tape was diminished by the defence's belated discovery that there were several similar recordings, one or more of which had been edited. Justice Paul banned publication of the recorded conversation and also decided that the tape was inadmissible because it had been edited. Nevertheless, the tape—or tapes—suggested that a more extensive series of events had taken place leading to Ummi's appearance in court than the evidence showed. While the recorded conversation was no smoking gun, it raised a host of questions which the trial never answered. This in no way helped Anwar's case but reports spread by his supporters of the existence of an Ummi tape with references to large sums of money and talk of killing Anwar's career further intensified public doubts about the fairness of the prosecution case against the former deputy prime minister.

By 5 January 1999, the government had finally conceded that Anwar was beaten on the night of his arrest. In a statement that followed investigations by a special police team, Attorney-General Mohtar Abdullah said he was satisfied that 'injuries on certain parts of [Anwar's] body were caused by police officers when the former deputy prime minister was in police custody'. He believed that the Royal Malaysia Police was 'fully responsible for the injuries to [Anwar] whilst in the legal custody of the police'. But the investigations had so far 'not identified the person or persons responsible for such injuries'. The admission, while expected, was not only severely embarrassing for the government but also a damaging blow to the image of law and order in Malaysia at a time when Anwar was claiming at his corruption trial that he was the victim of a political conspiracy. Mohtar's failure to announce a guilty party set off widespread talk of a cover-up since it seemed inconceivable that anyone could assault a high-profile prisoner at police headquarters without the knowledge of others.

Two days later, the police chief resigned. In a brief statement, Rahim Noor said he assumed 'full responsibility in respect of the matters' referred to by the Attorney-General. But it was another seven weeks before he confessed, at a Royal Commission appointed by the government soon after his resignation, that he personally had beaten Anwar. Even before his confession, the police—and, by extension, the government—had lost the trust of a wide swathe of Malaysians. Their disillusionment with the body of people commissioned to uphold law and order was intensified by the apparent protection of the person who committed the assault. Many people wondered whether the failure of any officer to finger the man widely believed to be the perpetrator reflected either fear of a powerful superior or a culture of silence towards transgressions within the force. The question was openly asked—but never answered—after five senior officers gave evidence at the Royal Commission about their involvement before and after the assault.

Rahim's admission that he assaulted Anwar while the former deputy prime minister was blindfolded and handcuffed on the night of 20 September was made through a lawyer, Teh Poh Teik, who said his client had 'acted under grave provocation'. The unheralded disclosure by the lawyer startled the commissioners and Anwar, who was appearing as a witness, although circumstantial evidence had been steadily mounting against Rahim. After a forensic doctor told the commission that the blows, which left the former deputy prime minister with his widely publicised black eye, could have been lethal, Teh stood up and suggested to Anwar that Rahim hit him because he was provoked. Anwar replied: 'I'm stunned. So I was right all along.' He then went on to say that there had been 'absolutely no conversation at all' in his cell at that time. Anwar denied the lawyer's suggestion that he had provoked the police chief by calling him the 'father of all dogs'. One of the commissioners, Judge Mahadev Shankar, asked Teh if his client was 'admitting that he has done this thing'. The lawyer answered: 'That is my instruction and that is my client's position.'

Called before the commission, Rahim said that the 'chaotic and frightening situation' in Kuala Lumpur on the day Anwar Ibrahim was arrested may have been partly responsible for his loss of control in assaulting the former deputy prime minister. Rahim painted a picture of a city on the brink of anarchy as he and his officers discussed plans to introduce a curfew and moves to call in the army and police reinforcements from other states. It was a more dramatic portrayal of events in the centre of Kuala Lumpur on 20 September, when Anwar had addressed the crowd of some 40 000 people at the National Mosque than earlier official reports.

The former police chief did not offer an apology or show any emotion as he described the assault, which he said had not been abetted, directed or assisted by anyone—'not even the PM'. Denying premeditation, Rahim said he and Anwar had been 'close friends'. He stated that he had entered Anwar's cell and was about to remove the blindfold when the prisoner called him the 'father of all dogs'. Rahim said he lost his control and sense of balance, adding: 'I slapped him, both on the left and right. He fell. I saw him fall on the slab.' He could not recall whether he had delivered 'other physical acts on him'. He told the commission that earlier in the day before Anwar was arrested, the former deputy prime minister had made 'fiery political speeches'. He said: 'We were practically caught with our pants down, to be honest with you, your lordships. We looked at the situation and uppermost in our minds was not to allow the riots in Jakarta to spill over into Kuala Lumpur at all costs.' It was an extraordinary disclosure of police ineptness and lack of foresight but Rahim may have felt it provided a vindication for his attack on Anwar. His claim that the attack was unpremeditated was refuted by the evidence of the five senior officers who said he had given signals for Anwar to be handcuffed and blindfolded before he entered the cell. Abu Talib Othman, counsel assisting the commission, said the attack was a 'clear and straightforward case of a calculated assault on a defenceless person'.

On 7 January 1999, Dr Mahathir appointed Foreign Minister Abdullah Badawi to the post of deputy prime minister, finally filling a cabinet vacancy left open since the sacking of Anwar. At the same time, he postponed the UMNO elections, due in June, until the following year. This meant that the post of deputy president previously held by Anwar would, for the time being, remain vacant. However, Dr Mahathir installed Badawi as his de facto party second-in-command by assigning him to undertake 'the duties of the deputy president'. This met to some degree the desire of senior party officials for the establishment of a line of succession without committing Dr Mahathir himself or the party to formally endorsing Badawi as the next leader. Analysts said the Prime Minister either wanted an interim period to assess for himself Badawi's capability to become the heir apparent or felt UMNO heavyweights needed time to accept the Foreign Minister as Anwar's replacement.

While some party officials had reservations about whether Badawi would make a good leader, the respected, likable and self-effacing former foreign minister, who was fondly known to the public as Pak Lah, would have been the people's choice in a popularity contest with UMNO rivals. He was untainted by either scandal or the UMNO bane of money politics. But senior UMNO figures were concerned that he might not be tough enough to keep the tight hand needed to control party factions and corruption. One top official said Badawi did not have the 'killer instinct' to lead a political party. A columnist writing in the *New Straits Times* said in an open letter to Badawi that while he 'had to maintain his amiable nature through thick and thin' from time to time he also needed 'to show the steel' in him.

On 7 January, Dr Mahathir handed over the finance ministry portfolio, which he himself had been holding, to good friend Daim, which, together with Daim's existing role as Minister of Special Functions and head of the committee overseeing the recovery of the economy, made him unquestionably Malaysia's economic czar. Daim was also UMNO treasurer.

On 13 January, the 45th day of Anwar's trial, the charges against him were altered radically by the prosecution with the judge's acquiescence, effectively reducing the onus of proof on the government. This amazing development, which the defendant's leading counsel described as unjust and highly prejudicial to the accused, came without warning. Anwar was originally charged with the corrupt practice of directing police Special Branch officers to obtain written statements from Azizan and Ummi denying sexual misconduct and sodomy 'committed' by the defendant for his advantage to 'protect himself from criminal action or proceedings'. In the amended charges, references to the *commission* of sexual misconduct and sodomy were changed to allegations of sexual misconduct and sodomy. The 'advantage' was now said to be to save himself from 'embarrassment'. The alterations removed the need for the prosecution to prove the sexual acts took place in order to obtain a conviction on the corruption issue at the heart of the charges. Defence team leader Aziz Addruse said the prosecution had smeared the reputations of Anwar and Shamsidar Taharin by seeking to prove they committed adultery and by introducing evidence intended to show that the accused had committed acts of sodomy with the driver Azizan. Now it was saying these were only allegations.

The following day, Justice Paul wiped from the trial record virtually all the evidence introduced by the prosecution to prove Anwar had been guilty of sexual misconduct and sodomy, ruling it now irrelevant. This meant the defence could not respond to this evidence in either its submissions to the court or by calling witnesses. The judge said that while the truth or falsity of the sexual allegations was of some importance to the original charges, it was no longer a 'constituent element'. He directed all evidence related to the sexual allegations to be struck out 'to avoid any prejudice to the accused'.

Malaysians found it mind-boggling that after being subjected in the media to a barrage of sexual allegations against Anwar in explicit language previously banned from publication they were now being told they were no longer relevant to his High Court trial. For two months, disclosures about alleged intimacies involving the former deputy prime minister and various partners had startled a community in which Malay Muslims' conservative moral attitudes and opposition to the open discussion of sexual matters was matched among many Chinese and Indian Malaysians. Many Malaysians agreed with Anwar's lawyers that the introduction of evidence now deemed irrelevant had only served to smear him. They also believed the trial had caused tremendous harm to the reputation of the country as well as the government. Based upon the evidence before the court, either the Deputy Prime Minister of the Government of Malaysia and deputy president of a party standing for the highest moral values of Islam had engaged in sexual orgies involving men and women; or some person or persons at a very senior level had concocted an elaborate plot, which included the planting of semen extracted from an innocent victim and bodily fluids from alleged partners on a mattress said to have been seized from a supposed love nest.

After Dr Mahathir sacked Anwar from cabinet, declaring him unfit to be a Malaysian leader, he said the trial would prove his point. But as the trial entered its final stages, throughout Malaysia, especially in rural areas of Peninsular Malaysia, many Malaysians remained unconvinced of Anwar's guilt. People returning to Kuala Lumpur from Kelantan and other northern states, after spending the Muslim Hari Raya holiday in their home towns and villages, reported that the Anwar trial had generated anti-government sentiment and signs of a shift by some former UMNO supporters to PAS. They said people's scepticism about the lurid testimony on Anwar's alleged homosexual and heterosexual affairs had only been deepened by the fact it had been declared irrelevant.

By now it was clear the only question likely to determine the judgment of Justice Paul was whether or not Anwar corruptly, by the definition of the law, used his position to have the police lean on Ummi and Azizan to procure him an 'advantage'. But the defence seemed more preoccupied with trying to persuade him to throw out the case on the grounds that the charges against Anwar had been fabricated as part of a political conspiracy, although the judge had firmly rejected their arguments as irrelevant. In both his trials, Anwar seemed to have decided that his conviction was a foregone conclusion. Therefore, he chose to make as much political capital as possible out of his court appearances by issuing statements intended to reach the public through the media and making allegations against his former colleagues as part of the case for the defence. But journalists covering both trials felt the high-powered team of top Malaysian lawyers failed to put enough effort into challenging key elements of the charges against their client because of their fixation with the conspiracy theory. They wasted their undoubted talents on arguing issues the judge was not prepared to consider. At one point, Justice Paul declared: 'Even if there was a political conspiracy, what is its relevancy to the charges against Anwar now?' In spite of this, defence lawyer Fernando went on to argue for some minutes that Ummi was 'used by part of this political conspiracy' and was 'the villain of the piece'.

Arguments more oriented to the charges may not have changed the outcome of the trials but to many lay observers the defence's position made it easier for the prosecution to obtain convictions. The prosecution hammered away at the point that Anwar tried to stop a police investigation into the allegations because it would cause deep embarrassment to the accused, who had 'projected himself as a righteous and religious person'. The chief prosecutor, Abdul Gani Patail, said that Anwar had used the Special Branch as his personal tool for his advantage. The officers had no choice but to accede to his instructions because he was the deputy prime minister. He had committed corrupt practices by abusing an instrument of the government that was committed to the protection of the security of the nation. He said: 'No country in the world could afford a political leader to use such instruments of the government for his personal gain.'

This was the nub of the case. So there was little surprise when Justice Paul ruled that Anwar had a case to answer and was called on him to enter his defence. The defence announced that it would be calling Dr Mahathir, Daim and Megat Junid as witnesses but later abandoned that intention, complaining that the Prime Minister had refused to be interviewed before his planned appearance. A face-to-face confrontation in the High Court between the Prime Minister and his former deputy would undoubtedly have been great theatre. It would have been the first meeting between them since 3 September when the UMNO supreme council expelled Anwar following his earlier sacking from the government. But neither the appearance on the witness stand of Dr Mahathir or other members of his cabinet would have helped Anwar's case since Justice Paul had shown clearly that he would not be moved by any conspiracy arguments.

Anwar, however, was determined to use his time as a defence witness to try to show that enemies in government had concocted the charges that landed him in court. He seized the opportunity aggressively and animatedly to attack Dr Mahathir and other senior figures, drawing applause from relatives and friends in the gallery until the judge threatened to clear the court. Under questioning by his leading counsel, Raja Aziz Addruse, Anwar said that in his role as chairman of the Cabinet Committee on Management and Good Governance he had caused displeasure among many parties. The committee received 'voluminous complaints of alleged government malpractices and corruption including accusations against ministers, government officials and even the Prime Minister himself'. He said senior government officials would come to him with complaints about corruption and other matters because there was a public perception that he would not allow a case to be closed. When Justice Paul called on Raja Aziz to show the relevance of his questions, he said his aim was to show the motive behind the conspiracy to bring Anwar to trial. He asserted that the case against Anwar was a frame-up 'instituted because of ill-will and because of bad motives caused by the accused performing his duty'.

Justice Paul said Raja Aziz's argument to introduce the conspiracy evidence from Anwar was 'based on wrong reasoning' and he disallowed further questions on the matter. Nevertheless, the defence kept coming back to its contention that Anwar was the innocent victim of the machinations of malevolent cabinet colleagues and the Prime Minister's political secretary, Abdul Aziz Shamsuddin, all of whom later dismissed his allegations.

Anwar said it was 'generally known' in UMNO that Abdul Aziz 'harboured enmity' towards him. He claimed that Dr Mahathir had apologised to him at a meeting in August 1997, for the involvement of his political secretary in the move to smear him with sexual allegations. Police Special Branch officers had alerted him to the 'seriousness and dimension' of the political campaign against him. They had impressed upon him that the involvement of Daim, Megat Junid and Abdul Aziz, who were known to be 'confidants of the PM', would certainly complicate their investigations. Describing the conspiracy argument as 'very fanciful', Justice Paul said the defence could adduce evidence to try to show a conspiracy by police to change their stand or create evidence against the accused, but he ruled that if there was any political conspiracy it was 'irrelevant'.

Justice Paul also instructed the defence to show, if it could, that Anwar did not use his position, as the charges stated, to direct police to obtain retractions of allegations against him of sexual misconduct. But Anwar and his lawyers ignored his advice. With his undeviating focus on the conspiracy theory, which the judge had ruled irrelevant, Anwar not only did nothing for his case, but virtually conceded an element of guilt concerning the charges against him. While denying that he had directed the police to trace Ummi and Azizan as quickly as possible and force retractions from them, he admitted that he told the officers to investigate the matter of the allegations thoroughly and to frighten the pair 'a little'. That was enough to support the charges and sink his defence.

Anwar may have failed to persuade Justice Paul to accept the conspiracy arguments he put forward to defend himself but he was having more success in winning the public to his side. His plaint before the court that he was 'helpless', following the judge's ruling that allegations of a political plotting against him were irrelevant, and his leading counsel's grievance that the defence was 'not being allowed to put its case', increased public sympathy for a man seen by many people to be more sinned against than sinning. However, in a court where the presiding judge had made it clear the issues boiled down to questions of law and relevancy, the lawyers' stubborn adherence to their original theme seemed self-defeating. Whatever the merit of his rulings, Justice Paul, who had written a book on evidence and was regarded as an authority on the subject, supported them with detailed references to previous cases and statutes. Anwar's lawyers made little effort to present counter-arguments and appeared to have lost their way from the time the prosecution amended the charges against Anwar.

For weeks the defence was also focused on disproving the allegations that Anwar had committed sodomy and had had an adulterous affair with the wife of his private secretary. The prosecution aimed to show the allegations supplied the motive for the four corrupt practices charges against Anwar while the defence sought to demonstrate the evidence against Anwar had been fabricated. Anwar's lawyers complained that the amendments to the charges had undermined the foundations of their case, which was aimed at demonstrating that police had fabricated the sexual misconduct evidence as part of a conspiracy to remove Anwar from the political scene. But in the new circumstances and having regard to the judge's stand on the conspiracy theory, many lawyers expressed surprise that the defence had not changed tack and argued the case on strictly legal issues.

In November 2000, Malaysiakini, an Internet news website, carried a critical examination of the Anwar's defence. The article was written by M. Bakri Musa, a US-based Malaysian surgeon and author of *The Malay Dilemma Revisited: Race Dynamics in Modern Malaysia*, and T. Melindah Musa, a Washington, DC lawyer. In the authors' assessment, the defence lawyers were 'uncoordinated', and 'like musicians in an orchestra without a conductor'. With the state throwing its massive resources into prosecuting Anwar, defending him demanded maximum commitment and effort. In a Malaysian trial where there was no jury, it was the judge who would ultimately render judgment and impose sentence. He was the one the lawyers had to convince, 'not the foreign observers in the gallery'. The article said Anwar's lawyers forgot that ultimately a judicial judgment was 'a very human process'. The writers also observed that Anwar's 'frequent court outbursts and juvenile tantrums' did not endear him to the judge.

As the trial drew to a close, it became increasingly evident that Justice Paul had narrowed the issue to whether or not Anwar had abused his position as deputy prime minister in contravention of the law. This left Malaysians puzzling over how a trial that began with the high drama, sexual shenanigans and political intrigue of a top-rating television soap opera could now be set to end with all the excitement of a weather report. Unlike members of the public, Anwar's seasoned lawyers should not have been surprised by developments. Even if they could not have persuaded Justice Paul to acquit Anwar, they could have, it seemed, laid better legal grounds for arguing his case in higher courts. The trial ended suddenly after a dispute between Anwar's lawyers and Justice Paul prompted the defence to seek the judge's disqualification—without success—and then refuse to make a final submission. It was another useless exercise by the defendant's team.

10 | Long jail terms end dazzling career

On 4 April, ten days before the scheduled announcement of the verdict, the former deputy prime minister's wife, Azizah, took the plunge into political life, launching the National Justice Party (Keadilan) which, notwithstanding its platform of liberal policies, had one real purpose—the release of her husband. The timing of the launch appeared to reflect a pessimism that the verdict would go against Anwar. For Azizah it was another major watershed in a life that had once centred on being the dutiful wife of the nation's number two leader and raising their six children. She handled the formalities of being Keadilan president well but proved inadequate to the task of settling differences between the factions that emerged in the party. Two years after its founding, moderate members began deserting the party, leaving it in the hands of a hard line element under Anwar's sway.

The launching of Keadilan coincided with the hospitalisation of the Prime Minister for treatment of a lung infection and bronchitis. Dr Mahathir's illness caused public concern that Malaysia might suddenly lose its Prime Minister and be shaken by a political crisis but he recovered quickly and was soon demonstrating his old vigour. He had been released from hospital but was still recuperating on

14 April when Anwar was brought to the High Court to learn his fate after his long and remarkable trial, which had engrossed and polarised the nation like no other event in Malaysia's history. Delivering his verdict, Justice Paul said that having 'meticulously considered the law and the facts on an overall basis', he found the prosecution had proved its case against the accused beyond reasonable doubt. Granted leave to make his own plea for a light penalty, Anwar instead began reading a written statement outlining yet once again his argument that he was the victim of a political conspiracy. The judge tried to stop him, stating that his statement should be made in a political forum, but Anwar pressed ahead. Declaring that he had 'no hope of justice', Anwar said the charges were part of a political conspiracy to destroy him and ensure Dr Mahathir's 'continued hold on power at whatever cost'. His statement served no useful purpose so far as his trial was concerned. Justice Paul said the offence was serious and struck at the very core of the administration of justice, adding: 'If some politicians are out to topple you it has no bearing in this case.'

He sentenced Anwar to six years imprisonment on each of the four charges but said that the terms should run concurrently. Assuming Anwar was given the customary one-third reduction for good behaviour his total time in jail would be four years. But he would be barred from sitting in parliament for another five years after his release. Justice Paul said the term of imprisonment would run from the previous day, so it did not include the six months Anwar had already spent in jail before and during his trial. The judge refused a defence application for a stay of execution and bail for Anwar pending an appeal. The sentence was longer than Anwar had expected. He reminded journalists that he had told them it would be two to four years, adding: 'But it doesn't make a difference.' One of his lawyers, Gurbachan Singh said the sentence was 'manifestly excessive', but it was not the heaviest Justice Paul could have imposed. The maximum jail term on each charge was fourteen years. Nevertheless, many people, including this writer, thought it was unreasonably severe, considering the nature of the offence. The 'corrupt practice' with which he was charged was a minor transgression compared with the widely accepted corruption rampant throughout all levels of the Malaysian government. It deserved no more than a slap on the wrist, not six years in jail.

A second trial was yet to come, but already commentators were writing off Anwar's political career. Government and opposition politicians alike were pessimistic about Anwar's chances of making a return to active politics. Several people drew a comparison with Harun Idris, another important UMNO figure, who was convicted of corruption in 1975. Describing Harun as an even more popular figure than Anwar, a veteran Malaysian journalist pointed out that many UMNO leaders strongly opposed his prosecution. He was pardoned after some years but never recovered his previous political prominence. UMNO sources said there could be a move to pardon Anwar if Dr Mahathir died or no longer controlled the party. But since the new leaders would not welcome a potential rival back into the party, Anwar would most likely, like Harun Idris, end up in the political wilderness. A senior UMNO politician observed: 'You do not invite a tiger into your tent.'

While Anwar's conviction and sentence did not lead to a massive public protest, the trial result and the astonishing events of the previous six months had produced a momentous change in the way many Malaysians viewed their government and its instruments of power and authority. When the Prime Minister met Malaysian students on a trip to London one of them boldly suggested that he should resign. Dr Mahathir told him and the others present that even if he was cursed he would not resign because he had 'a duty to perform'. The opposition party, PAS, was quick to capitalise on the feelings of suspicion and disgust towards the administration. The fundamentalist opposition party's leaders could normally draw large crowds of Malaysians to their ceramah (public meetings) but the numbers increased significantly in the wake of the trial verdict when they accorded Anwar the status of political victim and invited Azizah to join them as a featured speaker.

On 27 April, thirteen days after his corruption conviction, Anwar was back in court to face a charge of committing 'carnal knowledge against the order of nature'. In the High Court, Attorney-General Mohtar Abdullah leading the prosecution said the government would proceed with one charge of sodomy against

Anwar. Sodomy is an offence in Malaysia carrying a maximum sentence of 20 years and a caning. Mohtar asked the court to postpone consideration of the other four sodomy counts and one remaining count of corruption mentioned when a total of ten charges were preferred against the defendant following his arrest. Subsequently, after the government had obtained a conviction against Anwar in the second trial, it dropped all the other charges.

The prosecution elected to proceed with the sodomy charge in which the other person allegedly involved was Azizan, one of its key witnesses in the corruption trial. It chose not to go ahead with the counts involving four other people, three of whom, including Anwar's adopted brother, Sukma Darmawan, had publicly claimed they were coerced by police into falsely accusing Anwar of sodomising them. However, the government charged Sukma with sodomising Azizan and abetting Anwar to sodomise Azizan. Mohtar successfully applied for Sukma to be jointly tried with Anwar.

When the joint trial of Anwar and Sukma opened before Justice Ariffin Jaka on 7 June, the prosecution made its move to have the date of the alleged offences changed from May 1992 to between January and March 1993. This prompted the defence team to accuse it of abusing the court process and acting in bad faith. Declaring that Mohtar had decided to make the amendments after both defendants' had given notice of alibis showing the apartment in which the offences were alleged to have been committed was not completed by May 1992, Anwar's lawyers sought to have the charges thrown out. But Justice Ariffin rejected the defence argument and ordered the hearing to go ahead.

At the UMNO annual general assembly on 18 June, the first party congress since Anwar's sacking, Dr Mahathir launched a strong new attack on his former deputy, accusing him of trying to topple the administration with foreign support, in a reference to the events of 1998. He said that because of Anwar's 'betrayal', it was appropriate for him to have been sacked. Denying Anwar's claims that he was the victim of a conspiracy, he said: 'I did not victimise him, I did not conspire to stop him from becoming the UMNO president and Malaysian prime minister. His morals and behaviour prevented him from becoming UMNO president.' Asked at a press conference if he would recommend a pardon for Anwar, Dr Mahathir said: 'Anwar says he is innocent. How do you pardon an innocent man?'

In June, the Prime Minister and his staff moved into new quarters in a six-storey domed and impressive building in the centre of Putrajaya, the 4580-hectare new administrative capital, 40 kilometres south of Kuala Lumpur. Anwar claimed he had opposed such 'mega-projects' as Putrajaya but he had participated in their planning and, but for a major misjudgment, he could have been the first prime minister to work from the multibillion ringgit 'garden city' and reside in the grand official residence built there for the head of government. Instead, on 25 June about the same time as Dr Mahathir was being driven in a limousine from his old home in Kuala Lumpur to start his first day in his fancy new office at Putrajaya, Anwar was being taken in a police van from his cell in the Sungei Buloh prison to the High Court for the continuation of his sodomy trial.

At the hearing, after rejecting the defence's contention that it was obtained by police threats, Justice Ariffin allowed the prosecution to introduce as evidence Sukma's confession, which he had subsequently retracted. In the statement, Sukma, an Indonesian, said he had been placed under the care of Anwar's father while he studied in Malaysia. He said his homosexual relationship with Anwar started in 1976 or 1977, when he was still a teenager and they were sharing a room. It continued after Anwar was married. A summary of the contents appeared in the *New Straits Times* under the headline: 'Lurid details by Sukma on sex with Anwar'. This new attempt by the establishment to undermine sympathy for Anwar failed to overcome public scepticism about the judicial process.

The second trial moved along more rapidly than the first, with the prosecution building its case almost solely around the evidence of Azizan and closing its case in August. But interruptions due to the 1999 general election, holidays and procedural arguments resulted in the hearing dragging on into the middle of 2000. Justice Ariffin rejected a defence application for Azizan's evidence to be thrown out on grounds the witness had contradicted himself and lied to the court. The defence had moved to have Azizan's credibility impeached because in Anwar's earlier corruption trial he had said that he had not been sodomised after 1992. In the second trial, Azizan said he had meant he had not been sodomised in Anwar's house since that time. The prosecution argued that Azizan's explanation for his alleged contradiction was 'plausible', and Justice Ariffin said he was satisfied that the evidence of the witness was reasonable and acceptable. He said his credibility should not be challenged.

Justice Ariffin gave Anwar more leeway than the first judge to argue his conspiracy theory and attack former colleagues over alleged corruption. A defence witness, Raja Kamaruddin Wahid, who was a minor UMNO official, gave strong support to the defence argument that the charge against Anwar was fabricated, saying that on 26 June 1998, Abdul Aziz Shamsuddin, who was then Dr Mahathir's political secretary, told him about plans to destroy Anwar's reputation so he could never become prime minister. The witness said Abdul Aziz told him he was paying Azizan and Ummi Hafilda to make up stories about Anwar. He alleged Abdul Aziz told him he had wanted revenge against Anwar for a long time and the best way to topple him was by making up charges on sodomy and adultery. Raja Kamaruddin later 'realised that slander was a big sin' and 'asked guidance from God'. He then contacted Anwar with his story.

The trial was twice interrupted by questions over Anwar's health—first when a defence lawyer suggested the defendant had been poisoned with arsenic, and later when the former deputy prime minister complained of headaches. The arsenic incident, which ultimately became an embarrassment for the Anwar camp, had its genesis in a dramatic declaration to the court by defence lawyer—and opposition politician—Karpal Singh. He said that Anwar was suffering from arsenic poisoning and someone might be trying to murder him. Karpal Singh said a sample of Anwar's urine had been sent to a pathology laboratory in Melbourne in the assumed name of Subramaniam. Declaring that the sample showed a dangerous level of arsenic, 77 times a normal occurrence, Karpal Singh said Anwar was 'in jeopardy of his life' and called for an in-depth inquiry. He described the pathologist's report as 'significant', considering that Anwar had been beaten by the former police chief after his arrest a year ago, and said: 'It could well be that someone out there wants to get rid of him. It would be a shame if the conspiracy we have been referring to should include murder.' He then went on to say he suspected some people in high places were 'in all likelihood responsible for the situation'. These remarks later brought a sharp response from the government. It hit Karpal Singh with a charge of sedition, which carried a maximum penalty of three years' jail. However, the charge was eventually withdrawn.

Anwar's wife, Azizah, said at a press conference that the pathologist had told her the level of arsenic in her husband could not have been ingested accidentally. She said she was 'scared for his life'. The decision to test Anwar's urine came after he had experienced a series of symptoms suggestive of poisoning. Azizah said that from the beginning they had 'seen the existence of a conspiracy at the highest level' to silence Anwar's influence in politics but never expected that it would lead to 'a criminal act'. Justice Ariffin directed that the defendant be sent to hospital and the trial postponed until such time as doctors certified him fit. Keadilan and other opposition parties capitalised on Karpal Singh's sensational assertion in court to re-awaken waning public interest in Anwar's case and give a boost to their efforts to win voter support ahead of the forthcoming general election. A rally supporting a petition to the King for a royal inquiry drew thousands of people to the National Mosque. It ended in a violent clash between protesters and police and was followed by the arrest of opposition figures.

Having ceased to be surprised by the bizarre twists and turns of Anwar's two trials and many tribulations, Malaysians in the street expressed shock that there might be an attempt on his life but did not react with disbelief. They had been stunned and then numbed by the sacking and arrest of the second most powerful man in the country and the events that followed. They had stared at their television screens in amazement as the Prime Minister gave them specific information about the alleged sexual misconduct of his deputy prime minister and heir apparent, using words they had never heard broadcast before. They had read about the black eye that shook the nation and then learned that the chief of police had beaten Anwar after he was blindfolded and handcuffed in a cell in police headquarters. So many Malaysians were prepared to believe that someone had tried to poison Anwar. However, subsequent tests in Malaysia and overseas on urine and nail samples from the former deputy prime minister showed that his arsenic level was normal. Azizah said she wondered whether the samples sent to the laboratories belonged to her husband. She also said her husband's health had improved quickly because of the prayers offered by the people. But the government took great care to ensure the tests were carried out by responsible experts at home and abroad, leaving little doubt among even the most cynical journalists that the results were valid. The episode seriously damaged the credibility of Azizah, who had been regarded by members of the media as a believable source of information in the often-suspect Anwar camp. But by this time the opposition could make almost any unproved accusation against the government and have Malaysians believe it.

Dr Mahathir's frustration showed when, following the arsenic incident, his former deputy complained of persistent headaches. The former medical practitioner labelled the headaches 'a tactic of an expert liar' and lashed out:

> There's not a doctor in the world who can heal such a headache.
> Soon his supporters will get angry and riot again. Believe me, that
> is Anwar's way, lie to incite the people so he will become a hero.
> We'll find it difficult to counter the lies. But believe me, his whole
> life is a lie, pretending to be pious but practising disgusting activities.

In their final submission, the defence team described Azizan as unreliable, untrustworthy and lacking credibility. Lawyer Christopher Fernando said the prosecution had failed to prove its case beyond reasonable doubt and called for the acquittal of the accused. But the judge did not see it that way. On 18 October 1999, Justice Ariffin Jaka said he had given the evidence a 'maximum evaluation' before deciding that the prosecution had established its case against Anwar and co-defendant Sukma Darmawan beyond reasonable doubt. Rejecting a defence submission that it was a complicated case, he said it was an ordinary criminal case of sodomy under the penal code.

The bitter enmity existing between the two men who two years earlier were hailed as the 'perfect team' to lead Malaysia was reflected in Anwar's High Court testimony when he took the stand in his defence and public remarks by the Prime Minister around the same time. In a meeting with farmers in his home state of Kedah, which was broadcast over national television, Dr Mahathir said Anwar was previously his friend, whom he had brought into government and groomed to be deputy prime minister. But when he knew he was a homosexual he was not willing to allow him to be his successor. He said a person like that was 'not qualified to be even a junior leader, let alone the prime minister'. Addressing the court, Anwar named four 'master conspirators', including two cabinet ministers and Dr Mahathir's political secretary, as behind a plot to have him removed from power with fabricated charges. He also accused the Prime Minister of brushing aside corruption allegations against two ministers and a former state chief minister. Allowed to proceed in detailing his earlier claims that he was a victim of a conspiracy by people in the government who allegedly feared his reforming zeal, Anwar painted a picture of such extensive intrigue that one was left to wonder how the government ever managed to continue functioning. And in claiming to be a man of virtue surrounded by villains, the former deputy prime minister advanced an implausible scenario, given his comfortable establishment lifestyle from 1982 to 1998 and the wealth of his family.

Additionally, if there was a conspiracy within the government to destroy Anwar politically with false charges of corruption and sodomy, it was more likely to have been provoked by his blatant bid to seize the leadership from Dr Mahathir before he was ready to surrender it than by a crusade for reform. Nevertheless, his accusations pointed to tensions within the leadership of UMNO, which has always been a party riven with factions. Once again, he tore into Daim, who had recommended Anwar as his successor as Finance Minister in 1991 and praised him a few years later for his achievements in the job. According to the authors of the book *Daim: The Man Behind the Enigma*, which was first published in 1995, he said: 'I told [Anwar] that to be a good Finance Minister, one must work very hard and read a lot. He has done well. The economic growth shows it.' Anwar had paid tribute to Daim in his maiden budget speech in the Malaysian Parliament in November 1991, declaring that he had formulated the budget with confidence because of the strong economy he had inherited. Anwar said: 'At the onset, I therefore wish to express my gratitude to the former Minister of Finance, Tun Daim Zainuddin, whose determined efforts in introducing strong and bold measures strengthened the fundamentals in the economy.'

The former deputy prime minister and finance minister delivered an entirely different judgment on Daim in the High Court. But, as with Anwar's accusations against other former close associates, many of his claims sounded as fanciful and implausible as his earlier charge that Daim carried M$1 billion in cash on board an MAS flight to Switzerland. Anwar said there was 'bad blood' between him and Daim, who had allegedly advised Anwar to resign to avoid the embarrassment of charges being brought against him. He said he had told Daim: 'You mean you have the audacity to fabricate such malicious lies about my alleged corruption and sexual misconduct when it is public knowledge that you have squandered billions from the country? You have been using your private jet to bring in women via the VIP channel, bypassing the Customs and Immigration.' It was hard to imagine Anwar coming up with such a neatly constructed assault on Daim in the course of a conversation. The paragraph had the edge of a sound bite structured for public dissemination.

Justice Ariffin did not stop Anwar from bringing up the alleged taping of Ummi's conversations with Sarawak politician Sng Chee Hua in London. Stating that Ummi had telephoned Azizan from London and told him not to change his story and to 'continue with the plan', Anwar said this information came from Nor Azman Abdullah, Sng's assistant, who had allegedly recorded Ummi's conversations and given the tapes to the former deputy prime minister. According to Anwar, Nor said Daim secured a contract for Ummi in connection with the new Kuala Lumpur International Airport, which together with a cash payment of a reported M$2.5 million was a reward. Anwar brought up his conflicts with other previously mentioned foes or 'conspirators', including Megat Junid,

Abdul Aziz Shamsuddin, Rafidah Aziz and Rahim Thamby Chik. He said Rahim was 'extremely angry' with him after Anwar asked him to resign from his government and party posts over his alleged involvement with the 15-year-old girl.

In the wake of Anwar's evidence, the woman in the case, whose accusation five years earlier that she had had a sexual relationship with Rahim had destroyed his political career and led to the jailing of her defender Lim Guan Eng, admitted she had lied. Norhayati Yusof, now aged 20, called a press conference to announce that she had made a statutory declaration in 1998 denying her involvement with Rahim. She said she was disclosing this because the sex allegation was raised at Anwar's sodomy trial. Norhayati said she had been forced to lie by two men who taught her 'to fabricate a story' about a relationship with Rahim. The case took an even odder twist when her grandmother disputed Norhayati's revised version of events.

As it had in the first trial, the defence announced plans to call Dr Mahathir. But the judge said that the defence must show that the Prime Minister's evidence would be relevant to the case and after hearing argument ruled that he was not a material witness. Defence appeals against the ruling to the Court of Appeal and the Federal Court were unsuccessful. The prospect of Anwar's lawyers extracting any cogent information from Dr Mahathir that supported the conspiracy theory was always very unlikely. The defence move seemed mainly aimed at focusing public attention on the trial and renewing Malaysians' interest in Anwar's fate, which had been steadily waning.

On 17 and 18 July 2000, Anwar delivered a final address in his defence, declaring that the instrument of government was 'unfortunately used and abused' to fabricate charges against him. He urged Justice Ariffin to be 'guided by the law and the dictates of conscience'. The judge replied: 'You can rest assured that I will be guided by my conscience and judge the case based on evidence.' On 8 August Justice Ariffin convicted Anwar of sodomy and sentenced him to nine years imprisonment. He fixed the new sentence to begin when the former deputy prime minister completed the six-year term imposed on him at his earlier trial on corrupt practices charges. Sukma was sentenced to six years imprisonment and two strokes of the cane on each of the charges, his jail terms to be served concurrently.

If Anwar, who was then a few days away from his 53rd birthday, received the normal one-third remission for good behaviour on each sentence, he would be behind bars for a total of ten years from the date of his first conviction on 4 April 1999. On his release, he would be barred from standing for Parliament for another five years. While his age of 66 in April 2014 would not necessarily bar his return to politics, it seems likely the passage of time will have dimmed his aura as a potential leader and have brought to power a new government team with little reason to offer him a position.

The case against Anwar was seriously flawed. It was severely weakened from the beginning by the manner in which the prosecution scrambled around to find a year and month in which the alleged acts of sodomy could have been committed in the Tivoli Villas apartment and finally settled on a flexible time 'between January and March 1993' to guard against any new Anwar alibi. Azizan raised more questions than he answered with his floundering appearance on the witness stand. The government prosecutors made such a botched job of the sodomy charge they brought against Anwar that a lay person might think he deserved to go free. That was not the view of Justice Ariffin, who said he was satisfied the evidence did not support the defence argument that the charges were fabricated. He also said he was of the view that conspiracy was 'not an issue in this case' and was, therefore, irrelevant. The judge held that Azizan, the main prosecution witness, was cross-examined by the defence 'aggressively and extensively' and had 'come out unscratched'. His evidence was consistent with a confession by Sukma. Justice Ariffin characterised the letter in which Sukma withdrew his confession as 'an afterthought'. He said he was satisfied that the prosecution had proved its case against both accused beyond reasonable doubt.

The nine-year jail sentenced imposed by Justice Ariffin shocked observers from those Western countries where there are no legal prohibitions against consensual sexual acts between males but it was less than half Malaysia's possible maximum penalty of 20 years imprisonment. Anwar would have been aware of the harshness of the punishment for sodomy in Malaysia—an offence under both criminal and shariah law—and, therefore, in view of the allegations hanging over his head, he courted the disaster that befell him by not resigning from UMNO when he was given the opportunity and heading off overseas. It was a sorry end to what might have been a rewarding career if he had just bided his time and not chosen to challenge his mentor. Anwar's wife, Azizah, who had remained composed throughout both trials, was close to tears after the guilty verdict. She said it had been expected but the reality was painful. Riot police lined the streets around the court area and forced small groups of people to disperse. But the big turnout of demonstrators urged by Anwar supporters did not materialise.

Before sentencing Anwar, Justice Ariffin agreed to let him make his own mitigation plea. It turned out to be another fierce blast at Dr Mahathir but also included attacks on the Prime Minister's family and 'cronies' and the judiciary. Written in his cell before the verdict, it showed that Anwar had expected to be convicted. He defied repeated attempts by the judge to stop him from 'giving a lecture' and making a 'political speech'. Anwar said the judgment was 'unjust, disgraceful and revolting'. He ended by telling Dr Mahathir and 'his greedy cronies' to 'beware the wrath of the people'. It was his last angry cry before he was locked up for what ought to have been the most politically productive years of his life. But if he had any expectation that his allegations of corruption and cronyism in the government would be featured in the Malaysian media, he would have been disappointed. His emotional declaration from the dock was heavily edited in the main newspapers, taking up a few paragraphs beneath the judgment of Justice Ariffin.

The absolute bleakness of Anwar's future was reflected in the fact that not a single voice was raised publicly within the UMNO leadership to express either concern over the length of his sentence or sympathy for his plight. Notably, no one among the former ministerial colleagues who were on his winning UMNO team in the 1993 party elections commented on the outcome of the trial. Those who were once close to Anwar had all distanced themselves from him over the past two years and pledged allegiance to Dr Mahathir.

The only domestic expressions of concern over the sentence or sympathy for Anwar came from opposition parties, which had used his case to their political advantage. As the cell door closed behind him on his return to Sungei Buloh prison after sentence was passed, Anwar faced a long and lonely future in the isolation of the four walls confining him. He maintained an air of spirited defiance in public but one of his lawyers reported that from time to time he succumbed to a black depression. He never conceded in conversation that he had taken the wrong path. But, most certainly, his apparent belief that he could take on and defeat the system that had brought him to power was a serious misjudgment. It was one of many mistakes.

Anwar was doomed from the moment Dr Mahathir turned against him. He did not have the political acumen to defend himself and lost any hope of significant support when he demonstrated that in a contest with the master he was a mere novice. His first mistake was to allow himself to be lionised abroad for his pro-Western economic policies at the same time as his leader was being denigrated for denouncing foreign money-market speculators and to believe he could steer the economy away from the direction favoured by the Prime Minister. His second error was to misread the mood of the party in 1998 when he tried unsuccessfully to force his former mentor's retirement by drawing parallels between Indonesia under President Suharto and Malaysia under Dr Mahathir. The Prime Minister was incensed by these developments. He had tolerated Anwar's impatient manoeuvring for power from the time he made him Deputy Prime Minister because he thought he was the most qualified person to succeed him. He had also invested considerable time and effort into grooming Anwar for the top job and time was running out for him to find anyone else. But Anwar's attempt to take advantage of the regional economic crisis and his favourable standing with the West to further his political ambitions prompted Dr Mahathir to look at his heir apparent with a more jaundiced eye. He had dismissed speculation and rumours about Anwar's sex life in the past because vilification of adversaries was a feature of UMNO politics and because he did not want his judgment of his deputy to be proven wrong. Additionally, he was so conservative in his beliefs that he could not imagine that a man of Anwar's reputed piety, with a wife and six children, could be a practising homosexual. But now he began to listen to close associates and members of his staff who had been telling him that the sexual allegations made against Anwar a year earlier were true.

Dr Mahathir met Ummi and Azizan, who conveyed to him what they were later to tell the High Court. His revulsion at the revelations of Azizan was apparent when he gave a detailed account of a specific episode at a press conference. Dr Mahathir's traditional Malay abhorrence of homosexuality was reflected in his address at a function of Wanita UMNO, the women's wing of the dominant government party, a few days after Anwar's arrest: 'It is so disgusting to see a man hugging and kissing another man in public. So nauseating.' He also said a homosexual leader could not lead a country like Malaysia because he would be tempted to follow his lust, which could be manipulated by foreign powers. In November 2001, he declared, in an interview with BBC radio: 'The British people accept homosexual ministers but if they ever come here bringing their boyfriend along, we will throw them out. In this country a homosexual is not acceptable as the prime minister.' Defending the sacking of Anwar, he repeated his assertion that Malaysia could not have a leader who was a homosexual and added: 'So we had to take action.'

Having apparently concluded after interviewing Ummi and Azizan that he had been wrong about Anwar, Dr Mahathir would no doubt have felt mortified over his earlier rejection of reports advising him that the man he had brought into UMNO was a homosexual. This could have intensified his anger towards Anwar. In any case, the evidence he now had provided him with a reason to throw Anwar out of the cabinet. Additionally, if Ummi and Azizan were to be believed, Anwar had broken the law.

When Anwar chose to fight rather than go quietly his fate was sealed. Dr Mahathir's wrath towards his chosen heir was fierce and brooked no opposition from within the party. One of Malaysia's leading political analysts, who has close connections to people at the highest government level, was emphatic in telling me, 'The majority of Malaysians, the majority of people who count in UMNO did not want Anwar in jail. But no one was prepared to stand up to Dr M. They were afraid of him.' However, in his remorseless pursuit of Anwar, the Prime Minister suffered more harm to his standing than the man he sought to portray as an evil liar feigning piety. Anwar's aura of respectability and rectitude and the appalling actions of the state apparatus persuaded many Malaysians that the former deputy prime minister was the good leader and Dr Mahathir the bad.

Noted Malaysian author and social commentator Rehman Rashid had this to say during the first trial:

> Even if Anwar is guilty, this matter could and should have been conducted in a very different manner nonetheless, to preserve dignity, to save people's shame; above all to show that the answer to dishonourable deeds is honourable deeds; that the base are redeemed by the noble. Not by miming buggery before a live audience. Which leads me to conclude that Mahathir Mohamad has contempt for his people. Many have stood against him; none has prevailed. Whether they were institutions or individuals, their defeats have been total, crushing, humiliating. They have been consigned to political oblivion, reduced to non-existence.

Many Malays who had supported Dr Mahathir and UMNO had now lost confidence in both. They did not believe anything that the Prime Minister said and were ready to desert him and the party. They had become more attentive to the disparagement of Dr Mahathir by ulama in the mosques and by PAS at its public gatherings. Suddenly, the possibility that UMNO's 44-year reign as the dominant government party could one day end was no longer unthinkable.

11 | Foe's defeat comes at a cost

While Anwar paid a heavy price for his abortive bid to seize power from Dr Mahathir, the Prime Minister's political destruction of his protégé proved costly for him and his government. More seriously, it put in question the future stability of the country. Even before the second trial had run its course, public sentiment had turned so sharply against the government that the political landscape in Malaysia had been irrevocably changed. While Anwar might no longer have a political future, he was the catalyst for a monumental shift within the country which, if it continues unchecked, could see Malaysia transformed from a multicultural nation with a moderate Muslim majority into a hard-line Islamic state intolerant of non-Malays and other religions.

By the middle of 1999, election fever was spreading rapidly throughout Malaysia, although a date had yet to be fixed for the poll, which would be the first Malaysia-wide test of the popularity of the ruling National Front coalition since the nation was split by Anwar's sacking and arrest. The parliamentary term was not due to expire until April 2000, but the Prime Minister was expected to call the general election early to capitalise on signs of an improvement in the economy. Opposition party PAS had begun preparing for the election after officials at the grassroots level reported disillusionment of many Malays over the Anwar affair was turning them away from UMNO. Dr Mahathir accused the Western media of supporting the opposition and depicting him as a dictator who assaulted Anwar 'and made false accusations against him'. This, he claimed, gave rise to hatred against him and the government. The hatred was largely engendered by his treatment of Anwar but Dr Mahathir was slow to realise this. He had remarked in 1998 that many Malaysians did not believe the sexual allegations against Anwar but confidently forecast that he and the government would eventually overcome their scepticism. He was wrong, clearly underestimating the damaging effect of the dumping and jailing of his deputy. In June 1999, he said the Anwar affair had become 'a historical event which over time would be forgotten'. But in November, he felt constrained to warn UMNO members that if Anwar's lies and slander were not stopped they would 'feel the effect in the general election'. As a senior UMNO official noted, it was not proving easy to 'exorcise the ghost of Anwar'. Addressing party activists at the launching of a national campaign called Operation Destroy Slander, Dr Mahathir did not hide his frustration, declaring that it was 'difficult to counter lies and slander by a systematic liar like Anwar'.

While senior UMNO officials had reached a consensus that Dr Mahathir should be allowed to retire at a time of his own choosing, despite their feeling that he was an election liability, they wanted the succession set in stone so they could tell the grassroots that change was coming. Accordingly, they were annoyed by his statement to visiting African journalists that he would have to find a 'suitable time' to step down after the next general election, in remarks that made it clear he was not yet ready to entrust his job to Deputy Prime Minister Badawi. Dr Mahathir said it was not that easy to retire because his supporters and 'voters largely' kept telling him not to go. For that reason, he could not really say when he would quit as Prime Minister. He said he could not leave it to an 'inexperienced deputy' to manage the election as well as the party and government. After the election he would 'have to find a suitable time to retire'.

His reference to an 'inexperienced deputy' shocked Badawi and the rest of the top leadership. It left Malaysians wondering when the flawed system, for which they held him responsible, would be changed. With his reluctance to endorse Badawi as his successor and his growing personal involvement in every major area of government, Dr Mahathir showed that he no longer trusted anyone else to tackle the problems confronting Malaysia and thought that only he had the dedication and determination to realise his vision for Malaysia. But with time running out for him as each new birthday passed and Malays unresponsive—if not stubbornly resistant—to his efforts to remedy the religious and cultural shortcomings he outlined in *The Malay Dilemma* three decades earlier, he grew increasingly frustrated and irascible. This intensified the concern of his colleagues that UMNO would lose ground to the opposition until the party had a new leader. But it was another year before Dr Mahathir and other senior party leaders agreed on a time frame for him to retire and Badawi to take charge.

While there were signs of deep unease within UMNO, the Prime Minister appeared to feel that the improving economy would ensure the government's continuing strength at the election. As he marked his eighteenth year in office on 16 July, Dr Mahathir looked relaxed and confident in contrast with his tired and edgy appearance a year earlier when the economy was in recession and he faced a political challenge from Anwar. His spirits had been lifted by signs that Malaysia had weathered the Asian economic storm and was on the road to recovery and the virtual certainty that Anwar, whom he had deemed unfit to be a leader, would not in Dr Mahathir's time become prime minister. Additionally, he knew that no one in the party was prepared to question his authority. His radical capital controls, which had stabilised the currency and the stock market and boosted business confidence, had won grudging approval as a useful short-term move from foreign financial analysts who had initially condemned them. Fund managers who had treated Dr Mahathir like a pariah a year earlier scrambled for a share of Malaysia's US$1 billion global bond issue in May. The economy was heading for solid growth following a contraction of more than 7 per cent in 1998. With exports remaining strong throughout the recession and imports weak, Malaysia's foreign exchange reserves had soared to more than six months of retained imports. Basking in all the good economic news, Dr Mahathir sounded like a man who felt he had been vindicated and had even less reason than before to make concessions to his critics. He exulted: 'We have yet again proven the prophets of doom wrong.'

Two years earlier, when it was thought the winds of change stirred up by the Asian financial crisis might bring a fresh current of economic and political thinking to Malaysia, there was talk of a new era ahead under the liberal-sounding Anwar. Now, there was no such expectation. While some favoured chieftains of Malaysia Inc. companies had been financially bruised they still had a sympathetic government, which was determined to keep the existing system intact and the dreaded IMF at bay. In his regular column for Japan's *Mainichi Daily News*, Dr Mahathir again recited his argument that 'a company's failure is a national failure. When a company fails, governments get no money, employees suffer, as do consumers. So you cannot simply allow companies to fail, especially when it is due to no fault on their part, as in a recession.' Whether or not the argument was valid, his statements provided ammunition for the opposition to claim government policy was to bail-out friends of Dr Mahathir and Daim.

On 10 November, Parliament was dissolved and a day later Omar Hashim, chairman of the Election Commission, announced that Malaysians would go to the polls on 29 November. The legislative assemblies of the eleven states in peninsular Malaysia were also dissolved. (The Borneo states of Sarawak and Sabah hold their legislative assembly elections separately.) At stake were 193 parliamentary seats and 394 state seats. The National Front coalition, comprising UMNO, the Malaysian Chinese Association (MCA), the second biggest party in the National Front, the Malaysian Indian Congress (MIC) and some smaller parties, held 166 seats in the federal parliament and controlled all but one of the state assemblies. The single exception was the PAS-run state of Kelantan. PAS, the Democratic Action Party (DAP), Keadilan and the Malaysian

People's Party (MPP), joined together as the Alternative Front in a copycat combination of parties representing the main ethnic groups to try to achieve a better result than the 26 seats the opposition held in the old federal parliament. Azizah filed nomination papers to run as a Keadilan candidate for her jailed husband's parliamentary seat of Permatang Pauh, in Penang state, which Anwar had held for seventeen years.

The National Front coalition immediately went on the attack against the opposition with a series of hard-hitting newspaper advertisements linking it to violence and political insecurity. Opposition leaders retaliated, accusing the government of practising the 'politics of fear' and saying its political advertisements were the 'most incendiary, inflammatory and irresponsible' ever to appear in the country's election campaigns. A series of full-page pictures and captions promoting the coalition as a united group of parties standing for stability, security, progress and peace used press photographs taken during street demonstrations and rioting by Anwar supporters to contrast it with the opposition. One of the advertisements proclaimed, 'Don't let hatred win', over a picture of stone-throwing protesters. Another showed a car surrounded by demonstrators who had smashed its windows, with a television crew huddling inside. The message above it read: 'No to violence.' Despite clear indications that Dr Mahathir was more an encumbrance than an advantage, the National Front election manifesto omitted any new promises and focused on the Prime Minister's triumphant stand against the iniquitous West, as other countries in the region succumbed to its economic imperialism.

In my interview with Fadzil Noor at PAS headquarters in Alor Star, the capital of Kedah state, two weeks ahead of the election, during which he said the party would make Anwar Prime Minister if it won control of parliament (see Chapter 1), he predicted the defeat of the National Front in the Kedah, Perlis and Terengganu state polls. It was partly political hubris but PAS knew it was making gains against UMNO while the government party sensed it was losing ground in the north of Peninsular Malaysia. Dr Mahathir promised Kedah, his home state, Perlis and Terengganu would be given special attention, as he set out on a gruelling Malaysia-wide drive for votes. He also played down the impact of the Anwar affair on the coming poll, saying that he had faced a tougher election in 1990, two years after about 80 000 UMNO members, including cabinet ministers, had resigned to join the new party formed by Tengku Razaleigh. He noted that no ministers had supported Anwar with their resignations.

But a more important question than the lack of overt ministerial backing for Anwar was how much support or sympathy he had generated among Malay voters. PAS leaders were quick to seize the opportunity to exploit the split in the Malay community over the sacking of Anwar. In the days before his arrest, they shared the stage with him at public meetings where he denounced the government. Later, after he had been arrested and charged with corruption and sodomy, they supported his claim that he was the victim of a high-level political plot. When I talked with Fadzil he rejected the government allegation that Anwar was guilty of sodomy, declaring it was a conspiracy against him.

Two days before the election, Dr Mahathir paid a visit to Anwar's old constituency in an attempt to persuade voters to elect the UMNO candidate rather than Azizah. He told the Permatang Pauh constituents that Azizah was appealing to people's emotions, 'going around with her daughter crying and telling the women folk that she is without a husband and her children are without a father'. He urged voters not to be swayed by sadness or sympathy. It was a huge mistake. On election day, Permatang Pauh voters gave Azizah a resounding victory. With a 9000-vote majority, she delivered a crushing defeat to her National Front opponent, Ibrahim Saad, who was a former political secretary and boyhood friend of her husband.

Throughout the country, the Anwar factor and PAS's astute exploitation of Malays' discontent left UMNO badly battered. It was the worst showing of the dominant government party in Dr Mahathir's eighteen years in office. While the National Front succeeded in retaining control of parliament with a two-thirds majority, it suffered a drop in seats from 166 in the old house to 148 seats in the new; the opposition, on the other hand, increased its representation from 22 to 45. Three of the seats in the old parliament were held by independents and two were vacant. Four government ministers and four deputy ministers were defeated. Opposition gains in Malaysia are major achievements as parties must rely on meetings and hand-distributed pamphlets to get their messages across due to government control of the press and while the Internet has provided a new medium, it has a limited reach.

Dr Mahathir had to endure the humiliation of losing Terengganu state to PAS, which also retained control of neighbouring Kelantan. More unhappily for the Prime Minister, UMNO fared badly compared with the other government parties, with the number of its parliamentary representatives falling from 94 to 74. The non-Malay parties all did reasonably well. The MCA lost a modest four seats—from 31 to 27—while the MIC remained unchanged with seven and Gerakan, another Chinese party, improved its tally from five to seven. Together with those won by eight other National Front parties, the total number of non-UMNO seats in the National Front was now 74—the same as UMNO. In the old parliament the non-UMNO parties had 72 seats, compared with UMNO's 94. UMNO had not fared so badly since the 1969 election. Party officials disclosed that in 41 parliamentary constituencies with an 80 per cent predominance of Malays, UMNO won only 45.3 per cent of the popular vote.

Dr Mahathir did not distinguish between the components in the coalition, declaring after the election results were in that the National Front was clearly 'the choice of the people of Malaysia'. But, according to a party source, other senior UMNO officials were aghast at the outcome, regarding it as 'disastrous'. UMNO's poor result highlighted the deep split in the Malay community arising from the sacking and prosecution of Anwar and related developments, which had shocked people into a re-evaluation of the political system under which they lived. The voting also showed the divide was roughly geographical, with UMNO supporters predominant in the south of Peninsular Malaysia and PAS followers strong in the north.

PAS and three other opposition parties—Democratic Action Party (DAP), Keadilan and Malaysian People's Party (MPP)—had capitalised on sympathy for Anwar by nominating the former deputy prime minister as their Alternative Front choice for the next prime minister. The fundamentalist Islamic party was the chief beneficiary of the poll, securing 27 seats, compared with its previous eight. Party president Fadzil Noor was elected for the first time to parliament, where he became leader of the opposition. In addition to seizing control of Terengganu and tightening its grip on Kelantan, PAS made significant gains in two nearby states, Perlis and Kedah. As well as turning the Anwar affair to its advantage and questioning Dr Mahathir's Islamic credentials, PAS had one very effective promise: it told rural Malay voters that a vote for PAS was a passport to heaven and a vote for UMNO was the path to hell. Dr Mahathir's exhortations to Malays not to believe PAS's lies about him or their distortions of the teachings of Islam went unheeded. Throughout the election campaign he was a target of fierce criticism from PAS officials and their supporters among the ulama.

The alliance with PAS proved costly for the DAP, with many former Chinese supporters deserting the party over its union with fundamentalists proposing to turn Malaysia into an Islamic state. Veteran DAP leaders Lim Kit Siang and Karpal Singh lost their seats. Two years later the DAP seceded from the opposition alliance. The National Front was saved from a more serious electoral setback by the Chinese votes it received. Dr Mahathir had made a special pitch to the Chinese some weeks before the election, telling them how important they were. He persuaded leading Chinese organisations to come out publicly in support of the National Front, something they had never done before. A few days before the election he played host to Chinese Premier Zhu Rongji, whose visit concluded with a promise of large joint ventures. In speeches Dr Mahathir alluded to the 1969 racial riots in which Chinese were the main victims and drew parallels with the demonstrations by Anwar supporters in Kuala Lumpur and the violence in Jakarta before the fall of Indonesian President Suharto. In the week before the election, National Front advertisements, specifically directed at the Chinese, implied that violence, unrest and economic chaos would follow an opposition victory.

Dr Mahathir had even given a relatively mild response to an unprecedented Chinese call for a range of radical political and social changes, including an end to special Malay privileges. Casting aside the caution traditionally employed in discussions of race relations and other sensitive issues in Malaysia, eleven guilds and associations representing a large segment of the Chinese community presented a list of 'election requests' to political parties, which included a provocative proposal that the classification of Malaysians as bumiputras (Malays and other indigenous races) and non-bumiputras (all other races) should be discarded 'in stages'. They said 'affirmative action to help the underprivileged should be based on need and not on colour, creed and religion', alluding to the quota systems introduced under the 1972 New Economic Policy to ensure Malays could attend universities and find jobs without having to compete directly for positions with the economically and academically dominant Chinese. In seeking the removal of a cornerstone of the UMNO political programme, the Malaysian Chinese Organisations' Election Appeals Committee, known by its Chinese acronym Suqiu, was clearly emboldened by the anticipated significance of the Chinese vote in the impending general election. The comprehensive petition also called for 'independence of the judiciary', the abolition of the *Internal Security Act* and the adoption of a *Freedom of Information Act*. It said that press freedom should be ensured by the dropping of the requirement for newspapers to renew their permits annually. The text of the petition was run in full by all Chinese newspapers, many of which carried supportive editorials. The *Nanyang Siang Pau* said the petition was 'a total expression of the wish and aspirations' of the Chinese community.

Dr Mahathir accused Suqiu of blackmail and said it did not represent the Chinese community. He said the ruling National Front coalition wanted support that was unconditional, warning: 'Do not put pressure on us.' Considering the controversial content of the petition, his response was low key. But the outcome of the election, which had dramatically showed the erosion of support among Malays for UMNO, made it vital for the party to demonstrate more strongly its commitment to Malay welfare. Any indication that UMNO might be courting the Chinese risked further alienating Malays, who were sensitive to any signs they could lose their special privileges. PAS, which asserted it was the true defender of Malay rights, was ready to welcome Malays with open arms. Therefore, ten months after the election, when the Chinese media gave renewed attention to the Suqiu election list, Malay-language newspapers responded with a spirited defence of 'Malay rights'. Some 200 members of UMNO Youth demonstrated against the Suqiu proposals outside the Selangor Chinese Assembly Hall, which is the headquarters of a number of Chinese bodies. Dr Mahathir made an emotional declaration to representatives of Malay organisations that the government would 'not take one step backward' on the question of Malay rights. Then, in his National Day message, Dr Mahathir accused 'extremist' Chinese and Malay groups of threatening the nation's peace and harmony.

The Malay group he singled out, al-Ma'unah, a radical Islamic organisation seeking to overthrow the government by force, was undoubtedly extremist, but Suqiu certainly did not deserve the same classification. Dr Mahathir warned that the al-Ma'unah incident, in which members of the group were involved in an armed confrontation with security forces after seizing weapons from two army depots, and Suqiu's 'demands' could spark anarchy and chaos. He went further in vilifying Suqiu—and thereby a large segment of the Chinese community—declaring that their demands were 'not much different' from those made by the communist insurgents who fought against British and Malaysian forces in the 1950s and 1960s. He said the communists, most of whom were Chinese, wanted to 'totally abolish the special status of the Malays in Malaysia'. Dr Mahathir said the Chinese extremists made their 'absurd demands' after perceiving that the Malay-led government had become weaker. He issued a veiled warning that they might be arrested under the *Internal Security Act*.

His remarks exacerbated the feelings of Chinese that they were second-class citizens in their own country, notwithstanding the government's supposed support for multiculturalism. Adding to their unhappiness was the growing talk among senior UMNO officials that the only way for the party to win back the hearts and minds of the Malays who had defected to PAS was to demonstrate that it was more Islamic than its opponent. Many Chinese saw themselves caught in a country that could only become more Islamic under either PAS or UMNO and less accommodating to their lifestyles.

Many Chinese told me that if the situation became intolerable they would try to emigrate to Canada or Australia or any other Western country that would have them. They would at least ensure that their children did not have to live in a country that did not regard them as equal citizens. The general feeling of the community was reflected in a survey of Chinese students at the University of Malaya towards the end of 2000, which found that while 86 per cent were proud to be Malaysians, 66 per cent felt that they had been treated as 'second-class citizens'. This widespread sentiment signals a potentially serious problem for Malaysia, which could suffer a serious brain drain adversely affecting its future development.

Meanwhile, in the wake of the election, Dr Mahathir did nothing to mollify the party's critics. Although the defeat of four ministers and four deputy ministers gave him an opportunity to revamp his cabinet, he made only minor concessions to calls for new blood and stuck with long-time associates. He sounded resentful of the fact Malays had voted against him. In his regular article for the Japanese newspaper *Mainichi Daily News*, he said that 'quite a large number of Malays' had 'turned against UMNO' and complained that the Malay community had come to believe that nothing could 'diminish their dominant position in Malaysian politics'. So they saw no need to vote for UMNO. UMNO's commitment to the status quo was underlined on 3 January 2000, when the supreme council decided to propose that Dr Mahathir be re-nominated as president and Badawi be nominated for the post of deputy president. It also agreed that the two leaders should be elected unopposed at the party elections on 11 May.

Six weeks after the general election, in a move that was widely seen as a vindictive response to the opposition's gains, police arrested three prominent opponents of the government, including Karpal Singh, under the tough *Sedition Law*. Although Karpal Singh had lost his parliamentary seat he remained a vocal critic of the ruling National Front. He was charged over the remarks he had made in Anwar's trial suggesting people in high places were trying to poison the former deputy prime minister with arsenic. While his allegation was reckless to say the least, it was highly unusual for a lawyer to be prosecuted for a statement made in court while defending his client. The government eventually realised that it had stepped into a legal minefield after local and international legal bodies questioned the validity of its case and in January 2002, Attorney-General Abdul Gani Patail withdrew the charge just as a hearing was due to commence. The other two opposition figures arrested were Zulkifli Sulong, editor of the PAS newspaper *Harakah*, and Marina Yusoff, vice president of Keadilan. Zulkifli's arrest for allegedly publishing a seditious article followed repeated threats by government leaders to shut down *Harakah*, which had seen an increase in its circulation from about 75 000 copies to more than 300 000 since Anwar's arrest. The arrest warrant for Marina Yusoff was issued in connection with a speech in which she allegedly criticised the police over the 1969 racial riots. All three, whose alleged offences were committed during the bitterly contested campaign ahead of the election, were later released on bail.

The 1999 general election demonstrated that UMNO was in serious political trouble but virtually everything that Dr Mahathir did to try to remedy the situation only made it worse. While he had assured Malays UMNO would defend their privileges, he undermined any beneficial impact this may have had by delivering a harsh new attack on Malay attitudes in a question-and-answer session at the Young Malay Professionals Congress in Kuala Lumpur. In remarks guaranteed to alienate the community he needed to win over, he said Malays had to stop pleading for favours from the government if they were to survive in the economy of the new millennium. He said the culture of begging for aid, which was rampant among Malay business people, was a barrier to their economic progress. He urged Malays to give up their 'get rich quick' outlook, which led them to barter for cash the government contracts, import permits, taxi licences and other concessions they acquired under special privileges granted to indigenous Malaysians. Dr Mahathir said no one took up space allocated for Malays in shopping centres because too many people were 'looking for the easy way', rather than having to start up a business.

Meanwhile, Chinese Malaysians were outraged by a campaign conducted through *Utusan Malaysia* to reduce the number of Hong Kong and Taiwanese movies shown on a Malaysian television network. *Utusan* caused added tension within the Chinese community in December when it said the Suqiu proposals had 'made fire burn within Malays'. Amid this atmosphere of racial disharmony, the government's avowed aim to create a Malaysian identity for all races seemed increasingly a pipe dream. Dr Mahathir could probably afford not to worry too much about the Chinese, most of whom would continue to vote for the UMNO-led National Front as a less odious alternative than the PAS-led opposition (although Kedah Chinese turned against the government in a by-election in November). But without strong Malay support UMNO and the government would eventually fall. Nevertheless, Dr Mahathir continued his one-man campaign to pressure Malays into stiffening their sinews and casting off their old bad habits. In November 2000, Dr Mahathir provided more political ammunition for PAS and the religious leaders who detested him by condemning Malay students for spending too much time studying religion. He also said their achievements were below those of non-Malays. At the same time, he announced federal government plans to take over state-run religious schools to improve the academic achievements of their students. This move was aimed mainly at religious schools in opposition-controlled Kelantan, where, he said, 'children were taught to hate the federal government and the Prime Minister'. The state's PAS government said it would resist the move.

Dr Mahathir especially upset ulama with his remarks that Malay students failed their examinations because they were more interested in 'religion, protests and politics' than seeking professional knowledge. Targeting Malay students who took part in pro-Anwar demonstrations, he said: 'We see non-Malay students achieving success because they actually learnt, while the only learning the Malay students did was to tell the government how to run the country.' He also compared them adversely with the Chinese, saying that although non-Malays made up a smaller percentage of the student population, their achievements far outshone those of the Malays. Non-Malays scored most of the first-class passes while Malay students were 'happy with minimal results'.

When UMNO delegates gathered in Kuala Lumpur in May for the first annual general assembly of the new millennium (or, as sticklers for exactitude would insist, the last of the old), many Malaysians were hoping they would respond to calls by people inside and outside the party for change. The triennial election of office bearers in conjunction with the meeting provided an opportunity for the party to revamp the leadership, which was seen as essential to halting the erosion of its support among Malays. But there was little different about UMNO at the end of the convention. The party introduced no new major policies and added only a few new faces to the supreme council, its supervisory body.

The three new vice presidents were the same trio elected to those key posts in 1993, when they were associated with Anwar. They had all, of course, dissociated themselves from Anwar and pledged allegiance to Dr Mahathir. The election of Defence Minister Najib Tun Razak, 47, who had been a vice president since 1993 and garnered the most votes, had been expected. But second place went surprisingly to Muhammad Taib, 54, who had been a vice president and chief minister of Selangor, until he was charged with a currency offence in Australia in 1997 and investigated by the Malaysian authorities. He stepped down as chief minister and took leave from his UMNO position until he was cleared on both counts. He had not been considered a leading contender for vice president. The third successful candidate was also a former vice president, Muhyiddin Yassin, 53, Domestic Trade and Consumer Affairs Minister, who was defeated for the position in 1996.

The general assembly reconfirmed Dr Mahathir as party president and installed Badawi as party deputy president after it had been decided that neither leader should have to face a challenge. But the most Dr Mahathir was prepared to say about a future change in the top post was that 'one day' Badawi would lead the party. The Prime Minister said that he had 'not decided when to step down'. He seemed to imply that he might remain an influential political figure after retirement, like Lee Kuan Yew, Singapore's first prime minister, who has remained in cabinet as Senior Minister. Dr Mahathir said he was not immortal and could become sick or drop dead one day. But before retiring he wanted to make sure that UMNO accepted and fully respected the new leadership. He said:

'That is my job and I can't just let go of everything because I have retired.'

While the UMNO meeting was the occasion for much soul-searching over its losses in the November general election, the annual PAS assembly, or muktamar, in June, was a celebration of the opposition party's significant gains. The party underlined its triumph in the 1999 poll by holding the meeting in Kuala Terengganu, the capital of its newly won state. While elated by the party's improved showing, PAS speakers expressed concern over a threat by UMNO to force the party to change its name. The defection of Malays to PAS so rattled the dominant government party that much of its own annual convention was devoted to discussion on how to combat its opposition foe. It was disclosed that support for UMNO had declined within six identified groups—religious scholars, government servants, party members, intellectuals, teachers and youth. Delegates attacked PAS for using religion to win over voters and called for a ban on the use of the word 'Islam' in the names of political parties. Unsurprisingly, this proposal provoked an outcry from PAS leaders, whose public image as religious figures was fostered by the party's name. They had capitalised on the religious ring of Parti Islam se-Malaysia to promote themselves as more Islamic than their UMNO counterparts. PAS president Fadzil Noor warned that PAS members would react strongly to any attempt to force the party to drop the word 'Islam'. He said he could 'not guarantee they would remain calm'.

In September, the federal government acted suddenly to cut PAS off from an important source of finance. It announced that Terengganu would no longer have direct access to oil revenues paid to the old state government. The state had previously been receiving royalties amounting to 5 per cent of the earnings of Petronas, the national petroleum corporation, from oil and gas fields off the coast of the north-eastern state. But the government had been alarmed by the potential bonanza for PAS from sharp increases in oil prices which would have brought the Terengganu state government M$1 billion in 2000. The Finance Ministry said the state would now receive 'compassionate funding', which would be made in the form of a direct federal payment for specific projects.

Just a year after the general election, the opposition delivered another shock to the ruling National Front by seizing a Kedah State assembly seat which top National Front coalition leaders had campaigned hard to retain. The loss was especially embarrassing for Dr Mahathir, coming in his home state. The Lunas by-election, which was brought about by the assassination of the constituency's National Front representative, attributed by police to Islamic extremists, was won by a candidate of Keadilan but the real victor was PAS. The fundamentalist party succeeded in its aim of breaking the National Front's two-thirds stranglehold on the state assembly, which had allowed the government to make changes to the state constitution to entrench its position.

PAS and Keadilan reached agreement on a Malay candidate from the smaller party, although the DAP—the other main member of the opposition alliance—had wanted to continue its practice of running an Indian contestant against the Indian traditionally nominated by the National Front. The PAS–Keadilan arrangement angered the DAP but was an astute move. PAS and Keadilan saw the by-election as an opportunity to capitalise on the split among Malays over the treatment of Anwar by entering a Malay candidate. They further exploited the Anwar factor by choosing someone from Keadilan with close ties to the former deputy prime minister. When the opposition plastered the town of Lunas with the familiar pictures of a black-eyed Anwar ahead of the by-election, the National Front countered with posters bearing a portrait of Dr Mahathir. The move backfired. It merely served to reinforce the anti-government message of the Anwar photograph by drawing attention to the man whom many Malaysians held responsible for the beating of the former deputy prime minister by the police chief on the night of his arrest. Dr Mahathir had convincingly denied instigating or encouraging the brutality. But a large body of Malaysians either did not believe him or saw the black eye as a symbol of the injustice suffered by Anwar as a result of his sacking by the Prime Minister and subsequent imprisonment.

National Front officials apparently thought that the picture of Dr Mahathir, a son of Kedah and a parliamentary representative of the state, would influence the people of Lunas to vote for the coalition candidate. But putting Dr Mahathir in a popularity contest with Anwar in a multiracial electorate where the Prime Minister had split the Malay and Chinese vote by his words and deeds was a bad idea. The government spent M$15 million in a hectic programme of road repairing and mosque building in Lunas in the three and a half weeks between the death of the former state assemblyman and the poll to find a replacement, and sent top officials to support the National Front candidate. However, Lunas residents were unimpressed with the sudden investment of government funds, paying little attention to the National Front visitors from Kuala Lumpur but turning out in the thousands to hear speeches by PAS president Fadzil Noor, another son of Kedah, and other opposition leaders.

In addition to being hammered over the Anwar affair, Dr Mahathir was attacked for the government's action in ending the oil royalty payment to Terengganu. The opposition also capitalised on Chinese unhappiness over recent statements by the Prime Minister. In addition to his attacks on Suqiu, Dr Mahathir had accused a Chinese group of educationists of being chauvinistic and wanting to have 'everything Chinese', because of their opposition to his scheme to bring schools catering to Chinese, Malays and Indians together in a common compound. Sharir Samad, an outspoken UMNO veteran, who was a member of the party's supreme council, blamed the 'character' of Dr Mahathir for the National Front's defeat in Lunas. He said the Prime Minister displayed the 'old man sulking' syndrome in his criticism of the Chinese. The Keadilan candidate, Saifuddin Nasution, defeated the National Front candidate, S. Anthonysamy, by 500 votes. A year earlier, in the general election, the former Lunas assemblyman, Dr Joe Fernandez, won by 4700 votes.

The by-election result emphasised again the erosion of Malay support for the National Front and highlighted the possibility of Kedah falling into the hands of PAS, like Kelantan and Terengganu. However, Keadilan was unable to repeat the success in a Perlis by-election in January, 2002, because the party had been weakened by internal divisions, and because Chinese voters saw Dr Mahathir's Islamic moderation a safer choice than a PAS ally amid post-

September 11 fears of Muslim terrorism. Some Malays who had deserted UMNO returned to the fold. But PAS remains strong in the northern states, especially Kedah.

This was underlined in by-elections in July 2002, following the death of Fadzil Noor. While the National Front took back the federal parliamentary seat in Kedah won by the late PAS leader in 1999, it was defeated in the battle for the constituency he represented in the state legislative assembly. Moreover, the government coalition won the federal seat only narrowly, through the support of non-Malays and ethnic Thais, who are a prominent minority in Kedah. The defeated PAS candidate, Dr Mohamad Hayati Othman, actually received more Malay votes then Fadzil Noor. Dr Mahathir asserted that the National Front had made progress but conceded that Malay votes were 'split down the middle'.

A matter of concern in the Lunas by-election was the intrusion of racial and religious hatred into the campaign. Dr Fernandez was killed by members of a group said by police to have links to the al-Qaeda terrorist organisation of Osama bin Laden because of false allegations he was involved in converting Muslims to Catholicism. Anthonysamy was an Indian and a Catholic like the man he hoped to succeed. In the week preceding the election, posters circulated in the Lunas constituency carrying a doctored photograph of him in a priest's robe and wearing a crucifix. Whether the inflammatory posters were created by the opposition parties or a small faction among their supporters, they showed that a nastier element of politics was developing in Malaysia.

Dr Mahathir could no longer ignore the manifestations of disunity. As 2001 began, he warned of cracks in the nation that could lead to its collapse, and acknowledged that the split extended to the administration itself. In a speech to public servants, Dr Mahathir said there were signs among them of attempts to sow seeds of hatred towards the government. He said some public servants mistakenly thought the government was corrupt, practised cronyism and was against Islam. But while he repeatedly raised the alarm about the widespread antagonism towards the government he did not accept that he was a major part of the problem. Dr Mahathir had gone from being a leader who had been admired and respected for his achievements in the years from 1981 to 1997 to one who was now reviled by a large segment of the population. Farish Noor, a political scientist and historian, who has written extensively on Dr Mahathir's career, noted early in 2001 that the fact that the Prime Minister was more unpopular at that time than he had ever been was 'almost beyond dispute or question'.

Antagonism was not the only difficulty Dr Mahathir's government had to cope with in 2001. The preoccupation of the leadership with development in the boom years and the political and economic crises at the end of the 1990s meant little attention had been given to simmering social tensions. In crowded urban slums crime, corruption and racial strains built up into a potentially explosive mixture. But the authorities had been lulled into a belief that the long period of relative racial calm in the three decades since the riots of 1969 meant Malaysians had learned a lesson from that episode and were committed to living together in harmony. In fact, a new generation of Malaysians knew nothing of the terror of that time and were more segregated racially and more suspicious of their ethnically different neighbours than ever before. The government had not only failed to create a Malaysian identity but had aggravated the separateness of the races. With both UMNO and PAS engrossed in a battle for the hearts and minds of Malays, Chinese and Indians were left feeling increasingly insecure. In the wake of the Anwar affair, which had shattered public confidence in the administration, the police and the judiciary, the poor felt especially vulnerable.

In this climate of national uncertainty, the outbreak of racial violence that occurred in a pocket of poverty in Kuala Lumpur in March 2001 was bound to have occurred sooner or later. A minor argument led to a series of clashes between Indians and Malays, which resulted in six deaths over several days. The number of casualties, which included 50 people injured, was significantly fewer than in May 1969, but it alarmed the citizens of a nation which had managed to avoid such bloodshed for more than 30 years. Opposition officials and members of non-government organisations visited the area and discussed with residents steps that needed to be taken to overcome the tension between the races, reduce the rampant crime and improve living conditions. But government leaders sought to play down the racial nature of the violence, studiously refraining from categorising the incidents as confrontations between Malays and Indians. Dr Mahathir declared: 'There were no racial clashes but when people start spreading rumours that Indians are attacking Malays, then people come out and it happens.'

The media seemed unsure of how to handle the racial violence. In one report, the national newsagency Bernama referred to 'clashes between two groups of residents in Taman Desaria and areas adjacent to Jalan Klang Lama' and did not use the words 'Indians' or 'Malays'. However, Lee Lam Thye, a member of the National Unity Advisory Panel and former member of parliament called on the National Unity Department to investigate the incidents. He said Malaysians could not take inter-racial harmony in the multiracial nation for granted. The March racial clashes highlighted the growth of ethnic-based gangs, which were aggravating tensions in mixed-race squatter areas. Poverty, frustration over living conditions and the prejudices of people of different races and religions were causes of the initial racial skirmishes in the cluster of deprived kampungs south of the Federal Highway, which carries commuters between the city centre and the comfortable condominiums of Petaling Jaya. Later, however, pitched battles were fought between members of Indian and Malay gangs. Homes in the kampungs ranged from shacks to low-cost terrace houses. Nearby were high-rise apartments of middle-class Malaysians. Most of the people living in the worst conditions were Indians who had migrated to the city from rubber and oil palm estates, where their race had provided the labour since the early days of British colonial rule. Gang-instigated violence was common in the area, and local storekeepers had complained of having to pay protection money to both Malay and Indian groups. The most active gangs were made up of young Indian men who had turned to crime after failing to find work on their arrival in the city from the rural estates where they were raised. Indians were the principal members of several major Malaysian criminal groups, such as the Steyr Gang, named for an automatic weapon that was part of their armament. According to a study on violent crime by police in Kuala Lumpur, 38 Indian gangs with 1500 members were responsible for a majority of criminal activities in the country. A senior police officer told reporters that although Indians were the third largest race after the Malays and Chinese, they committed the most crimes.

In the same week that Kuala Lumpur police were investigating the involvement of Indian and Malay gangs in the capital's outbreak of racial unrest, their Malacca counterparts arrested 121 Chinese allegedly taking part in a triad initiation ceremony near the town of Jasmin. The Malay, Chinese and Indian gangs reflected the polarisation of the three main communities in Malaysian society. Social workers said Chinese secret societies capitalised on concerns of Chinese about their minority status and Malay political dominance, providing them with a protective big brother. Eleven of the Chinese taken into custody were students ranging in age from thirteen to eighteen. Police said they were being initiated into the Red Face Society, which has links to Hong Kong.

Utusan Malaysia attacked me for reporting that the racial disturbances had created a climate of fear, but one Malaysian newspaper commentator—with the clout to be outspoken—took a similar approach. In a *New Straits Times* column written as a letter to politicians, Abdullah Ahmad, executive director of The New Straits Times Press (Malaysia) Berhad, said that the violence left many people 'angry, very fearful and disappointed'. They were angry, he said, because the acts of senseless individuals almost led to widespread violence, and fearful because a 'repeat of the bloody May 13, 1969, riots could send the whole country reeling into anarchy and untold misery'. He also said people were disappointed that despite repeated pleas, the authorities had not continued development in the affected area after building some low-class flats. He said: 'Only those who went through the ugly 1969 racial riots could really understand why many of us are really fearful of the potentially explosive situation there.' While today the authorities were talking about massive development, the people had heard this before and he was not sure they would believe it this time. Some serious work needed to be done if the different ethnic groups in Malaysia were to 'live harmoniously, without bloodshed, without violence'.

Indian community leaders and politicians called for urgent action to help the poor of their race. The news editor of the *Sun* newspaper, K. Baradan, directly attributed the neglect of Indians to the government and the Malaysian Indian Congress (MIC), the number three party in the National Front coalition, and highlighted the disparities between the Malays, Chinese and Indians. He said the Malay community was supported by 'huge infusions of funds', while the Chinese, with their talent and networking, took maximum advantage of education and economic liberation. But for the Indian poor, who were the underclass within the Indian minority, neglect was 'the order of the day, both by the government and the MIC'. Baradan said every scheme to help the Indian poor that had come from the Indian leadership had 'somehow floundered, lost steam or become hijacked by a callous breed of bureaucrats who had somehow bled the schemes to death'.

With the commentaries of Baradan and Abdullah Ahmad, the press appeared finally to have sloughed off the self-censorship apparently gripping it in the early stages of the March incidents. But the generally cautious attitude of the media to major national stories turned Malaysians to alternative sources of information. At the same time, the government's repeated failure to be honest and transparent with the public further undermined its standing. Together the media and government created an environment that benefited the opposition.

12 | Clinging to power

In his speech at the opening of the UMNO annual general assembly on 21 June 2001, Dr Mahathir delivered his most devastating critique of Malays since he wrote *The Malay Dilemma*. Delegates were exasperated by his return to an old refrain which they did not want to hear. They had hoped he would put before them a vision of the nation's future under UMNO that would rekindle public faith in the party and at the same time firmly declare his plans for retirement while endorsing his successor. But his address reflected an obsession with the past and his intense frustration over having failed to mould Malays into the people he wanted them to be. He was saying, in effect, that his efforts over 30 years had been fruitless.

This may have been disheartening for him but his language was disquieting to UMNO officials who knew it would only further alienate the Malays whom they were trying to woo back to the party. The more frustrated Dr Mahathir became the blunter was his message. Malays, especially young Malays, resented and rejected his scathing remarks. To make matters worse, Dr Mahathir, who was just over three weeks away from chalking up twenty years as Malaysia's leader, let it be known at a press conference that he was not likely to step down soon, although he conceded that 'lots of people' did not like him. When he was asked about his retirement plans, he said it was a very difficult question to answer. He said that while some people would like to see him 'disappear or disintegrate', there were others who insisted that he should stay on. He added that he had to 'find the right time to step down'.

In his address, Dr Mahathir demonstrated his stubborn commitment to what most other people saw as a lost cause. Commenting on the low grades of Malay children, which rendered many of them 'unqualified to enter universities if not for a special quota', he said many of them were 'lazy and uninterested in studying'. They preferred to loaf around and were upset if their laziness was mentioned. He compared Malay children—and their parents—adversely with 'non-Malays' (meaning Chinese), who regarded 'seeking knowledge as noble' and looked up to those who were knowledgable. Chinese parents and teachers paid 'serious attention towards education of their children and the young', while Malays did not really emphasise the acquisition of knowledge and Malay parents did not force their children to study. Dr Mahathir said Malays were so 'impatient to become rich' they would sell 'every opportunity and allocation given to them', including company shares, licences, permits and contracts. The only business in which they participated was 'selling their special privilege'. Without government assistance, they would fail in all areas. Without positive discrimination by the government, only 20 per cent of those entering universities would be Malays. Without government intervention in favour of Malays, the positions of vice chancellors, professors and lecturers would be held by non-Malays and not monopolised by Malays as they were today.

Dr Mahathir went on to say that after 43 years of independence Malays were 'still weak in all areas'. He said they were 'weak economically, unknowledgeable, and not smart'. They were easily bribed, became drug addicts and suffered from AIDS. They accepted this because they would 'be protected by the Malaysian Government'. He declared: 'We topple, steal and we will do anything to achieve our great dreams.' When I asked Dr Mahathir whether his harsh words might be counterproductive politically, he said some people would 'feel unhappy about it' because they did not like to be told the truth, but he suspected that many people would heed the warning. As a leader he had to lead. He had to tell people this was the way to go. It was too bad if some people did not like it and the party lost votes. He asserted: 'If they don't want to vote for me, what can I do.'

In his speech, Dr Mahathir devoted a considerable amount of time to talking about the past rather than focusing on the present and the future. He said Malays had forgotten how they were once colonised and despised because they were factionalised and disunited. They had 'forgotten their strength and success, when they were once united and had fought hard against the British and had achieved independence'. The Malay struggle, of course, was not a war of independence, like the bitter conflict between the Indonesians and the Dutch, but a bloodless battle (excluding the violence of early years) through political manoeuvring and public demonstrations to pressure the British into a post-colonial government acceptable to the Malays. Nevertheless, Dr Mahathir painted the British as conniving, dangerous adversaries brought to their knees by the people whom the Prime Minister otherwise seemed intent on maligning. He said: 'The British, a world power, who had just won the war, who were so cunning and skillful, were forced to bow to the Malays who were united in a political party [UMNO] they had newly established.'

It was a remarkable speech, highlighting how removed Dr Mahathir was from the priorities of most other Malaysians. While the establishment media does not regularly provide an insight into popular opinion because it usually steers away from lively political debate, letter-writers have found an alternative public forum in Malaysiakini, a website providing provocative and controversial Malaysian news and commentary. Soon after the 2001 UMNO general assembly, Malaysiakini carried a letter from a Malay describing the Prime Minister as a man 'full of bitterness', who blamed the woes of UMNO and the government on everyone, including foreigners, the opposition and Malays, but never on himself or the party he leads. The race as a whole had 'lost a lot of ground' since he became Prime Minister. Malays had been 'grievously let down' through corruption and cronyism by 'the very party that was formed to protect them'. Addressing the Prime Minister, the writer said: 'You don't make yourself great by making others small. Today, you are a powerful hero, tomorrow? Dear Mahathir, when will you wake up?'

It was the kind of moderate criticism you could hear often from Malays in their homes—and even at government receptions, uttered in a low voice by disaffected department heads or Wisma Putra (Foreign Ministry) officials. Milder in tone than the frenzied attacks of the opposition and inveterate Mahathir-haters, the grievances of these middle-class Malaysians highlighted the shift in attitude by a large section of the public which had once been supporters of the Prime Minister. Their antipathy towards Dr Mahathir was intensified by the fact that pro-government media references to Dr Mahathir were unfailingly fawning. Even more obnoxious to many Malaysians was the effort by members of Dr Mahathir's retinue to create a personality cult around the Prime Minister. Ironically—considering Beijing had supported a communist insurgency in Malaysia for many years—the image-makers seemed to have been inspired by the Chinese Communist Party propaganda machine that glorified Mao Zedong from the 1950s to the 1970s. A 1999 seminar on The Thoughts of Dr Mahathir echoed the title of the famous 'little red book' containing the reflections of Chairman Mao, which millions of Red Guards held in their hands like a religious text in the 1960s as they wreaked destruction throughout China. The seminar was organised by a group of 'academicians, businessmen and politicians' and was opened by Abdullah Badawi, who explained that the Prime Minister's thoughts as a leader had brought about many changes in the country.

Badawi officiated at two other events in 1999 celebrating the achievements of Dr Mahathir. The first was the launching of a CD-ROM called 'Mahathir, CEO Malaysia Inc', to highlight the role of the Prime Minister 'in the planning and implementation of Malaysia's economic development'. The occasion was organised by the Asian Strategy & Leadership Institute (ASLI), the president of which is Dr Mahathir's son Mirzan. The Deputy Prime Minister also presided at a ceremony to introduce an album of 'patriotic songs' dedicated to Dr Mahathir, at which Badawi declared that the government welcomed efforts to foster love for the country's leaders. At both the seminar and the patriotic songs happening, Badawi said it was not true that Dr Mahathir was a dictator. It was an odd declaration, indicative of the mood of the time and reflecting the low esteem in which the Prime Minister was held by many Malaysians. As part of this bid to boost his image, the Information Ministry also arranged for the production of a sixteen-episode drama for television based on the life of the Prime Minister. The M$450 000 series, called 'The Unfinished Struggle', featured a 'Dr Kamal' who 'starts as a simple kampung (village) doctor but eventually brings his vision of change to the nation's political arena'. Malaysians joked that it would become a never-ending series as Dr Mahathir continued to postpone his departure from office.

The cult of personality reached an intensity in 1999 ahead of the general election, when Dr Mahathir was coming under heavy attack on opposition websites, where he was portrayed as maha zalim, or very tyrannical. And it continues unabated even though he has announced his plan for retirement. Malay culture, with its feudal traditions, accords respect to a long-serving leader, whose status is reinforced by his durability. But the orchestrated adulation of Dr Mahathir goes beyond the praise bestowed on earlier prime ministers. Hardly a day passes without a front-page story in national newspapers reporting Dr Mahathir's latest pronouncement. He comments regularly, in speeches and at press conferences, on a wide range of topics, including politics, the economy, race and religion, and almost every word is published in the press. His image is omnipresent. Every public appearance rates a photograph in newspapers and coverage on television. His face, with its familiar half smile, gazes down from walls in government offices. The evening television news is preceded by a clip of patriotism-stirring scenes of famous landmarks, national parades, athletic endeavours and heroic achievers, interspersed with shots of the Prime Minister and his wife, Siti Hasmah.

It all adds up to the kind of attention usually paid to leaders who need propping up because they came to power without due democratic process. But Dr Mahathir has been elected to parliament from a constituency in his home state of Kedah at regular five-year intervals with a comfortable majority despite the animosity he inspired among many Malaysians. He has been reconfirmed as UMNO president at every triennial party election since he first assumed the post. Dr Mahathir, or his minders, apparently feared that the vilification of the opposition would undermine his remaining support and set out to try to counter the 'lies and slander' of the political enemy and the disenchantment of citizens. But the extravagant praise of the nation's leader made him look like the omnipotent pharaoh PAS held him to be. It also made many Malaysians receptive to PAS's claim that Dr Mahathir was helping his family enrich themselves at the expense of the state in the same way Indonesian President Suharto's sons and daughters grew wealthy through government contracts and their father's position.

Dr Mahathir's children's business deals have certainly been modest compared with the extensive involvement of the Suharto family in a wide range of enterprises, but the 1998 arrangement under which Petronas, the national oil company, purchased the shipping assets of the Prime Minister's oldest son, Mirzan, as the recession began to bite gave life to a host of unfounded rumours about Mahathir family nepotism. Despite claims that the shipping transaction was a practical commercial arrangement, the fact that cash-rich Petronas was under the direct control of the Prime Minister's Department convinced many Malaysians that it was the bailout claimed by the opposition and a favour for Mirzan. The problem Dr Mahathir faced was that people who disliked him for one reason or another—including his heavy sarcasm, his complaints about public ingratitude, his habit of lecturing Malays, Chinese and almost everybody else—were prepared to believe everything bad said about him. He made it easy for the opposition by taking no action to prevent the recurrence of the kind of controversial deals that had attracted strong criticism of Malaysian business practices. The long-running saga of Daim protégé Halim Saad's difficulties, arising out of the impact of the 1998 recession on debt-burdened Renong was a case in point. The buyback of Malaysian Airlines from Tajudin Ramli, another Daim friend, at more than twice the market valuation, was another. Dr Mahathir denied that any of the deals that attracted criticism were bailouts but they were added to his enemies' long list of alleged wrongdoings, damaging his image and benefiting the opposition.

While acknowledging that many people do not like him, he has made no serious effort to change what they regard as his aggravating ways. His address to the UMNO annual general assembly in 2001 demonstrated that there were two Mahathir's. One was the visionary leader with a grand plan to turn Malaysia into a developed nation by the year 2020. The other was a man so riven by resentment over his early experiences in life that he was consumed by the desire to create a super-Malay, whom the dastardly West would never be able to subjugate. Tunku Abdul Rahman, Malaysia's first prime minister, who did not like Dr Mahathir, said he had an inferiority complex. The British-educated Tunku was an Anglophile while Dr Mahathir was very much an Anglophobe. There was another important difference between the two men. Dr Mahathir was the first UMNO president and prime minister who was not from one of the royal families or the Malay aristocracy. Tunku's aristocratic bearing and charm endeared him to the British, who treated him with respect and courtesy. By contrast, Dr Mahathir, as a struggling doctor in the poor state of Kedah, endured the belittlement that was standard in relations between British officials and ordinary Malays. His anger grew with every slight he suffered, leaving him with bitter memories which influenced him in all his relations with the West.

His unrelenting outrage was reflected in an article he co-wrote with a journalist of *Mainichi Daily News* and in a speech at UMNO's annual general assembly in 1998. In the *Mainichi* article, he recalled that when he was young, Malays had to call all Europeans masters. 'We were always regarded as inferior to them. I always resented having to call other people master. I think in my own country I should be the master.' At the UMNO meeting, he said he was proud when he saw Malays getting rich. With a dash of hyperbole, he stated: 'Once upon a time all of us only swept the streets.' He said he had lived under four colonial regimes, experiencing British rule before and after the Second World War and subjugation by the Japanese and the Siamese during it. Japan gave Siam four states, including Kedah, where the young Mahathir resided. Dr Mahathir said he observed how Malays who did not show respect to the Japanese army were forced to hold rocks over their heads and witnessed a Siamese soldier kick an old Malay man when he did not get off his bicycle during the playing of the national anthem of Siam. But it was the British who earned his greatest ire. 'I was around during the British Empire. We did not have a shred of dignity. We were not allowed to do this or that. Almost everything we could not do.'

Dr Mahathir declared in a speech at a conference in Namibia in July 1998, that he was neither a racist, 'anti-white or anti-European'. But his fiercest hostility is reserved for white Western nations and their leaders. Along with Britain and the United States of America, Australia, its prime ministers and its journalists have been subjects of his most unrestrained diatribes. His outbursts are surprising because among the tens of thousands of Malaysians who have studied in Australia, members of the armed forces who have had close cooperation with their Australian counterparts since in-dependence, and senior officials of the diplomatic corps who have been posted to Canberra, the goodwill towards Australians is over-whelming. Dr Mahathir's opposition to any Australian involvement in South-East Asian and East Asian cooperative agreements meant that possible advantages to the region of Australia's participation in the development of new trade and business initiatives were lost. He firmly blocked Australia from participating in the ASEAN-Europe Union dialogues, although other leaders in South-East Asia thought a Europe–ASEAN–Australia discussion group was worth exploring. The depth of Dr Mahathir's prejudiced view of Australia was most clearly reflected in his reaction to events in East Timor in 1999. He was incensed by what he saw as Australia's intrusion into a regional dispute which he believed fell under the aegis of ASEAN. He lashed out at Australia after it was put in charge of an international peace-keeping force, which he had wanted to be restricted to ASEAN units under Malaysian command, saying Australians really loved it when they had 'the chance to pressure [and] condemn their neighbours'.

Dr Mahathir has also demonstrated a less than even-handed approach when dealing with Muslim and non-Muslim tragedies. While he repeatedly called for foreign intervention to stop Serb atrocities against Muslims in Kosovo, he was silent on the slaughter of men, women and children in predominantly Christian East Timor by militia units loyal to Indonesia, a nation with a mainly Muslim population. If the multinational force led by Australia had not moved in when it did, the pro-integration militias' slaughter of opponents and burning of villages would have continued. But Dr Mahathir criticised the 'rather heavy-handed' way Australian troops operated in East Timor, accusing them of 'pointing guns at almost everybody'. He said rather naively that Malaysian soldiers would have tried 'to contact the groups and tell them that it was not worthwhile to fight'. Nobel Peace Prize laureate and East Timorese leader Jose Ramos Horta was under no illusions about the position of Dr Mahathir's Malaysia on East Timor. He said he was totally opposed to Malaysia leading the UN peacekeeping efforts, adding that it was 'always on the side of Indonesia'. In an article for the *Mainichi Daily News*, Dr Mahathir said the West seized the opportunity presented by the economic and political turmoil in Indonesia to 'break up' the country, adding that Australia was the 'main beneficiary' of this.

In April 2000, in an interview with Australia's SBS television while he was attending a Group of 77 summit in Cuba, Dr Mahathir made a harsh, unprovoked attack on Australia and Australian Prime Minister John Howard, saying he was not welcome in Malaysia. His accompanying remarks highlighted his implacable animosity towards Malaysia's neighbour to the south. It was not the first time he had attacked an Australian prime minister. Robert J. Hawke attracted his censure for describing the death sentence imposed on two Australian drug traffickers as barbaric, and Paul Keating upset the Malaysian Prime Minister by calling him recalcitrant for not attending the first APEC summit. Howard had earned Dr Mahathir's ire by joining other Western leaders in expressing concern about Anwar's arrest and trials. Coming from the leader of a country, which, he liked to recall, had once practised a White Australia policy, these comments had the same effect upon him as the slights he had experienced under British colonialism. He was clearly so embittered by them that they may well have affected his judgment on matters related to Australia.

Strangely for a man who was a medical doctor, he has often seemed to be more motivated by passionately held beliefs than cold logic. This has not affected Malaysia much where foreign relations of the commercial kind were concerned, since nations trading with his country and Western corporate chiefs operating Malaysian factories have been pragmatic enough to ignore the vitriol issuing from the Prime Minister's Department as long as the goods were flowing. But his obstinacy on the need to change Malay culture and stubborn insistence on personally pursuing this goal despite every indication that it was unattainable threatened to undermine his aim of making Malaysia a developed nation of moderate modern-thinking Muslims by driving Malays into the PAS fundamentalist camp. Instead of concentrating his political efforts on winning the hearts and minds of Malays, he persisted in beating his head against the brick wall of their recalcitrance and making himself an easy target for opposition claims he was not a true Malay. It was his Indian blood, they said. And instead of using his skill and experience to further reduce Anwar's influence in UMNO, which had been diminished by his inept push for power in 1998, Dr Mahathir let his anger towards his ungrateful protégé provoke him to seek his political destruction and thereby turned him into a martyr.

At the same time as the standing of Dr Mahathir was plummeting in 1999 and 2000, the image of UMNO was taking a battering. A new spate of corruption stories were circulating, highlighting the party's failure to clean out crooked officials and eliminate money politics. At UMNO general assemblies Dr Mahathir repeatedly pleaded with members not to use their positions or links to senior officials to make themselves rich and not to try to buy their way into top posts with bribes, often weeping in the process. But his teary appeals neither moved greedy UMNO members nor attracted the sympathy of Malaysians, since he took no action against leading personalities widely believed to be dishonest. It was hard to take seriously Dr Mahathir's emotional denunciations of money politics and petty corruption in a political environment that accepted rupiahs flowing like rivers of gold into the coffers of government parties, public works contracts going to relatives and friends of senior figures and the cosy cooperation of the leadership with a coterie of corporate chiefs. Many Malaysians, who had followed the curious twists of government–corporate collaboration, seen money changing hands during elections and experienced corruption in government departments, were convinced the leaders and officials of UMNO were venal. This sentiment has provided fertile ground for PAS to win the support of Malays, many of whom found it easy to believe the opposition's exaggerated portrayal of the Prime Minister as a pharaoh.

Dr Mahathir was no dictator but he certainly had extraordinary powers and only had himself to blame for the low regard in which UMNO was held by the public. If he wished, he could have shaken up the party thoroughly, earning himself some respect from Malaysians in the process. But he had his mind on other matters, such as the unwillingness of Malays to develop a strong work and study ethic like the Chinese. Unfortunately, the strength of his authority—together with a feudal Malay reluctance to remove a veteran leader—deterred his colleagues from suggesting it would be better for the party and the country for him to step aside and let Abdullah Badawi take the helm. UMNO provides the mechanism for leaders to be changed through elections but the procedure followed has been for a prime minister to choose his successor by appointing a deputy. The first prime minister, Tunku Abdul Rahman, made way for his number two, Abdul Razak. Upon Razak's death, the Deputy Prime Minister, Hussein Onn, took his place. In 1981, Hussein Onn retired, passing the baton to his deputy, Dr Mahathir. Dr Mahathir, like his two predecessors, was subsequently confirmed as the nation's leader through his election as UMNO president. But the party's right to change presidents was underlined by the 1987 challenge by Tengku Razaleigh Hamzah, who came close to defeating the sitting Prime Minister and UMNO president, Dr Mahathir.

However, after the crushing blows that fell upon Anwar, the senior figures who might have led a push against the president were held in check by fear of their leader. Dr Mahathir had given the Home Affairs portfolio, with its draconian apparatus of security forces and controls, to Badawi but he could take it back at any time. Abdullah Ahmad, *New Straits Times* executive, columnist and former political secretary of the second prime minister, Abdul Razak, wrote that Dr Mahathir enlarged the presidential prime ministership started by his former boss. 'The power of the prime ministers of Malaysia and Singapore, and Senior Minister Lee Kuan Yew, is awesome, not only over their colleagues but also over their respective peoples.'

Dr Mahathir has proved himself to be a ruthless politician. He has no time for either government supporters or members of the opposition who stand in his way. In March 2001, speaking informally to reporters in the lobby of parliament, he railed against the opposition, declaring that it was a stumbling block to every development proposed by the government. He has never hesitated to use the *Internal Security Act* against his enemies, although he won the applause of liberals with his release of detainees when he first came to power. A major sweep of a host of people across the political spectrum in 1987 prompted Tunku Abdul Rahman to offer a critical comment to a British newspaper. Malaysia's first prime minister declared: 'This is becoming more or less a police state. I never dreamt they would resort to those methods of dealing with our citizens. The opposition has the right to talk against the government. Now he [Dr Mahathir] has arrested all of them.'

In *The Malay Dilemma* published in 1970, a younger and more radical Dr Mahathir delivered a stinging attack against Tunku Abdul Rahman and his government. He wrote: 'But power corrupts and the near-absolute power that the Alliance [coalition of UMNO and other parties] obtained corrupted the thinking of the leaders almost absolutely.' The government, he wrote, was 'openly contemptuous of criticism'. Taking aim at Tunku Abdul Rahman, Dr Mahathir stated: 'The Prime Minister in particular became so powerful both by virtue of his office and by popular acclaim that the party became subservient to his person.' But Tunku Abdul Rahman, whom Abdullah Ahmad described as an 'old-school prime minister', never exercised power as flagrantly as Dr Mahathir. UMNO is more subservient to its present leader than it has been to any other prime minister. Many critics of Dr Mahathir say that just as Tunku Abdul Rahman's administration had lost touch with the masses and was surprised by the May 1969, riots, the present government shows little understanding of the grievances of Malaysians. Dr Mahathir's critics also say that he was never a real revolutionary because he held to conservative views which still guide him and render him an obstacle to the political reform Malaysia needs. They point to his remark in *The Malay Dilemma* that in itself the feudalist inclination of the Malays was not damaging. 'It makes for an orderly law-abiding society.'

A senior UMNO figure who has worked closely with Dr Mahathir paid tribute to his vision and the intensity of his spirit but faulted him on the manner in which he had 'trampled on a lot of people's feet'. He said this was because of his 'confrontational, uncompromising, I'm-always-right stance'. Dr Mahathir would 'never apologise for mistakes' because this would be interpreted as a weakness.

Dr Mahathir showed the tough spirit of a potential leader early in his political career and was more tenacious in pursuing his goals than his contemporaries. It marks him apart from most other Malaysian politicians, including those who have come close to becoming president of UMNO and prime minister. Tengku Razaleigh challenged him for the party leadership and continued to fight him from outside UMNO for several years. But Tengku Razaleigh finally returned to UMNO and while making it known that he would like to succeed Dr Mahathir has not actively confronted him a second time. A Malaysian whom many people think should have been prime minister conceded that he was 'not prepared to go for the kill'. Musa Hitam, who headed Malaysia's Human Rights Commission from 1999 to 2002, was elected UMNO deputy president in 1981 when Dr Mahathir was elected president. He became Deputy Prime Minister under the new Prime Minister but resigned in 1986 over 'differences' with Dr Mahathir. He later supported Tengku Razaleigh's bid to replace Dr Mahathir at the 1987 UMNO elections but was defeated when he tried to retain his deputy presidency. He told me he agreed with the *Asian Wall Street Journal* when it said 'the trouble with Musa Hitam' was that he was 'never the type to go for the jugular'. Musa said: 'I'm not prepared to play dirty, it's as simple as that. As a democrat I think that shouldn't be the attitude.' While he was a good Muslim in the sense that he believed in takdir (fate), at the same time he believed in what he called 'positive fatalism', meaning that he tried his best. He said: 'If I reach there, I reach there; if I don't, so be it.' Musa once remarked that one of the problems of people who got into politics was 'their inability to get out of politics'.

Dr Mahathir is clearly more hard-nosed than Musa. His background may have something to do with that. He was brought up in an environment where he was pushed to be an achiever. He was the youngest in a family of six boys and three girls. His father was the founder and first headmaster of the Sultan Abdul Hamid College in Alor Star, which Mahathir attended. He said: 'My father was very strict and serious about studies.' His schooling was interrupted by the Japanese occupation. The college reopened on 15 October 1945, after being closed for 1390 days. Mahathir bin Mohamad Iskandar was among the students who learned with the reopening of their school that they had passed the Junior Cambridge Examination, which they had sat in December 1941. In the post-war years, he edited the college publication and was chairman of the Literary and Debating Society. A fellow student recalled that he 'organised the debates and talks of the society with efficiency'. By then he was 20 and showing a strong political consciousness. Although still at school, he became involved in the campaign against the British proposal for a Malayan Union, which Malay nationalists opposed. Writing under the pen-name of C. H. E. Det, he was a regular contributor to the Sunday edition of the *Straits Times*. Many of the views expressed in these articles were expanded in *The Malay Dilemma*. In 1947 he was admitted to the King Edward VII College of Medicine at the University of Malaya in Singapore. After an internship at the Penang General Hospital he set up his own practice in Alor Star. But he maintained his political enthusiasm, joining UMNO and then standing for parliament in the 1964 general election, in which he won the Kota Star Selatan seat. He was defeated in the next general election in 1969 but in 1974 won the Kedah seat of Kubang Pasu, which he has retained at every subsequent poll. In the 1960s and early 1970s, his outspoken criticism of the ruling elite, his attacks on Chinese control of the economy and championing of Malay rights made him a hero of the nationalists and student radicals—the very sections of the community who now despise him. The 13 May 1969 riots prompted Dr Mahathir to tackle the leadership head-on in an open letter to the then Prime Minister, Tunku Abdul Rahman, criticising government policies. He was expelled from UMNO in September 1969, and not re-admitted to the party until March 1972, a year after Razak replaced Tunku Abdul Rahman as president.

The Malay Dilemma upset the UMNO hierarchy even more than the open letter to Tunku Abdul Rahman. However, in the wake of the May 1969 riots the leadership realised something had to be done to assuage the despair of many Malays. To this end, the New Economic Policy introduced measures providing the kind of 'constructive protection' for the Malay community that Dr Mahathir called for in his book. But Dr Mahathir went much further than proposing efforts to give Malays greater equality with Chinese, shocking colleagues with his destructive analysis of Malayan culture. He said the proposition that only the fittest would survive did not apply in Malaya, where 'no great exertion or energy was required to obtain food'. The hot, humid climate was not conducive to either vigorous work or even to mental activity and most people were 'content to spend their unlimited leisure in merely resting or in extensive conversation with neighbours and friends'. By contrast, the life of the Chinese people was 'one continuous struggle for survival'. Additionally, the Chinese did not have the Malay 'partiality towards in-breeding'. Chinese avoidance of marriage within the same clan resulted in the reproduction of the 'best strains and characteristics which facilitated survival'. The young Dr Mahathir wrote that the Malays, 'whose hereditary and environmental influence had been so debilitating, could do nothing but retreat before the onslaught of the Chinese immigrants', who were 'hardened and resourceful'. Before long the 'industrious and determined immigrants' had displaced the Malays in petty trading and all branches of skilled work. He further emphasised the detrimental effect of in-breeding by comparing rural Malays, whom, he said, preferred to marry relatives, with town Malays, whose inter-racial marriages 'enriched Malay stock'. With this reference to Malays who married non-Malays, he put himself, with his Indian heritage, on a higher plane than other members of the Malay community. Today, nationalists extol the importance of racial purity and decry Dr Mahathir for his mixed blood.

Dr Mahathir called for an equality that must mean 'a gain for the have-nots and a loss for the haves' to overcome Malay frustration and bitterness, which had led to the May 1969 riots. Noting that educationally Malays were far behind other communities, he advocated 'special provisions' to help them, as well as employment opportunities to overcome the discrimination 'in commercial and business circles controlled by non-Malays'. In remarks that many Chinese have regarded as an alarming early insight into his thinking, Dr Mahathir also placed in question the right of Chinese and other non-Malays to be in Malaya. He said Malays were the rightful owners of Malaya and if citizenship were conferred on other races it was because Malays consented to this. He added: 'That consent is conditional.'

In his 'introduction' to *The Malay Dilemma*, Dr Mahathir said general disapproval greeted his submission at a seminar held in Kuala Lumpur in 1966 that hereditary and environmental influences were among the factors responsible for the poor examination performance of Malay students, because it was thought he was implying that Malays were by nature inferior and that this inferiority was hereditary and consequently permanent. He wrote: 'This is not what the writer implied or concluded. The intention was to spotlight certain intrinsic factors which retard the development of the Malays, particularly those which can be corrected.' Today, he is still seeking to correct these factors, with virtually no success. Returning to his theme of Malay laziness in an interview with the Mingguan Malaysia newspaper in June, 2002, he said: 'I have failed in achieving the most important thing: how to change the Malays.' A few days later, on 20 June, in his opening speech to the 2002 UMNO general assembly he said he was disappointed because he had achieved too little from his 'principal task' of making Malays a successful, respected and honourable race. He added: 'I beg your forgiveness because I have failed. I pray that from among the Malays, there will emerge a leader capable of changing certain characteristics of the Malays.' Then, in his closing speech, he caused pandemonium when he tearfully announced his resignation. He later agreed to stay on until October 2003, when Abdullah Badawi will become head of government, with the expectation of subsequently being elected UMNO president. Dr Mahathir's efforts are clearly frustrating him and having a destructive impact on Malays at a time when the nation is already sharply divided.

13 | Terrorists at the gates

Parti Islam se-Malaysia (PAS), the opposition party that wants to turn Malaysia into a fundamentalist Islamic state, has undergone a remarkable transformation in a few years. Until recently, it was regarded as a party with a limited following of rural voters in thrall to its religious leaders, which was unlikely to duplicate elsewhere its victory in Kelantan, the country's poorest state. However, it has emerged as a significant political organisation with growing support among young urban Malays in addition to its kampung base, which has a strong chance of achieving power throughout the northern half of Peninsular Malaysia and, eventually even the possibility of winning control of the federal parliament. Its threat to UMNO prompted Abdullah Ahmad to warn in his *New Straits Times* column: 'PAS is no longer a blustering provincial party with no real strength; it is a terrifying force now and in future.' PAS has cleverly capitalised on every misstep of Dr Mahathir, especially his merciless destruction of Anwar and his controversial remarks about Malays and religion, which it has turned against him. For example, the party says his plans for the federal government to take over state-run religious schools where, he claims, PAS supporters teach children to hate him, demonstrate that he is an enemy of Islam.

But PAS has also benefited from an Islamic resurgence through-out South-East Asia which has radicalised a swath of Muslims across South-East Asia and created an unlikely alliance of US-hating mujahideen which includes young affluent Malays, anti-government guerillas in Indonesian Aceh and the southern Philippines, and savage Christian-killers in the Maluku islands of Indonesia. Malays with this new Islamic consciousness—born-again Muslims—have gravitated to PAS. Within PAS many of them have evolved into dangerous extremists eager to join the holy warriors of the region.

Until recently PAS did not actively cultivate other races but, recognising how events have given it greater potential to challenge the National Front, it has sought to portray itself as an acceptable option for non-Malays. However, the party has run into difficulties in reconciling the moderate face it presents to the Chinese and Indians of Malaysia with the hardline pronouncements of senior party officials. Moreover, the cornerstone of PAS's political plat-form—and the ultimate reason for the party's existence—is its goal of making Malaysia a state in which a Middle-Eastern-style unfor-giving Islam permeates and controls every institution. Shariah (Islamic) law would have supreme authority. The Muslim moder-ation of Dr Mahathir would be dead. Abdul Hadi Awang, who became PAS chief on the death of Fadzil, Chief Minister of Terengganu, has twice tried to introduce into parliament a bill to make apostasy a capital offence for Muslims. Since all Malays are deemed to be Muslims at birth, the law would apply to any member of the race wishing to take up another religion or to no longer be a practising Muslim. While the PAS bid to introduce the death penalty for people who renounce their Islamic faith has been blocked by the National Front, it has put pressure on UMNO to defend its declared role as the legitimate representative of followers of Islam in Malaysia. Many UMNO officials believe it should be less moderate in its interpretation of Islam to counter PAS efforts to impugn the government party's Islamic credentials.

Seeking to rebut PAS's denigration of UMNO, Dr Mahathir has said the world acknowledge Malaysia as a Muslim nation and many other Islamic governments regard it as the best model for them.

However, PAS has successfully kept UMNO on the defensive. The opposition party has repeatedly criticised UMNO for using its constitutional powers to prevent the implementation of legislation passed in PAS-controlled Kelantan that would introduce the traditional shariah penalties for offenders, such as cutting off the hands of thieves and stoning adulterers. Kelantan Chief Minister Nik Aziz Nik Mat has accused UMNO of rejecting the Koran and the reported sayings of the Prophet Mohamad, while Fadzil Noor said ulama who supported UMNO were 'mute satans' for not speaking out against the Prime Minister. Hadi Awang issued an amanat (decree), declaring that all members of UMNO were infidels, or non-believers. He also tried unsuccessfully to table in federal parliament a bill to 'control and restrict' the propagation of religions other than Islam, prompting angry protests from followers of other faiths. After Terengganu fell to PAS in the 1999 general election, Hadi Awang announced the state would follow Kelantan in imposing the harsh hudud punishments for offences against Islamic law and also introduce the first PAS state's dress code, requiring Malay women to wear the face-encircling tudung and cover all other parts of their bodies except the hands. Terengganu also banned women from taking part in Koran-reading competitions, which are a major activity in Malaysia. Harun Taib, chairman of the state Education and Religious Law Implementation Committee, said that a woman's voice, like most of her body, was aurat, or taboo, and should not be heard by anyone outside her family.

Addressing Muslims at one of his weekly religious meetings in Kota Baru, the state capital, Kelantan's Chief Minister Nik Aziz, who is known among Malays as Tok Guru, or venerable teacher, said women were the main cause of 'social ills and moral decadence'. He asserted that the people most responsible for vice and other problems were young women fond of wearing attire that exposed their bodies. He said the way they dressed invited men to rape or molest them. They usually wore revealing clothing on Saturdays, the main shopping day in the state. He was apparently referring to Chinese or Indian women since Malays are bound by the state's dress code for Muslims. He said: 'It is on this day that we can see many young women wearing blouses which expose the navel. Even a Tok Guru can be weakened watching them.' His comments outraged women's groups. Non-Muslims have often poked fun at the pronouncements of Nik Aziz, who has banned many forms of entertainment, directed supermarkets to set up separate male and female checkout counters and recommended that government offices employ 'less beautiful' women to protect men from temptation. But within PAS anything said by the man who is the party's spiritual adviser is taken seriously. This includes his declaration that the party would introduce legislation in federal parliament to enforce the hudud penalties 'when' it came to power. The states of Kelantan and Terengganu are providing an example of the kind of nation Malaysia would become if PAS did succeed in gaining control of the federal parliament.

PAS claims it opposes Islamic extremism but some members have turned up in regional radical groups while others have been linked to the al-Qaeda terrorist group associated with Osama bin Laden, members of which carried out the September 11, 2001, attacks on the World Trade Centre and Pentagon. While UMNO, during its unbroken period since independence as the dominant government party, has taken a moderate stand on most Islamic issues, Malaysia has produced a variety of religious extremists over the years. They have ranged from the belligerent to the benign, the latter including a group called al-Arqam which had thousands of followers in cities and kampungs, in the army and government before it was banned. It was led by a charismatic Malaysian who built up an international business empire and lived in luxury in Thailand until he returned to Malaysia to face arrest.

Of more concern to the authorities has been the emergence of cults that have clashed violently with Malaysian security forces. On 16 October 1980, eight Muslim extremists were shot dead by police after an armed band led by a self-styled Messiah from Cambodia stormed a police station at Batu Pahat, in Perak. Twenty-three police officers and civilians were injured in the attack. On 19 November 1985 four police officers and fourteen followers of an extremist cult died in a five-hour police operation against the group at Baling in Kedah, a state next to Perak. Police arrested 159 people, including women and children, who were members of the cult.

In mid-2000, a group called al-Ma'unah, led by an Islamic zealot who convinced his followers he was invulnerable to bullets, launched an audacious but ill-conceived plan to overthrow the government. First, fifteen members of the group dressed as soldiers carried out the biggest seizure of military weapons in Malaysia's history, driving away from two army camps in Perak state with 100 M16 rifles and a score of other weapons, including machine guns and grenade launchers, together with enough ammunition to wage a small war. They then used an army radio transmitter to call for the ouster of Dr Mahathir and his government and the establishment of an Islamic state but appeared to have no clear plan for future action. The fifteen men who carried out the raid on the army camps ended up with eleven more al-Ma'unah members holed up on a hilltop in an area of jungle and orchards near the town of Sauk, the leader's home town, in Perak, where they were surrounded by more than 1000 police officers and soldiers supported with heavy weapons and armoured vehicles. During a tense four-day confrontation, the rebels killed two hostages before finally surrendering to police. A score of other members were rounded up and arrested. As the media expressed concern about the growth of 'radical Islam' in Malaysia, officials said there were more than 40 such 'deviationist groups' in the country. But there were some especially alarming features about al-Ma'unah. The cult had attracted affluent professionals and senior military men. The leader was a former army private, while numbered among his followers were a captain and warrant officer from the armed forces.

The al-Ma'unah group was founded in September 1998, the month of Anwar's sacking, by Mohamad Amin Razali, who took for himself the title of Sheikh. This was the name by which the former deputy prime minister was known when he was a fiery Islamic radical. Amin was influenced not only by Anwar but also by an earlier Islamic hero, Ibrahim Libya, a cult leader who claimed mystical powers and was killed in the 19 November 1985 shoot-out with police at Baling. At the time, Amin, then 15, was a student at the Lanai religious school, near Baling. With others of his age, he became an acolyte of Ibrahim Libya. Many of his student friends were arrested but Amin escaped the dragnet. At the age of 16, he went to Indonesia, where he studied under a Javanese mystic called Ibnu Abbas, who, according to Amin, authorised him to open a school in Malaysia to spread the teachings of al-Ma'unah. He did not set up his school until September 1998, when he was 28. Malaysia was in ferment over the sacking of Anwar, who was idolised by young Malay Muslims. It was the right time for a Malay dressed in flowing robes and turban, with bushy eyebrows, a thick Zapata-style mustache and goatee, who claimed martial-arts skills and magical powers, to present himself as a Muslim leader with the same nom de guerre as Anwar. On 28 December 2001, he was sentenced to die by hanging after being found guilty of treason. Amin and his followers generated widespread sympathy among the Islamic clergy, many of whom refused to deliver an official sermon condemning al-Ma'unah and other deviant religious groups, using their mosques instead to denounce the Mahathir government as un-Islamic.

The al-Ma'unah affair demonstrated that there was a fine line between fundamentalism and extremism within the Malay Muslim community. Many members of the cult, which claimed to have more than 1000 followers in Malaysia and abroad, were also members of PAS. Fadzil Noor distanced the party from the 'incorrect' Islamic practices of al-Ma'unah but said there would be no investigation into whether his members were involved in the cult. Other PAS leaders cast doubt on the official version of events, suggesting the government wanted to instil fear in the non-Muslim community so they would not support the opposition party.

With extremist religious views and bigotry thriving beneath the appearance of a nation committed to Islamic moderation and toler-ance of other faiths, it was probably not surprising that Malaysia, found itself along with other South-East Asian nations, facing an even greater threat to racial and religious peace in 2001. It came from Muslims drawn to the annihilation-of-the-West theme of the Saudi Arabian supporter of 'blessed terrorism' Osama Bin Laden. He already had a following in the region before members of his movement used airline jets as guided missiles on September 11, 2001 to destroy the twin towers of the US World Trade Centre and attack the Pentagon. One of his earliest and closest South-East Asian connections was with the Abu Sayyaf Islamic rebels in the

Philippines, who were responsible for a series of kidnappings in the Philippines and a raid on a Malaysian resort in 2000. Osama's emissaries have also been active in establishing links with radical Islamic groups in Indonesia, and until recently an al-Qaeda leader was using Malaysia as a base to coordinate the group's regional activities.

The successful terrorist assault on the commercial heart of the United States immediately increased the number of Osama's admirers in South-East Asia. Even moderate Muslims put as much blame on US policies as the perpetrators for the carnage. The blow to the United States gave a subliminal lift to the spirits of many Muslims depressed by the ummah's (Muslim community's) subservience in a world dominated by Americans and Europeans—although few would admit this. More seriously, it radicalised those who were merely conservative while inspiring those already radical to offer themselves as martyrs to the cause.

In November Osama appealed to Muslims to rise up against such enemies of Islam as the 'Australian crusader forces'—an apparent reference to the Australian troops sent to help the United States in its Afghanistan campaign. He denounced both the United Nations and Australia over the separation of 'a part of the Islamic World', East Timor, from Indonesia (ignoring the fact that most East Timorese were Christians). Then in January 2002, Singapore's Ministry of Home Affairs disclosed that the Australian High Commission was among targets for bomb attacks by Singaporean terrorists who had trained in Afghanistan at Osama's al-Qaeda camps. Their plans were uncovered when US forces seized al-Qaeda documents and a video in Afghanistan.

These developments came amid signs of growing Islamic militancy throughout the region to Australia's north and as radical elements in Malaysia were linking up with similarly minded Muslims in Indonesia and the Philippines. The Malaysian link to Osama was the Kumpulan Mujahideen Malaysia (Islamic Warriors Group of Malaysia), or KMM, some of whose adherents were also members of PAS. At the same time as KMM was coming under the spotlight, a split was deepening in the Anwar camp's party, Keadilan, between moderate officials and a hardline faction favouring the use of mosques and Islamic radicalism to rally popular support for a street struggle to overthrow the government.

The leader of the militant faction, Mohamad Ezam Noor, who had been Anwar's political secretary and had begun dressing and acting like the young radical version of his mentor, was arrested in 2001 under the *Internal Security Act*. As a result, he was accorded the same martyr status as Anwar and like him became a hero of young Malays studying in Malaysian religious schools, among whom are the terrorists of the future. In the current environment, PAS, the religious schools and the mosques are all breeding grounds for young Malays eager to fight for Osama or any like-minded fanatic.

The existence of KMM came to light as a result of a botched bank raid in Kuala Lumpur in May 2001, in which one man was shot dead and two others wounded. The robbery was intended to provide funds for the group. Police alleged members were also responsible for the unsolved murder six months earlier of Dr Joe Fernandez, the Kedah state politician gunned down as he was caught in a traffic jam. (Fernandez had been a target of rumours that he was spreading Christianity among Muslims.) KMM was also linked to the bombing of a church and a Hindu temple and an attack on a police station. Nine people were arrested and a cache of arms seized.

In August 2001, another ten alleged KMM members were arrested, including Nik Adli Nik Aziz, a former religious teacher and son of PAS spiritual adviser and Kelantan State chief Nik Aziz Nik Mat. Nik Adli's father had demonstrated his radical leaning by describing the September 11 attacks on the United States as the 'will of Allah' and urging Muslims to help and support Taliban-controlled Afghanistan in its fight against the United States. The authorities accused Nik Adli, who was said to be the leader of the group, of seeking to 'topple the government through an armed struggle and replace it with a pure Islamic state comprising Indonesia, Mindanao and Malaysia'. He denied the charges and his father accused the government of seeking to destroy PAS. While the Malaysian government undoubtedly made political capital out of the exposure of KMM's activities, there was no doubt about the group's existence or that it had links with extremists in Indonesia.

There have been a number of credible reports identifying KMM as part of the Osama network in the region and linking it also to the Indonesian group Laskar Mujahideen, which has been responsible for the worst of the jihad against Christians in north Maluku. Malaysian members of KMM have reportedly taken part in attacks on Christians in Ambon, the Maluku capital, in conjunction with Laskar Mujahideen. The Malaysia–Indonesia link was further confirmed by the arrest of a Malaysian KMM member in Jakarta on 1 August 2001, when a bomb he was carrying went off prematurely outside a shopping mall.

In January 2002, Malaysian police chief Norian Mai announced the arrest of thirteen men who were said to be members of a new wing of KMM with suspected links to Zacarias Moussaoui, the French Moroccan charged in the United States over his alleged involvement in the September 11 attacks. According to Malaysian immigration records, Moussaoui had visited Malaysia between 4 and 15 September and again on 5 October 2000. The police disclosed that one of the September 11 suicide hijackers, Khalid al-Midhar, was videotaped in Kuala Lumpur nine months before the terrorist attack. The arrests brought to 38 the number of alleged KMM members detained. They include businessmen, teachers, bank employees and taxi drivers.

Norian Mai said police seized training manuals and studies of militant movements in the Philippines, Chechnya, Afghanistan and Indonesia. Other documents contained instructions on guerilla warfare, map-reading and the use of firearms, and information about procedures used in protecting armouries. He said the authorities believed both KMM wings were established and controlled by the same three 'directing figures' from Indonesia, whom he identified as Indonesian Mujahideen Council head Abu Bakar Bashir and two religious leaders (ulama). Abu Bakar and one of the ulama were 'still at large' while the second, Mohamad Iqbal Rahman, had been arrested in Malaysia in June 2001.

Two days after Norian's announcement, Singapore's Ministry of Home Affairs announced the arrest of fifteen suspected terrorists, some of whom, it said, had been trained in al-Qaeda camps in Afghanistan. They were arrested by agents of the Internal Security

Department, who seized from their homes detailed information on bomb-making as well as photographs and video footage of surveillance carried out on potential targets. A Home Ministry official said the principal targets of the terrorists were the US Embassy and members of the US armed forces visiting Singapore, but they also included the British High Commission and the Australian High Commission. Most of those arrested were members of an organisation called Jemaah Islamiah, the leaders of which had links to Malaysia's KMM and the three Indonesians named by Kuala Lumpur. Singapore Deputy Prime Minister Tony Tan noted that Singapore was facing a new type of international terrorism which was strategic in outlook, and much more dangerous and sustained than the one-off terrorist attacks carried out in the past by disparate groups.

The war on terrorism, depicted by Osama Bin Laden as a war on Islam, accelerated the shift away from Islamic moderation in Malaysia and provided new incentives for radical elements in Indonesia and the Philippines. There is strong reason to believe that the kind of Islamic radicals who were Osama's followers will continue to emerge in Malaysia, Indonesia and the Philippines with aspirations to launch a regional holy war aimed at creating a South-East Asian Islamic state. The ripening conditions for increased radicalism in Indonesia, which has the world's largest Muslim population, were highlighted in a survey conducted towards the end of 2001 by the Centre for Research on Islam and Society in the Syarif Hidayatulah Islamic State Institute in Jakarta and published in *Tempo* magazine. It showed a rise in religious fervour and a fall in tolerance for other religions among Indonesian Muslims.

Fear of the Muslim militancy as displayed in the September 11 attacks and Malaysia's home-grown KMM caused some Malaysians who had been critics of Dr Mahathir to view him with new enthusiasm because of his moderate Islamic stance. The Chinese-led opposition Democratic Action Party finally severed its uneasy alliance with PAS and Keadilan, ending any chance of cooperation between the three parties in elections. There were signs of a resurgence in National Front support in two by-elections. But the shift back to the government parties was mainly among some moderate

Muslims, Chinese and Indians, who, while they may have gone through a period of Mahathir-hating, were never serious opposition voters. Many Malays responded less to September 11 and its implications of a frightening global terrorism threat than to the subsequent bombing of Afghanistan, which prompted an anti-American frenzy. PAS led the condemnation of the United States, with Fadzil Noor calling the Americans 'war criminals'.

The Ulama Association of Malaysia condemned the US bombing of Afghanistan as an act of aggression against Islam and urged Muslims to wage a jihad, or holy war, against the Americans. Abdul Ghani Samsudin, head of the organisation of Muslim clerics, said that a jihad was necessary to defend Afghanistan and Muslims worldwide. Muslims should be prepared to sacrifice their lives in the holy war. For Malays the proclamation of the ulama had the binding force of a fatwa—a religious decree. Dr Mahathir's cautious remarks that Malaysians should not involve themselves in the Afghanistan war were seen as un-Islamic by comparison.

Dr Mahathir failed to take a clear-cut position, leaving himself open to criticism from the West and Islamic activists. He condemned the September 11 attacks but expressed his opposition to the war in Afghanistan, saying the main victims were innocent people and the fighting would not eradicate the roots of terrorism. At a meeting of the Organisation of Islamic Conference in Kuala Lumpur in April 2002, Dr Mahathir angered many delegates by defining both Israeli soldiers who killed civilians and Palestinian suicide bombers as terrorists. However, in a later interview with Bernama he said the Palestinian bombers had no choice. It was legitmate for them to use terror against those using terrorism against them. Nevertheless, he was welcomed to Washington by President George Bush in May as an opponent of terrorism (although the American leader said the US had not changed its position that Anwar was a political victim who should be released from jail). But his chummy get-together with Bush harmed him at home, where the opposition savagely attacked him for consorting with the man they accused of being a friend of the Israelis and foe of the Palestinians.

Dr Mahathir cannot hope to stem the flow of Malay voters to PAS by linking the party to terrorism. PAS merely continues to attack his Islamic credentials. It has mastered the art of using religion to further its political interests. UMNO, it asserts, is a party of infidels. Its leader is a pharaoh wasting the people's money. The men who lead PAS, by contrast, are Islamic clerics, who speak the word of God. A vote for PAS is a passport to heaven. Dr Mahathir is only too aware of what he is up against. In an interview with the *New Sunday Times* in July 2001 he showed his frustration, when he said: 'If I say this is white but a religious man says that this is black, then this is black because the tok guru says it's black.'

Some UMNO officials are convinced the party must abandon moderation for a more conservative brand of Islam. This will not happen while Dr Mahathir is in power but future leaders may attempt to compete with PAS on its fundamentalist terms. This could slow or stop Malaysia's march to developed nation status. It could also provide further encouragement—beyond that now existing—for some Malays to embrace extremist ideas. As one Malaysian political analyst said, UMNO could never out-PAS PAS. In any move in this direction would merely give a stamp of approval to the PAS agenda of creating an Islamic state.

PAS might not in the near term win control of the federal parliament because if UMNO feels its political control is threatened it can always increase the number of constituencies in the southern states of Peninsular Malaysia and the Borneo states of Sarawak and Sabah, where it remains strong, to ensure its parliamentary majority. But there is a definite possibility of PAS gaining control of more northern states and even ending up running the top half of the peninsula. From such a large base, it could exercise significant influence over the rest of Malaysia and provide a haven for Islamic extremists. UMNO would be reluctant to take action against it for fear of increasing sympathy for the opposition party.

Over the longer term, UMNO's voting power seems likely to decrease steadily, until even the rejigging of constituencies will not help it survive. While UMNO can continue for the time being to rely on votes of Chinese—and to a lesser extent Indians—the demographic trends suggest this situation will be short-lived. The Centre for Malaysian Chinese Studies has signalled concern over the race's future. It says that while Malaysian Chinese made up 37 per cent of the population 40 years ago, their proportion has fallen to just under 26 per cent today. It forecast a drop to around 20 per cent in the next 20 years. Other studies suggest that Chinese will account for just 15 per cent of Malaysia's population by 2020. Malays and other indigenous people, who make up more than 60 per cent of Malaysia's 23 million people, are increasing in number by almost 5 per cent annually. At the same time, the Chinese birth rate is static or declining. The Indian segment of the population has fallen from about 10 per cent to 7 per cent in recent years.

If PAS maintains its growth in terms of Malay voters, it will eventually have enough support to overthrow UMNO and be in a position to turn Malaysia into an Islamic state. The Islamic resurgence in South-East Asia has certainly benefited PAS but Dr Mahathir bears the main responsibility for the dramatic shift in allegiance among many Malays from UMNO to the opposition party. They have deserted UMNO in protest against his divisive policies and unwelcome pronouncements. A Malaysia that is politically stable and on close and cordial terms with Singapore could be a major stabilising force in the region, providing moral support to moderate elements in Indonesia and acting as economic role model for Thailand and the Philippines. At the same time, it could encourage less advanced ASEAN members such as Vietnam, Laos and Cambodia to take pragmatic measures towards their development. But a nation in which an Islamic party tolerant of Muslim extremists controls a large portion of the country and is chipping away at the parliamentary majority of the moderate federal government will engender regional instability by causing worries about its future and its potential as a base for terrorists. In the past, UMNO was prepared to allow leaders of the Moro Islamic Liberation Front, a Muslim rebel group fighting a guerilla war against the Philippines government, to find refuge in Malaysia. PAS can be expected to be even more welcoming to Islamic revolutionary movements such as the Acehnese independence fighters from Indonesia's northern Sumatra. That is of special concern to Singapore which has had many differences with the UMNO-led government, has been labelled by conservative Muslims as the 'Israel of South-East Asia' and has openly worried about the possibility of PAS coming to power.

Dr Mahathir's dramatic and emotional announcement of his resignation at the 2002 UMNO general assembly, which he later retracted after colleagues pleaded with him not to step down, was dismissed as play-acting by PAS official Hatta Ramli and other opposition leaders. Hatta said it was a desperate attempt to fish for sympathy ahead of the next election. But a leading Malaysian political analyst said that while Dr Mahathir had often used histrionics as a political tool, this time his display of emotion seemed involuntary, brought on by the momentous nature of what he was saying. However, his announcement appeared to have been timed to have the maximum impact. The analyst believed Dr Mahathir had decided to retire after concluding that he was not going to change Malay culture, however long he stayed in office, and that it would be better for him to go while he could still orchestrate the transfer of power. It seemed that Dr Mahathir had finally resolved to give his full support to Badawi as his successor after some earlier hesitation and was concerned that when he resigned his deputy might be challenged for the top posts. The threat of Dr Mahathir's sudden departure so alarmed his colleagues, who feared it could be destabilising, that he was able to secure their support for an orderly transition in a fixed time frame. Dr Mahathir's decision to retire seems final. But before his resignation announcement he had been acting like a man who planned to hang on until death or illness ended his reign.

In December 2001, in an interview with Bernama, the national news agency, Dr Mahathir backed away from an earlier declaration that his current term as prime minister would be his last. Speaking of the next election—due by the end of 2004—he said: 'I am 76. The desire to ensure [the National Front coalition's] success is there, but [the National Front] can achieve success even if I do not contest or am no longer the leader.' Then, he added: 'This is a possibility but in certain situations if I am required to contest, I will contest.' What he seemed to be saying was that he was keeping his options open and might decide to remain in office beyond the next election, which he expected the National Front to win.

But Dr Mahathir's retirement and the transfer of power to Badawi, together with the installation of Najib Razak as the new deputy, now seems assured. Najib, who won the most votes in the part election for the three vice presidential posts in 2000—ahead of Muhyiddin Yassin and Muhammad Taib—was endorsed by Dr Mahathir in July 2000 as the next deputy prime minister to 'prevent a tussle' for the post. He said Najib was 'the best candidate in terms of seniority and most experience in the government'. I was told Najib supported Badawi as Dr Mahathir's successor in the expectation he would be made deputy prime minister and UMNO deputy president. My source said Najib was prepared to see Bawadi serve no more than two terms before he succeeded to the top positions.

This source also said that the future leadership would have to do something about Anwar. 'You just cannot let it go. The ghost of Anwar is with us, it will not go away.' The big challenge, according to this source, will be how to deal with him. A pardon is out of the question because he would then 'join the political fray'. Neither would the leadership want simply to release him from prison because then he would be 'a free-floating agent'. The source stated: 'He can join PAS [or] he can go back to UMNO and then he can say, "Excuse me, you are sitting on my seat".' He suggested the way out would be to find a job for him abroad, perhaps with the United Nations or some other international agency. But people I have spoken to who have worked with Anwar did not think he would accept such an outcome. They have predicted he would be so bitter and angry it would be difficult for the UMNO leadership to find a solution that would not see him trying to seize control of the country. PAS, meanwhile, will be working steadily to make itself the major party in Malaysia.

Abdullah Badawi faces the daunting task of having to deal with the Anwar problem, persuade Malays alienated by Dr Mahathir to return to the UMNO fold and convince Chinese and Indians that he has their interests at heart. He will also have to show that he is his own man. As Dr Mahathir's deputy he has parroted the Prime Minister on some issues, either out of conviction or in order to keep on the right side of his boss. As the next prime minister and president of UMNO, Abdullah Badawi will be a markedly different leader from Dr Mahathir. He will be diplomatic where Dr Mahathir is outspoken. He will be soothing where the present Prime Minister is abrasive. He will also, unless his nature changes in the job, be less authoritarian. Badawi, who is 14 years younger than Dr Mahathir, was a well-respected and well-liked foreign minister before he was appointed Deputy Prime Minister and Home Minister. He maintained close and cordial relations with his Pacific counterparts from Australia to Japan. He previously held the education and defence portfolios.

In a country where many senior figures have been accused of corruption, linked to sex scandals or alleged to have abused their official powers, Abdullah Badawi is Mr Clean to his colleagues and the general public, among whom his Pak Lah (Uncle Abdullah) nickname reflects an admiration other leaders do not command. He spent the late 1980s in the political wilderness after supporting Tengku Razaleigh Hamzah's unsuccessful challenge to Dr Mahathir for the UMNO presidency in 1987. But he returned to cabinet in 1991 and has been a Mahathir loyalist ever since. Analysts say he will have to toughen his approach in the top job but will come to it with an important asset. He has a religious background which will help him combat the claim by PAS that it is more Islamic than UMNO. Pak Lah's father was a religious teacher and his grandfather, Abdullah Fahim Ibrahim, was a highly regarded ulama. Badawi pursued Islamic Studies at the University of Malaya. However, he has reassured Chinese and Indians concerned that UMNO would embrace Islamic radicalism to recapture the territory it lost to PAS that his party has a moderate religious stance which is suitable for multiracial Malaysia. He has promised UMNO would oppose religious extremism.

The most important question for the future is whether he can stand up to PAS and keep his colleagues in line, maintaining the Islamic moderation favoured by Dr Mahathir. His success or failure will determine whether his government can not only withstand the pressures for Malaysia to become more fundamentalist but also demonstrate the strength and stability to act as a core force in countering the efforts of militants to turn South-East Asia into a radical

Islamic region dedicated to the destruction of the infidels in its neighbourhood. He will take control of a government that has lost the confidence of a large proportion of the people and a party in which corruption is pervasive and selflessness rare. Both the government and UMNO need a drastic overhaul to restore their credibility with the public if Badawi is to have any hope of preventing a further weakening of the parliamentary power of the National Front and the destabilising impact of an increasingly vigorous PAS.

The quality of his leadership will be important not only in determining the future of Malaysia but also in influencing developments elsewhere in South-East Asia. He must be a strong, able prime minister if the legacy of Dr Mahathir is not to lead to the unravelling of the region. UMNO officials can be expected to resist any change in the party's traditional practices of patronage and money politics. Self-interest among Badawi's colleagues will be a major obstacle for him to overcome, if indeed he has the will to try to change the system. Peace and progress in South-East Asia may well depend on his resourcefulness and stamina in putting Malaysia's house in order.

Index

Abdul Aziz Hussin 138
Abdul Aziz Shamsuddin 95, 96, 163,
    171, 176
Abdul Gani Patail 136, 144, 148, 161,
    193
Abdul Gani Samsudin 231
Abdul Malek Ahmad 147
Abdul Rahim Ghouse 98, 126, 129
Abdullah Fahim Ibrahim 236
Abu Bakar Bashir 229
Abu Talib Othman 158
Affifuddin Omar 72, 73
Afghanistan 227, 229, 231
Ahmad, Abdullah 202, 203, 215, 221
Ahmad Mohamad Don 80
AIDS Council of Malaysia 21
Ainum Mohamad Saaid 147, 148
Akbar Khan 82
Albright, Madeline 6, 56, 141
Alternative Front 186, 188
Amin, Mohamad Razali 225
Amir Muhammad 132
Ananda Krishnan 33
Anwar, Ibrahim
    50 Dalil 65–7, 76, 79, 80, 85–6, 98,
        114, 152
    alteration of charges 159–61

anti-government agitation 96
arrest 10, 98, 110, 112–13, 155,
    157, 182
arsenic poisoning 172, 173, 192
on ASEAN 5
assault 98, 109, 111, 118, 120–2,
    155–8, 172
call for resignation 79
character 2, 17, 18–19, 23, 65–7,
    79, 88–9, 99
charged 119–20, 168–9
conspiracy against 65–7, 93–5, 96,
    105, 108, 144, 155, 156, 161, 162,
    163, 167, 172, 174
on corruption, cronyism and
    nepotism 60, 61–2, 67, 72, 102,
    108
dismissal 85–8, 92, 99
DNA matching 152–3
education 12
and economy 40, 45, 46, 47, 48,
    51–2, 54, 59–60, 74, 76, 77, 81
on financial crisis 52
and foreign governments 126,
    141–2
health 172–3
and IMF 45, 54, 59–60, 81

imprisonment 53, 177–8
invitation to resign 90
and interest rates 60
on Islamic Law 20–2, 33
leadership challenge 9–10, 26–8,
    31–2, 48–9, 72, 92, 182
media support 42–3
morality issue 65–7, 79, 85–6,
    88–9, 92, 96–7, 99–100, 104–18,
    123–4, 134–5, 137, 172, 173–4
PAS 13, 31, 91, 99
on patriotism 56
Permatang Pauh Declaration 101
political career 12–16, 18, 21–30,
    31, 39–40, 49–50, 57, 67, 72,
    73–4, 75, 76, 85–6, 93, 99, 100–1,
    124, 125, 177, 179
popularity 86–7
prison conditions 140
relationship with Abdul Aziz 96
relationship with Mahathir 11–12,
    14, 25–30, 31–2, 33, 39, 40–1, 42,
    48–9, 50, 54, 55, 57, 62–3, 64–5,
    69, 71, 72–3, 75, 76, 77, 87, 90,
    92, 99–100, 113–15, 117, 130,
    139, 173–4, 176, 178, 179, 180–1,
    182
sacking 40, 85–8, 90, 182
sacking and reaction of foreign
    governments 92
secret tapes 155
sentenced 167, 176–8
sexual allegations 65–7, 79, 85–6,
    88–9, 92, 96–7, 99–100, 104–18,
    123–4, 134–5, 137, 149–65,172,
    173–4, 176, 180
support for 8, 42–3, 87, 88, 92–3,
    99, 124, 129–30, 140, 141, 163,
    178–9
trial 80, 89, 125, 132, 134–48, 167,
    168–81
UMNO 13–14, 15, 22, 23–4, 27,
    85, 87, 88, 90, 178, 213
Vision Team 23, 24, 25, 53
Anwar, Marzuki 24
Aquino, Corazon 127
Ariffin, Justice 169, 175, 176, 177,
    178

Asia Pacific Economic Cooperation
    (APEC) 125, 140–3, 212
Association of South-East Asian
    Nations (ASEAN) 3, 5, 6, 32–3,
    38, 55, 73, 77, 211
Axworthy, Lloyd 141
Azahar Mohamad 144
Aziza see Wan Aziza Wan Ismail
Azizan Abu Bakar 40, 106, 114, 134,
    137–8, 139, 149–51, 159, 170, 172,
    175, 177, 180
Azmin Ali 66, 135, 150
Azwan Ali 135

Badawi, Abdullah 6, 24, 29, 77, 79,
    87, 99, 125, 142, 158, 183, 184, 192,
    195, 207, 208, 214, 215, 220, 234,
    235–6, 237
Bank Negara 4, 35, 36, 37, 40, 46, 51,
    59, 60, 61, 63, 80–1, 82
banks 44, 51, 52, 59
beauty pagent incident 20–1, 33
Berjaya Group 34
Bin Laden, Osama 224, 226–7, 230
Burma 3, 6, 38
Burma Solidarity Movement 99
Bush, George 231

Cambodia 3, 5
Camdessus, Michel 4, 45, 59, 60
Central Limit Order Book (CLOB)
    81–2
Chandra Muzaffar 101
Chang, Victor 17
Chia Thye Poh 7
China 5, 6, 207
Chinese Malaysians 15, 17, 56, 58,
    189–94, 198, 202, 203, 222
Chretien, Jean 140
Commonwealth Games 60, 100, 110
Corporate Debt Restructuring
    Committee 35
cronyism 60, 61–2, 65, 67–9, 71–2,
    102, 108

Daim Zainuddin 9, 14, 34–5, 36, 41,
    45–6, 54, 57, 59, 61, 73–4, 75, 95,
    117–18, 135, 159, 163, 174–5, 209

Democratic Action Party (DAP) 53, 99, 124, 185, 188, 230
democracy 131

East Timor 212
economy 31, 33–8, 41, 43–6, 47, 51–2, 54, 57–60, 69–71, 74, 76, 77, 78–9, 80, 81, 82–4, 184–5
 see also financial crisis; National Economic Action Council (NEAC); New Economic Policy (NEP)
Eizenstat, Stuart E. 6
Ekran Berhad 33, 34
elections 185–203
Estrada, Joseph 121, 127, 140
European Community 5
European Union 2, 3
Eusoff Chin 136, 146, 147
Ezam Mohamad Noor 126, 226, 228

Fadzil Noor 12, 13, 91, 186, 189, 196, 199, 222, 223, 226, 231
Fauzi Abdul Raham 62
Fernandez, Joe 198
Fernando, Christopher 151, 173
financial crisis 31, 33–8, 41, 44, 51–2, 54, 59–60, 64, 82–4, 185
Fong Wen Phak 80
foreign governments 126–7, 140, 141–3, 212
foreign interference in Malaysia 4–5, 52, 126–8, 140, 141–2

gangs 201–3
Gates, Bill 2
Gazprom 7
Ghafar Baba 9, 14–15, 22, 23–4, 26, 48, 58–9
Gore, Al 142, 143
Gurbachan Singh 154–5, 167

Habibie, J.B. 56, 121
Hadi Awang, Abdul 222, 223
Halim Saad 33, 34, 35, 36, 209
Hamdan Taha 68
Hanif Omar 116
Harun Hashim 143
Harun Idris 168

Harun Taib 223
Hasnah, Judge 124
Hassan Marican, Mohamad 36
Hatta Ramli 234
Hawke, Robert J. 212
Hiebert, Murray 145
Horta, Jose Ramos 212
Howard, John 212
Hun Sen 3
Hussein Onn 214

Ibrahim Saad 187
Indian Malaysians 200–2, 222
Indonesia 3, 4, 9, 10, 17, 21, 37, 44–5, 54–6, 64, 73
interest rates 59, 60–1
Internal Security Act 12, 53, 76, 86, 89, 101, 105, 111, 113, 122, 123, 128, 129, 131, 138, 147, 150, 154, 190, 191, 215, 228
International Monetary Fund (IMF) 2, 4, 9, 39, 41, 42, 44, 45, 49, 54, 55, 57, 59–60, 70, 80, 81, 185
Iran 7
Ishak Baharom 20, 21
Islamic radicalism 10, 13
Islamic Law 20–2, 31, 33, 222, 223–30
Islamic Youth Movement of Malaysia (Abim) 12
Ismail Kassim 74
Israel 7

Japan 5
Jayakumar, S. 77, 78
Jemaah Islamiah 230
Johan Jaafar 75

Kadir Jasin 43, 55, 59, 118
Kamarudin Ali 111
Kamaruddin Jaafar 117
Kapal Singh 171–2, 189, 191
Keating, Paul 212
Kedah Ulama Association 101
Kuala Lumpur Stock Exchange (KLSE) 81, 82
Khalid Jafri 65, 80
Klang Valley 52

Konsortium Perkapalan Berhad (KPB) 36
Kuala Lumpur 2, 16, 22
Kuala Lumpur International Airport 117, 175
Kumpulan Mujahideen Malaysia (KMM) 227, 228, 229, 230

Land and General 35
Laos 3
law, Malaysian 52–3
Lee Kuan Yew 6, 7, 122–3, 215
Lee Lam Thye 201
Libya, Ibrahim 225
Lim Guan Eng 53, 145, 176
Lim Kit Siang 147, 148, 189
Lim Kong Boon 152, 153
Lingam, V.K. 146

Mahathir, Dr
   on ASEAN 5
   call for resignation 57
   character 1–2, 205–6, 210, 211–12, 213–14
   and Chinese population 189–92
   on cronyism 70, 71
   and economy 3–4, 8–9, 40–2, 47, 54, 57–9, 71, 74, 78–9, 80, 82, 184–5
   education 217–18
   and financial crisis 36, 41, 52, 185
   and foreign governments 126–7, 140–3, 212
   and foreign interference 4–5, 52, 126–8, 141, 183
   health 8
   and IMF 39, 42, 44, 57
   and interest rates 59, 60–1
   on Islamic Law 20–1
   leadership 69, 72–3, 76, 79, 87, 102, 124, 181, 183, 192, 195–6, 199, 204–10, 212–20
   and media 42–3
   and PAS 31, 209, 221–2, 231–4
   relationship with Anwar 11–12, 14, 25–30, 31–2, 33, 39, 40–1, 42, 48–9, 50, 54, 55, 57, 62–3, 64–5, 69, 71, 72–3, 75, 76, 77, 87, 90,

92, 99–100, 113–15, 117, 130, 139, 173–4, 176, 179, 180–1, 182
   relationship with Abdul Aziz 96
   relationship with Zahid 70–1
   on sexual allegations against Anwar 112
   on terrorism 231
   Thailand 'land-bridge' 40–1, 43
   and UMNO 87, 180–1, 195–6, 204, 206, 209, 213, 214, 216, 232–7
   US relations 4–5, 6, 7–8, 142–3
   defence of Suharto 55
   on Soros 38
Mahathir, Marina 21
Mahathir, Mirzan 24, 36–7, 209
Mahathir, Mokhzani 44, 71
Malaysia Airlines (MAS) 33, 35, 209
Malaysia International Shipping Corporation (MISC) 36
Malaysian Chinese Association (MCA) 185, 188
Malaysian Chinese Organisations' Election Appeals Committee (Suqiu) 190, 191, 198
Malaysian Indian Congress (MIC) 185, 188, 203
Malaysian People's Party (MPP) 186, 188
Malaysian relations with Singapore 77–8, 81–2
Malaysian Resources Corporation Berhad 117
Malaysia–Thailand 'land-bridge' 40–1, 43
Malott, John 8
Manjeet Singh 144
Marina Yusoff 193
media 42–3, 53, 55, 75, 131
   Western 128–9, 183
   see also newspapers
Megat Junid Ayob 95, 96, 97, 135, 163, 175
Mohamad Dzaiddin Abdullah 146–7
Mohamad Hayati Othman 199
Mohamad Iqbal Rahman 229
Mohamad Rodwan 153
Mohamad Said Awang 137, 138, 139

Mohtar Abdullah 79–80, 89, 136–7, 148, 156
Moro Islamic Liberation Front 233
Muhamad Ahmad 101
Muhammad Muhammad Taib 23, 25, 195, 235
Muhyiddin Yassin 23, 25, 29, 195, 235
Multimedia Super Corridor (MSC) 2, 32, 33
Munawar Anees 101, 104, 105–6, 114, 115, 121
Musa Hassan 152
Musa Hitam 48, 87, 216, 217
Muslim/Hindu conflict 52

Najib Tun Razak 23, 25, 39, 86, 195, 235
Naluri 36
National Economic Action Council (NEAC) 9, 45, 74, 82
National Front coalition 3, 51, 74, 182, 185, 186, 189, 190, 197, 203, 222, 230
National Justice Party 19, 101, 166
National Unity Advisory Panel 201
Navaratnam, Ramon 142
Nazri Abdullah 43, 75
Nazri Aziz 31
Netherlands East Indies 17
New Economic Policy (NEP) 58, 70, 190
newspapers 33, 38, 40, 42–3, 75, 104–5, 116–18, 128–9, 131, 145, 149, 193, 210
Nik Adli Nik Aziz 228
Nik Aziz Nik Mat 223, 224
Norian Mai 229
Norzielah Jalil 95, 135
Norhayati Yusof 176
Nallakaruppan, Solaimalai 76–7, 88, 89, 144, 152
Nural Izzah 127

Omar Hashim 185

Paal, Douglas 126
Palestinian cause 7
Parti Islam se-Malaysia (PAS) 12, 13, 19, 31, 48, 74, 91, 99, 124, 129, 168, 181–9, 191, 196, 197, 213, 221–3, 230
Paul, Justice Augustine 124–5, 127, 136, 139, 144–5, 147, 159, 163–4
Penang 52
Perlis 74
Permatang Pauh Declaration 101
Petronas 7, 36, 196, 209
Peremba 34–5
Philippines 3
Projek Lebuhraya Utara Selatan (PLUS) 35
protests 129–30

Qian Qichen 6

Rafidah Aziz 24, 29, 141, 176
Rahim Noor 86, 98, 101, 102, 109, 111, 116, 139, 156–7
Rahim Thamby Chik 23, 25, 53, 176
Rahmat, Mohamed 26, 27
Rais Yatim 87, 146
Raja Aziz Addruse 120, 146, 153, 159, 162
Raja Kamaruddin Wahid 171
Razak Baginda, Abdul 86–7, 214, 215
Rehman Rashid 181
Renong Group 33, 35
riots 58, 109, 130, 201–3
Rizal, Jose 15
Royal Commission 109, 122, 172
Rubin, Robert 126
Russia 5
Ruslan Kassim 98, 126, 129
Rustam Sani 18, 101

Sahidan Kassim 74
Saifudin Nasution Ismail 126, 198
Samsudin Abu Hassan 35
Sanusi Junid 24, 28, 73, 79
Selemat, Salamon 28
Selangor 20–1, 33
Shamsidar Taharin 139, 150, 152, 154, 159
Silicon Valley 2
Sime Bank 51
Singapore 3, 6–7, 77–8, 81–2
Siti Hasmah 208

Siti Zahara Sulaiman 29
Sng Chee Hua 155, 175
Soros, George 3–4, 5–6, 7, 38, 39
South-East Asia 2, 3, 4, 16, 19, 31,
  33–5, 50
Stock Exchange of Singapore (SES)
  81
Suharto, President 4, 9, 44, 54–5, 56,
  64, 73, 91, 189
Sukarno 16–17
Sukma Darmawan 98, 104, 105, 106,
  115, 121, 169, 170, 173, 177
Sungei Buloh Prison 53
Surin Pitsuwan 77

Tajudin Ramli 33, 34, 35, 36, 45, 209
Tan, Vincent 33
Tanjong Pagar 78
Tengku Razaleigh Hamzah 28–9, 39,
  47–8, 58, 87, 99, 187, 214, 216, 236
Thailand 2, 3, 31, 37, 44
Third Asia Oil & Gas Conference 60
Ting Pek Khiing 33, 34
Tivoli Villa 89, 135, 151–2, 177
Tunku Abdul Rahman 210, 214, 215,
  218

Ulama Association of Malaysia 231
Ummi Hafilda Ali 40, 95, 106, 114,
  134–5, 137, 138–9, 149, 150–1,
  153–5, 159, 171, 175, 180
United Engineers (Malaysia) (UEM)
  35–6
United Malays National Organisation
  (UMNO) 8–10, 13–19, 22–9, 31,
  33, 35, 47–8, 52, 55, 61, 64–5, 67,
  68, 85, 87–8, 90, 123, 124, 126, 143,

168, 178, 181, 183, 187, 188, 190,
  191, 192, 195–6, 204, 213, 214, 216,
  221–3, 232–7
and Mahathir 87, 180–1, 195–6,
  204, 206, 209, 213, 214, 216,
  232–7
Veterans Club 59
United States 1, 2, 3, 4, 5, 6, 7, 8, 17,
  56, 141, 142–3, 227, 231
Urban Development Authority 34
Utusan Melayu Group 75

Vietnam 3

Wain, Barry 57
Wan Azmi Hamzah 35
Wan Azizah Wan Ismail 20, 21, 22,
  91–2, 101, 109, 110–11, 120, 141,
  166, 172, 178, 180, 186, 187
water shortages 51–2
Wolfowitz, Paul 126
women's rights 20, 33
Wong Chun Wai 131
World Bank 2, 4, 49, 54
Wexler, Robert 7, 8

Yacob Karim, Mohamad 105, 114

Zacarias Moussaoui 229
Zahid Hamidi 10, 28, 29, 31, 61, 62,
  65, 67, 68, 71, 72, 75, 102
Zain, Mat 121
Zainuddin Maidin 62, 75
Zainur Zakaria 105, 144–5, 146, 147,
  149
Zeti Akhtar Aziz 80
Zulkifli Sulong 193